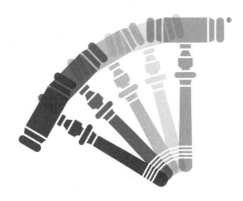

Casenote® Legal Briefs

EMPLOYMENT LAW

Keyed to Courses Using

Rothstein and Liebman's
Employment Law

Seventh Edition

Wolters Kluwer

Law & Business

Copyright © 2011 CCH Incorporated. All Rights Reserved.
www.wolterskluwerlb.com

Published by Wolters Kluwer Law & Business in New York.

Wolters Kluwer Law & Business serves customers worldwide with CCH, Aspen Publishers, and Kluwer Law International products.

No part of this publication may be reproduced or transmitted in any form or by any means, electronic or mechanical, including photocopy, recording, or any information storage and retrieval system, without permission in writing from the publisher. For information about permissions or to request permission online, visit us at *wolterskluwerlb.com* or a written request may be faxed to our permissions department at 212-771-0803.

To contact Customer Service, e-mail customer.service@wolterskluwer.com, call 1-800-234-1660, fax 1-800-901-9075, or mail correspondence to:

Wolters Kluwer Law & Business
Attn: Order Department
P.O. Box 990
Frederick, MD 21705

Printed in the United States of America.

1 2 3 4 5 6 7 8 9 0

ISBN 978-1-4548-0785-8

About Wolters Kluwer Law & Business

Wolters Kluwer Law & Business is a leading global provider of intelligent information and digital solutions for legal and business professionals in key specialty areas, and respected educational resources for professors and law students. Wolters Kluwer Law & Business connects legal and business professionals as well as those in the education market with timely, specialized authoritative content and information-enabled solutions to support success through productivity, accuracy and mobility.

Serving customers worldwide, Wolters Kluwer Law & Business products include those under the Aspen Publishers, CCH, Kluwer Law International, Loislaw, Best Case, ftwilliam.com and MediRegs family of products.

CCH products have been a trusted resource since 1913, and are highly regarded resources for legal, securities, antitrust and trade regulation, government contracting, banking, pension, payroll, employment and labor, and healthcare reimbursement and compliance professionals.

Aspen Publishers products provide essential information to attorneys, business professionals and law students. Written by preeminent authorities, the product line offers analytical and practical information in a range of specialty practice areas from securities law and intellectual property to mergers and acquisitions and pension/benefits. Aspen's trusted legal education resources provide professors and students with high-quality, up-to-date and effective resources for successful instruction and study in all areas of the law.

Kluwer Law International products provide the global business community with reliable international legal information in English. Legal practitioners, corporate counsel and business executives around the world rely on Kluwer Law journals, looseleafs, books, and electronic products for comprehensive information in many areas of international legal practice.

Loislaw is a comprehensive online legal research product providing legal content to law firm practitioners of various specializations. Loislaw provides attorneys with the ability to quickly and efficiently find the necessary legal information they need, when and where they need it, by facilitating access to primary law as well as state-specific law, records, forms and treatises.

Best Case Solutions is the leading bankruptcy software product to the bankruptcy industry. It provides software and workflow tools to flawlessly streamline petition preparation and the electronic filing process, while timely incorporating ever-changing court requirements.

ftwilliam.com offers employee benefits professionals the highest quality plan documents (retirement, welfare and non-qualified) and government forms (5500/PBGC, 1099 and IRS) software at highly competitive prices.

MediRegs products provide integrated health care compliance content and software solutions for professionals in healthcare, higher education and life sciences, including professionals in accounting, law and consulting.

Wolters Kluwer Law & Business, a division of Wolters Kluwer, is head-quartered in New York. Wolters Kluwer is a market-leading global information services company focused on professionals.

Format for the Casenote® Legal Brief

Nature of Case: This section identifies the form of action (e.g., breach of contract, negligence, battery), the type of proceeding (e.g., demurrer, appeal from trial court's jury instructions), or the relief sought (e.g., damages, injunction, criminal sanctions).

Palsgraf v. Long Island R.R. Co.

Injured bystander (P) v. Railroad company (D)

N.Y. Ct. App., 248 N.Y. 339, 162 N.E. 99 (1928).

Party ID: Quick identification of the relationship between the parties.

Fact Summary: This is included to refresh your memory and can be used as a quick reminder of the facts.

NATURE OF CASE: Appeal from judgment affirming verdict for plaintiff seeking damages for personal injury.

FACT SUMMARY: Helen Palsgraf (P) was injured on R.R.'s (D) train platform when R.R.'s (D) guard helped a passenger aboard a moving train, causing his package to fall on the tracks. The package contained fireworks which exploded, creating a shock that tipped a scale onto Palsgraf (P).

Rule of Law: Summarizes the general principle of law that the case illustrates. It may be used for instant recall of the court's holding and for classroom discussion or home review.

🏛 RULE OF LAW
The risk reasonably to be perceived defines the duty to be obeyed.

FACTS: Helen Palsgraf (P) purchased a ticket to Rockaway Beach from R.R. (D) and was waiting on the train platform. As she waited, two men ran to catch a train that was pulling out from the platform. The first man jumped aboard, but the second man, who appeared as if he might fall, was helped aboard by the guard on the train who had kept the door open so they could jump aboard. A guard on the platform also helped by pushing him onto the train. The man was carrying a package wrapped in newspaper. In the process, the man dropped his package, which fell on the tracks. The package contained fireworks and exploded. The shock of the explosion was apparently of great enough strength to tip over some scales at the other end of the platform, which fell on Palsgraf (P) and injured her. A jury awarded her damages, and R.R. (D) appealed.

Facts: This section contains all relevant facts of the case, including the contentions of the parties and the lower court holdings. It is written in a logical order to give the student a clear understanding of the case. The plaintiff and defendant are identified by their proper names throughout and are always labeled with a (P) or (D).

ISSUE: Does the risk reasonably to be perceived define the duty to be obeyed?

HOLDING AND DECISION: (Cardozo, C.J.) Yes. The risk reasonably to be perceived defines the duty to be obeyed. If there is no foreseeable hazard to the injured party as the result of a seemingly innocent act, the act does not become a tort because it happened to be a wrong as to another. If the wrong was not willful, the plaintiff must show that the act as to her had such great and apparent possibilities of danger as to entitle her to protection. Negligence in the abstract is not enough upon which to base liability. Negligence is a relative concept, evolving out of the common law doctrine of trespass on the case. To establish liability, the defendant must owe a legal duty of reasonable care to the injured party. A cause of action in tort will lie where harm,

though unintended, could have been averted or avoided by observance of such a duty. The scope of the duty is limited by the range of danger that a reasonable person could foresee. In this case, there was nothing to suggest from the appearance of the parcel or otherwise that the parcel contained fireworks. The guard could not reasonably have had any warning of a threat to Palsgraf (P), and R.R. (D) therefore cannot be held liable. Judgment is reversed in favor of R.R. (D).

DISSENT: (Andrews, J.) The concept that there is no negligence unless R.R. (D) owes a legal duty to take care as to Palsgraf (P) herself is too narrow. Everyone owes to the world at large the duty of refraining from those acts that may unreasonably threaten the safety of others. If the guard's action was negligent as to those nearby, it was also negligent as to those outside what might be termed the "danger zone." For Palsgraf (P) to recover, R.R.'s (D) negligence must have been the proximate cause of her injury, a question of fact for the jury.

Concurrence/Dissent: All concurrences and dissents are briefed whenever they are included by the casebook editor.

▶ ANALYSIS

The majority defined the limit of the defendant's liability in terms of the danger that a reasonable person in defendant's situation would have perceived. The dissent argued that the limitation should not be placed on liability, but rather on damages. Judge Andrews suggested that only injuries that would not have happened but for R.R.'s (D) negligence should be compensable. Both the majority and dissent recognized the policy-driven need to limit liability for negligent acts, seeking, in the words of Judge Andrews, to define a framework "that will be practical and in keeping with the general understanding of mankind." The Restatement (Second) of Torts has accepted Judge Cardozo's view.

Analysis: This last paragraph gives you a broad understanding of where the case "fits in" with other cases in the section of the book and with the entire course. It is a hornbook-style discussion indicating whether the case is a majority or minority opinion and comparing the principal case with other cases in the casebook. It may also provide analysis from restatements, uniform codes, and law review articles. The analysis will prove to be invaluable to classroom discussion.

Quicknotes

FORESEEABILITY A reasonable expectation that change is the probable result of certain acts or omissions.

NEGLIGENCE Conduct falling below the standard of care that a reasonable person would demonstrate under similar conditions.

PROXIMATE CAUSE The natural sequence of events without which an injury would not have been sustained.

Issue: The issue is a concise question that brings out the essence of the opinion as it relates to the section of the casebook in which the case appears. Both substantive and procedural issues are included if relevant to the decision.

Holding and Decision: This section offers a clear and in-depth discussion of the rule of the case and the court's rationale. It is written in easy-to-understand language and answers the issue presented by applying the law to the facts of the case. When relevant, it includes a thorough discussion of the exceptions to the case as listed by the court, any major cites to the other cases on point, and the names of the judges who wrote the decisions.

Quicknotes: Conveniently defines legal terms found in the case and summarizes the nature of any statutes, codes, or rules referred to in the text.

Wolters Kluwer Law & Business is proud to offer *Casenote*® *Legal Briefs*—continuing thirty years of publishing America's best-selling legal briefs.

Casenote® *Legal Briefs* are designed to help you save time when briefing assigned cases. Organized under convenient headings, they show you how to abstract the basic facts and holdings from the text of the actual opinions handed down by the courts. Used as part of a rigorous study regimen, they can help you spend more time analyzing and critiquing points of law than on copying bits and pieces of judicial opinions into your notebook or outline.

Casenote® *Legal Briefs* should never be used as a substitute for assigned casebook readings. They work best when read as a follow-up to reviewing the underlying opinions themselves. Students who try to avoid reading and digesting the judicial opinions in their casebooks or online sources will end up shortchanging themselves in the long run. The ability to absorb, critique, and restate the dynamic and complex elements of case law decisions is crucial to your success in law school and beyond. It cannot be developed vicariously.

Casenote® *Legal Briefs* represents but one of the many offerings in Legal Education's Study Aid Timeline, which includes:

- *Casenote*® *Legal Briefs*
- *Emanuel Law Outlines*
- *Examples & Explanations* Series
- *Introduction to Law* Series
- Emanuel *Law in a Flash* Flash Cards
- Emanuel *CrunchTime* Series

Each of these series is designed to provide you with easy-to-understand explanations of complex points of law. Each volume offers guidance on the principles of legal analysis and, consulted regularly, will hone your ability to spot relevant issues. We have titles that will help you prepare for class, prepare for your exams, and enhance your general comprehension of the law along the way.

To find out more about Wolters Kluwer Law & Business's Study Aid publications, visit us online at *www.wolterskluwerlb.com* or email us at *legaledu@ wolterskluwer.com*. We'll be happy to assist you.

Get this Casenote® Legal Brief as an AspenLaw Studydesk eBook today!

By returning this form to Wolters Kluwer Law & Business, you will receive a complimentary eBook download of this Casenote® Legal Brief and AspenLaw Studydesk productivity software.* Learn more about AspenLaw Studydesk today at *www.wolterskluwerlb.com.*

Name	Phone ( )
Address	**Apt. No.**
City	**State** **ZIP Code**
Law School	**Graduation Date** Month _____ Year _____

Cut out the UPC found on the lower left corner of the back cover of this book. Staple the UPC inside this box. Only the original UPC from the book cover will be accepted. (No photocopies or store stickers are allowed.)

Attach UPC inside this box.

Email (Print legibly or you may not get access!)
Title of this book (course subject)
ISBN of this book (10- or 13-digit number on the UPC)
Used with which casebook (provide author's name)

Mail the completed form to: Wolters Kluwer Law & Business
Legal Education Division
130 Turner Street, Bldg 3, 4th Floor
Waltham, MA 02453-8901

* Upon receipt of this completed form, you will be emailed a code for the digital download of this book in AspenLaw Studydesk eBook format and a free copy of the software application, which is required to read the eBook.

For a full list of eBook study aids available for AspenLaw Studydesk software and other resources that will help you with your law school studies, visit *www.wolterskluwerlb.com.*

Make a photocopy of this form and your UPC for your records.

For detailed information on the use of the information you provide on this form, please see the PRIVACY POLICY at *www.wolterskluwerlb.com.*

A. Decide on a Format and Stick to It

Structure is essential to a good brief. It enables you to arrange systematically the related parts that are scattered throughout most cases, thus making manageable and understandable what might otherwise seem to be an endless and unfathomable sea of information. There are, of course, an unlimited number of formats that can be utilized. However, it is best to find one that suits your needs and stick to it. Consistency breeds both efficiency and the security that when called upon you will know where to look in your brief for the information you are asked to give.

Any format, as long as it presents the essential elements of a case in an organized fashion, can be used. Experience, however, has led *Casenote® Legal Briefs* to develop and utilize the following format because of its logical flow and universal applicability.

NATURE OF CASE: This is a brief statement of the legal character and procedural status of the case (e.g., "Appeal of a burglary conviction").

There are many different alternatives open to a litigant dissatisfied with a court ruling. The key to determining which one has been used is to discover *who is asking this court for what.*

This first entry in the brief should be kept as *short as possible.* Use the court's terminology if you understand it. But since jurisdictions vary as to the titles of pleadings, the best entry is the one that addresses who wants what in this proceeding, not the one that sounds most like the court's language.

RULE OF LAW: A statement of the general principle of law that the case illustrates (e.g., "An acceptance that varies any term of the offer is considered a rejection and counteroffer").

Determining the rule of law of a case is a procedure similar to determining the issue of the case. Avoid being fooled by red herrings; there may be a few rules of law mentioned in the case excerpt, but usually only one is *the* rule with which the casebook editor is concerned. The techniques used to locate the issue, described below, may also be utilized to find the rule of law. Generally, your best guide is simply the chapter heading. It is a clue to the point the casebook editor seeks to make and should be kept in mind when reading every case in the respective section.

FACTS: A synopsis of only the essential facts of the case, i.e., those bearing upon or leading up to the issue.

The facts entry should be a short statement of the events and transactions that led one party to initiate legal proceedings against another in the first place. While some cases conveniently state the salient facts at the beginning of the decision, in other instances they will have to be culled from hiding places throughout the text, even from concurring and dissenting opinions. Some of the "facts" will often be in dispute and should be so noted. Conflicting evidence may be briefly pointed up. "Hard" facts must be included. Both must be *relevant* in order to be listed in the facts entry. It is impossible to tell what is relevant until the entire case is read, as the ultimate determination of the rights and liabilities of the parties may turn on something buried deep in the opinion.

Generally, the facts entry should not be longer than three to five *short* sentences.

It is often helpful to identify the role played by a party in a given context. For example, in a construction contract case the identification of a party as the "contractor" or "builder" alleviates the need to tell that that party was the one who was supposed to have built the house.

It is always helpful, and a good general practice, to identify the "plaintiff" and the "defendant." This may seem elementary and uncomplicated, but, especially in view of the creative editing practiced by some casebook editors, it is sometimes a difficult or even impossible task. Bear in mind that the *party presently* seeking something from this court may not be the plaintiff, and that sometimes only the cross-claim of a defendant is treated in the excerpt. Confusing or misaligning the parties can ruin your analysis and understanding of the case.

ISSUE: A statement of the general legal question answered by or illustrated in the case. For clarity, the issue is best put in the form of a question capable of a "yes" or "no" answer. In reality, the issue is simply the Rule of Law put in the form of a question (e.g., "May an offer be accepted by performance?").

The major problem presented in discerning what is *the* issue in the case is that an opinion usually purports to raise and answer several questions. However, except for rare cases, only one such question is really the issue in the case. Collateral issues not necessary to the resolution of the matter in controversy are handled by the court by language known as *"obiter dictum"* or merely *"dictum."* While dicta may be included later in the brief, they have no place under the issue heading.

To find the issue, ask *who wants what* and then go on to ask *why did that party succeed or fail in getting it.* Once this is determined, the "why" should be turned into a question.

The complexity of the issues in the cases will vary, but in all cases a single-sentence question should sum up the issue. *In a few cases,* there will be two, or even more rarely, three issues of equal importance to the resolution of the case. Each should be expressed in a single-sentence question.

Since many issues are resolved by a court in coming to a final disposition of a case, the casebook editor will reproduce the portion of the opinion containing the issue or issues most relevant to the area of law under scrutiny. A noted law professor gave this advice: "Close the book; look at the title on the cover." Chances are, if it is Property, you need not concern yourself with whether, for example, the federal government's treatment of the plaintiff's land really raises a federal question sufficient to support jurisdiction on this ground in federal court.

The same rule applies to chapter headings designating sub-areas within the subjects. They tip you off as to what the text is designed to teach. The cases are arranged in a casebook to show a progression or development of the law, so that the preceding cases may also help.

It is also most important to remember to *read the notes and questions* at the end of a case to determine what the editors wanted you to have gleaned from it.

HOLDING AND DECISION: This section should succinctly explain the rationale of the court in arriving at its decision. In capsulizing the "reasoning" of the court, it should always include an application of the general rule or rules of law to the specific facts of the case. Hidden justifications come to light in this entry: the reasons for the state of the law, the public policies, the biases and prejudices, those considerations that influence the justices' thinking and, ultimately, the outcome of the case. At the end, there should be a short indication of the disposition or procedural resolution of the case (e.g., "Decision of the trial court for Mr. Smith (P) reversed").

The foregoing format is designed to help you "digest" the reams of case material with which you will be faced in your law school career. Once mastered by practice, it will place at your fingertips the information the authors of your casebooks have sought to impart to you in case-by-case illustration and analysis.

B. Be as Economical as Possible in Briefing Cases

Once armed with a format that encourages succinctness, it is as important to be economical with regard to the time spent on the actual reading of the case as it is to be economical in the writing of the brief itself. This does not mean "skimming" a case. Rather, it means reading the case with an "eye" trained to recognize into which "section" of your brief a particular passage or line fits and having a system for quickly and precisely marking the case so that the passages fitting any one particular part of

the brief can be easily identified and brought together in a concise and accurate manner when the brief is actually written.

It is of no use to simply repeat everything in the opinion of the court; record only enough information to trigger your recollection of what the court said. Nevertheless, an accurate statement of the "law of the case," i.e., the legal principle applied to the facts, is absolutely essential to class preparation and to learning the law under the case method.

To that end, it is important to develop a "shorthand" that you can use to make marginal notations. These notations will tell you at a glance in which section of the brief you will be placing that particular passage or portion of the opinion.

Some students prefer to underline all the salient portions of the opinion (with a pencil or colored underliner marker), making marginal notations as they go along. Others prefer the color-coded method of underlining, utilizing different colors of markers to underline the salient portions of the case, each separate color being used to represent a different section of the brief. For example, blue underlining could be used for passages relating to the rule of law, yellow for those relating to the issue, and green for those relating to the holding and decision, etc. While it has its advocates, the color-coded method can be confusing and time-consuming (all that time spent on changing colored markers). Furthermore, it can interfere with the continuity and concentration many students deem essential to the reading of a case for maximum comprehension. In the end, however, it is a matter of personal preference and style. Just remember, whatever method you use, underlining must be used sparingly or its value is lost.

If you take the marginal notation route, an efficient and easy method is to go along underlining the key portions of the case and placing in the margin alongside them the following "markers" to indicate where a particular passage or line "belongs" in the brief you will write:

N   (NATURE OF CASE)
RL   (RULE OF LAW)
I   (ISSUE)
HL   (HOLDING AND DECISION, relates to the RULE OF LAW behind the decision)
HR   (HOLDING AND DECISION, gives the RATIONALE or reasoning behind the decision)
HA   (HOLDING AND DECISION, APPLIES the general principle(s) of law to the facts of the case to arrive at the decision)

Remember that a particular passage may well contain information necessary to more than one part of your brief, in which case you simply note that in the margin. If you are using the color-coded underlining method instead of marginal notation, simply make asterisks or checks in the margin next to the passage in question in the colors that indicate the additional sections of the brief where it might be utilized.

The economy of utilizing "shorthand" in marking cases for briefing can be maintained in the actual brief writing process itself by utilizing "law student shorthand" within the brief. There are many commonly used words and phrases for which abbreviations can be substituted in your briefs (and in your class notes also). You can develop abbreviations that are personal to you and which will save you a lot of time. A reference list of briefing abbreviations can be found on page xii of this book.

C. Use Both the Briefing Process and the Brief as a Learning Tool

Now that you have a format and the tools for briefing cases efficiently, the most important thing is to make the time spent in briefing profitable to you and to make the most advantageous use of the briefs you create. Of course, the briefs are invaluable for classroom reference when you are called upon to explain or analyze a particular case. However, they are also useful in reviewing for exams. A quick glance at the fact summary should bring the case to mind, and a rereading of the rule of law should enable you to go over the underlying legal concept in your mind, how it was applied in that particular case, and how it might apply in other factual settings.

As to the value to be derived from engaging in the briefing process itself, there is an immediate benefit that arises from being forced to sift through the essential facts and reasoning from the court's opinion and to succinctly express them in your own words in your brief. The process ensures that you understand the case and the point that it illustrates, and that means you will be ready to absorb further analysis and information brought forth in class. It also ensures you will have something to say when called upon in class. The briefing process helps develop a mental agility for getting to the *gist* of a case and for identifying, expounding on, and applying the legal concepts and issues found there. The briefing process is the mental process on which you must rely in taking law school examinations; it is also the mental process upon which a lawyer relies in serving his clients and in making his living.

Abbreviations for Briefs

acceptance	acp	offer	O
affirmed	aff	offeree	OE
answer	ans	offeror	OR
assumption of risk	a/r	ordinance	ord
attorney	atty	pain and suffering	p/s
beyond a reasonable doubt	b/r/d	parol evidence	p/e
bona fide purchaser	BFP	plaintiff	P
breach of contract	br/k	prima facie	p/f
cause of action	c/a	probable cause	p/c
common law	c/l	proximate cause	px/c
Constitution	Con	real property	r/p
constitutional	con	reasonable doubt	r/d
contract	K	reasonable man	r/m
contributory negligence	c/n	rebuttable presumption	rb/p
cross	x	remanded	rem
cross-complaint	x/c	res ipsa loquitur	RIL
cross-examination	x/ex	respondeat superior	r/s
cruel and unusual punishment	c/u/p	Restatement	RS
defendant	D	reversed	rev
dismissed	dis	Rule Against Perpetuities	RAP
double jeopardy	d/j	search and seizure	s/s
due process	d/p	search warrant	s/w
equal protection	e/p	self-defense	s/d
equity	eq	specific performance	s/p
evidence	ev	statute	S
exclude	exc	statute of frauds	S/F
exclusionary rule	exc/r	statute of limitations	S/L
felony	f/n	summary judgment	s/j
freedom of speech	f/s	tenancy at will	t/w
good faith	g/f	tenancy in common	t/c
habeas corpus	h/c	tenant	t
hearsay	hr	third party	TP
husband	H	third party beneficiary	TPB
injunction	inj	transferred intent	TI
in loco parentis	ILP	unconscionable	uncon
inter vivos	I/v	unconstitutional	unconst
joint tenancy	j/t	undue influence	u/e
judgment	judgt	Uniform Commercial Code	UCC
jurisdiction	jur	unilateral	uni
last clear chance	LCC	vendee	VE
long-arm statute	LAS	vendor	VR
majority view	maj	versus	v
meeting of minds	MOM	void for vagueness	VFV
minority view	min	weight of authority	w/a
Miranda rule	Mir/r	weight of the evidence	w/e
Miranda warnings	Mir/w	wife	W
negligence	neg	with	w/
notice	ntc	within	w/i
nuisance	nus	without	w/o
obligation	ob	without prejudice	w/o/p
obscene	obs	wrongful death	wr/d

Work and Law

Quick Reference Rules of Law

Bammert v. Don's Super Valu, Inc.

Fired employee (P) v. Employer (D)

Wis. Sup. Ct., 646 N.W.2d 365 (2002).

NATURE OF CASE: Appeal of dismissal of wrongful termination case.

FACT SUMMARY: Karen Bammert (P) was fired after her police-officer husband arrested her employer's wife for drunk driving.

RULE OF LAW

A state's public policy does not protect an at-will employee who is fired in retaliation for the acts of his or her non-employee spouse.

FACTS: Karen Bammert (P) worked at Don's Super Valu, Inc. in Menomonie, Wisconsin, for 26 years. Her husband was a police officer for Menomonie. The grocery store was owned by Don Williams, whose wife Nona was arrested for drunk driving in June 1997. Bammert's (P) husband participated in the arrest by administering a Breathalyzer test. Shortly after the arrest, Bammert (P) was fired. She sued for wrongful discharge, arguing that she was fired in retaliation for her husband's participation in the arrest. The state trial court dismissed the suit for failure to state a claim, and the appeals court affirmed. Bammert (P) argued that her lawsuit was justified on public policy grounds, even though she was an at-will employee. She pointed to two public policies that she said were implicated here. First, she said, Wisconsin law prohibits the operation of a motor vehicle while under the influence of an intoxicant. Second, state statutes encourage the preservation of the family, society, the state, morality, and civilization, she argued.

ISSUE: Does a state's public policy protect an at-will employee who is fired in retaliation for the acts of his or her non-employee spouse?

HOLDING AND DECISION: (Sykes, J.) No. A state's public policy does not protect an at-will employee who is fired in retaliation for the acts of his or her non-employee spouse. In general, employees are terminable at will, and can be fired for any reason or for no reason at all. In *Brockmeyer v. Dun & Bradstreet*, 335 N.W.2d 834 (1983), the Wisconsin Supreme Court adopted a public-policy exception that allows suit when the discharge is contrary to a fundamental and well-defined public policy as evidenced by existing law. Under *Brockmeyer*, a plaintiff stating a claim for wrongful discharge must identify a constitutional, statutory, or administrative provision that clearly articulates a fundamental and well-defined public policy. If a plaintiff can identify such a policy, and shows that it was violated, then the burden shifts to the employer to show just cause for the termination. Case law since

Brockmeyer has cautioned against interpreting the public policy exception too broadly, emphasizing that the exception is narrow. Bammert's (P) argument that the exception should be expanded to encompass her case was therefore rejected. As it stands, the public-policy exception applies to discharges in retaliation for the fulfillment of an affirmative obligation that the law places on the employee. Extending it to discharges for fulfillment of an affirmative obligation that the law places on a relative of an employee would go too far, and have no logical stopping point. Affirmed.

DISSENT: (Bablitch, J.) Wisconsin's public policy encouraging the vigorous enforcement of the law is well established. A police officer must be able to make an arrest without worrying that his or her spouse will be fired because of the arrest. The public-policy exception should be narrowly expanded to encompass retaliatory firing in response to a police officer's lawful actions in his or her capacity as a police officer.

ANALYSIS

The court noted that, while Bammert's (P) action was unsustainable, her firing was "reprehensible." The court did not want to extend the public policy exception to her case because of worries about a slippery slope—not knowing where to draw the line in these types of cases. But it did seem to indicate a desire to rule in Bammert's (P) favor.

Quicknotes

AT-WILL EMPLOYMENT The rule that an employment relationship is subject to termination at any time, or for any cause, by an employee or an employer in the absence of a specific agreement otherwise.

The Development of Employment Law

Quick Reference Rules of Law

Lemmerman v. A.T. Williams Oil Co.

Injured child employee (P) v. Employer (D)

N.C. Sup. Ct., 350 S.E.2d 83 (1986).

NATURE OF CASE: Appeal from dismissal of action for damages for personal injury.

FACT SUMMARY: Injured when doing odd jobs while at work with his mother, Shane Tucker (P) filed suit, alleging that, although paid for the work he did, he was not an employee under the terms of the Workers' Compensation Act, therefore giving the court subject matter jurisdiction.

🏛 RULE OF LAW
The court lacks subject matter jurisdiction where a statute provides that its remedies shall be an employee's only remedies against his employer for claims covered by the statute.

FACTS: Because his mother had no one to care for him while she was at work as a part-time cashier at a combination store and service station, eight-year-old Shane Tucker (Shane) (P) went to work with her. While there, he performed odd jobs for which the store manager paid him. When he slipped and fell on the sidewalk on A.T. Williams Oil Company's (Williams) (D) property, cutting his hand, Shane (P) and his mother filed this action, seeking damages for medical expenses, lost wages, and pain and suffering. Lemmerman (P) was appointed guardian ad litem for Shane (P), who contended that he could not have been an employee under the terms of the Workers' Compensation Act because the store manager did not comply with certain procedural formalities. Williams (D) asserted that Shane (P) was its employee as defined by the Act and that the Industrial Commission accordingly had exclusive jurisdiction over the claim. The trial court concluded that Shane (P) was an employee of Williams (D), and dismissed Shane's (P) action for lack of subject matter jurisdiction. The court of appeals affirmed.

ISSUE: Does the court lack subject matter jurisdiction where a statute provides that its remedies shall be an employee's only remedies against his employer for claims covered by the statute?

HOLDING AND DECISION: (Frye, J.) Yes. The court lacks subject matter jurisdiction where a statute provides that its remedies shall be an employee's only remedies against his employer for claims covered by the statute. The trial court made findings and concluded that Shane (P) was an employee injured within the course and scope of his employment with Williams (D) as defined in the Act. This issue is not affected by the fact that a minor, Shane (P), may have been illegally employed because N.C.G.S. § 97-2(2)

(1985) specifically includes within its provisions illegally employed minors. Further, failure to follow technical procedures is not controlling on the issue of whether an employer-employee relationship exists. The evidence amply supports the trial judge's findings that the manager, who had the authority to hire and fire employees, hired Shane (P) to do odd jobs as needed in Williams's (D) service station/store. Affirmed.

DISSENT: (Martin, J.) Shane (P) was on the premises, not as an employee of Williams (D), but because it was necessary in order for his mother to work. While on the premises, he sometimes performed menial tasks for the manager, who sometimes would give the boy something for his work. This was not enough to classify Shane (P) as an employee.

▶ ANALYSIS

Because workers' compensation precludes damage awards, injured individuals sometimes argue that they are independent contractors who can sue in tort rather than employees limited to workers' compensation relief. It seems clear here since Williams (D) was asserting that Shane (P) was an employee, while Shane (P) was contending he was not an employee, that the potential award under the jurisdiction of the court was greater than that under the Industrial Commission. However, commentators have asked if it is appropriate for an eight-year-old, who is too young to be a legal employee, to be limited to workers' compensation? It is unclear whether any consideration was given for the applicability and/or effect of any child-labor statutes in North Carolina to this case.

━■━

Quicknotes

EMPLOYEE An individual who performs work at the direction of another pursuant to an express or implied agreement between the parties and in exchange for compensation.

GUARDIAN AD LITEM Person designated by the court to represent an infant or ward in a particular legal proceeding.

INDEPENDENT CONTRACTOR A party undertaking a particular assignment for another who retains control over the manner in which it is executed.

SUBJECT MATTER JURISDICTION The authority of the court to hear and decide actions involving a particular type of issue or subject.

Continued on next page.

WORKERS' COMPENSATION ACT A statute making the employer strictly liable to an employee for injuries sustained by the employee in the course of employment. The compensation scheduled under the Act is an exclusive remedy, barring any common-law remedy that the employee may have had.

■━■

McAuliffe v. Mayor & City of New Bedford

Former policeman (P) v. Mayor and city (D)

Mass. Sup. Jud. Ct., 29 N.E. 517 (1892).

NATURE OF CASE: Petition for mandamus to restore a city employee's job.

FACT SUMMARY: When he was removed from the police force for allegedly violating city regulations forbidding solicitation of money for political purposes, McAuliffe (P) sought to be reinstated in his job.

🏛 RULE OF LAW
No member of the police department shall be allowed to solicit money or any aid, on any pretense, for any political purpose whatever.

FACTS: McAuliffe (P) was removed from his position as a policeman in New Bedford by the Mayor (D) on a finding that he had violated a department rule prohibiting any member of the police department from soliciting money or aid for any reason for any political purpose. There was additional evidence that McAuliffe (P) had been a member of a political committee, which was also prohibited by the regulations. Under the regulations, members of the police force held office during good behavior until removed by the Mayor (D) for cause deemed by him sufficient, after due hearing. McAuliffe (P) filed a petition for mandamus for reinstatement. He argued that the Mayor's (D) finding did not warrant the removal, that the part of the rule violated was invalid as an invasion of McAuliffe's (P) right to express his political opinions, and that a breach of it was not a cause sufficient under the statutes. He further argued that he did not have due hearing.

ISSUE: Shall a member of the police department be allowed to solicit money or any aid, on any pretense, for any political purpose whatever?

HOLDING AND DECISION: (Holmes, J.) No. No member of the police department shall be allowed to solicit money or any aid, on any pretense, for any political purpose whatever. There is nothing in the Constitution or the statute to prevent the City (D) from attaching obedience to this rule as a condition to holding the office of policeman and making it part of the good conduct required. McAuliffe (P) may have a constitutional right to talk politics, but he has no constitutional right to be a policeman. There are few employments for hire in which the servant does not agree to suspend his constitutional rights of free speech as well as of idleness by the implied terms of his contract. The servant cannot complain, as he takes the employment on the terms that are offered him. On the same principle the City (D) may impose any reasonable condition upon holding offices within its control. McAuliffe (P) received notice of the rule violation, he attended on notice a hearing, where he asked for no specifications and offered no evidence. Moreover, McAuliffe (P), having had notice of the proceedings, must be taken to have known their possible consequences. Petition dismissed.

▶ ANALYSIS

About 17 percent of American workers are employed by federal, state, and local governments today. Civil service laws control selection procedures through the use of competitive examinations and merit systems. Federal employees are covered by Title VII, the federal law proscribing a broad range of discriminatory employment practices under § 717; state and local government employees were brought under the general coverage of Title VII with the 1972 amendments.

Quicknotes

CONDITION OF EMPLOYMENT A requirement necessary in order for an individual to obtain or maintain employment.

MANDAMUS A court order issued commanding a public or private entity, or an official thereof, to perform a duty required by law.

TITLE VII OF THE CIVIL RIGHTS ACT OF 1964 Law prohibiting discrimination in employment on the basis of race, color, religion, sex, and national origin.

Rutan v. Republican Party

State employees (P) v. State government governing political party (D)

497 U.S. 62 (1990).

NATURE OF CASE: Appeal from dismissal of employment-discrimination action based on political affiliation.

FACT SUMMARY: Rutan (P) and four others protested employment decisions made by the governor of Illinois based solely on a state employee's affiliation or non-affiliation with the Republican Party (D), the party in power.

RULE OF LAW

The First Amendment forbids government officials from promoting, transferring, recalling, or hiring public employees solely on the basis of their support of the political party in power, unless party affiliation is an appropriate requirement for the position involved.

FACTS: On November 12, 1980, the governor of Illinois issued an executive order proclaiming a hiring freeze for every agency, bureau, board, or commission subject to his control. Exceptions would be permitted only with the governor's express permission. In reviewing an agency's request that a particular applicant be approved for a particular position, the governor's office looked at whether the applicant voted in Republican primaries in past election years, provided financial or other support to the Republican Party (D) and its candidates, promised to join and work for the Republican Party (D) in the future, and was supported by Republican Party (D) officials at state or local levels. Rutan (P) and four others filed suit, alleging that the governor was using his office to operate a political-patronage system in support of the Republican Party (D), the party in power. The Republican Party (D) contended that employees' First Amendment rights were not infringed because they had no entitlement to promotion, transfer, or rehire, and that the decisions did not chill the exercise of protected belief and association by public employees. The claims of Rutan (P) and three others were remanded by the court of appeals and one other was dismissed. This appeal followed.

ISSUE: Does the First Amendment forbid government officials from promoting, transferring, recalling, or hiring public employees solely on the basis of their support of the political party in power, unless party affiliation is an appropriate requirement for the position required?

HOLDING AND DECISION: (Brennan, J.) Yes. The First Amendment forbids government officials from promoting, transferring, recalling, or hiring public employees solely on the basis of their support of the political party

in power, unless party affiliation is an appropriate requirement for the position required. [In a footnote, the Supreme Court explained that these cases came to it in a preliminary posture and the question was limited to whether the allegations made by Rutan (P) stated a cognizable First Amendment claim, sufficient to withstand the Republican Party's (D) motion to dismiss under Federal Rules of Civil Procedure 12(b)(6). Such a motion alleges that the party or parties bringing suit have failed to state a claim upon which relief may be granted.] The Republican Party's (D) assertion that at-will employees have no entitlement to continued employment has been rejected by this Court before and is beside the point. Further, its argument as to a chilling of belief and association is not credible. Employees who find themselves in dead-end positions due to their political backgrounds are adversely affected. They will feel a significant obligation to support political positions held by their superiors and to refrain from acting on the political views they actually hold in order to move up the career ladder. Employees who do not compromise their beliefs stand to lose the considerable increases in pay and job satisfaction attendant to promotions and even their jobs if they are not rehired after a "temporary" layoff. These are significant penalties and are imposed for the exercise of rights guaranteed by the First Amendment. Unless these patronage practices are narrowly tailored to further vital government interests, they impermissibly encroach on First Amendment freedoms. There is no such government interest here. A government's interest in securing effective employees can be met by discharging, demoting, or transferring staff members whose work is deficient. All parties have stated claims on which relief may be granted. The Seventh Circuit is affirmed insofar as it remanded the claims of Rutan (P) and three others. Its decision to uphold the dismissal of another claim is reversed. Affirmed in part; reversed in part; and remanded.

CONCURRENCE: (Stevens, J.) If a legislative enactment denying public employment to nonmembers of the majority party is unconstitutional—as it clearly would be—an equally pernicious rule promulgated by the executive must also be invalid.

DISSENT: (Scalia, J.) One need not believe that the patronage system is necessarily desirable, but merely that it is a political arrangement that may sometimes be a reasonable choice within the judgment of the people's elected representatives.

Continued on next page.

▶ *ANALYSIS*

The rule announced in the instant case was first formulated by the Court in two of its prior decisions: *Elrod v. Burns*, 427 U.S. 347 (1976), and *Branti v. Finkel*, 445 U.S. 507 (1980). In *Elrod*, the Court decided that a newly elected Democratic sheriff could not constitutionally replace certain office staff with members of his own party "when the existing employees lack or fail to obtain requisite support from, or fail to affiliate with, that party." The Court, in *Branti*, prohibited a newly appointed Democratic public defender from discharging assistant public defenders because they did not have the support of the Democratic Party. Although the rule in those cases involved discharge or a threat to discharge public employees, the Court here extended that rule to cover promotions, transfers, and recalls.

■■■

Quicknotes

ENTITLEMENT A right or interest that may not be denied without due process.

FIRST AMENDMENT The First Amendment to the United States Constitution prohibiting Congress from enacting any law respecting an establishment of religion, prohibiting the free exercise of religion, abridging freedom of speech or the press, the right of peaceful assembly and the right to petition for a redress of grievances.

PATRONAGE The act of public officials who grant public offices and honors.

■■■

Campbell v. General Dynamics Government Systems Corp.

Employer (D) v. Employee (P)

407 F.3d 546 (1st Cir. 2005).

NATURE OF CASE: Action to compel arbitration.

FACT SUMMARY: A company president implemented a new dispute-resolution policy through e-mail without notifying employees that the new policy compels arbitration and forecloses their access to courts to address their grievances.

🏛 **RULE OF LAW**
A mass e-mail to employees announcing a new dispute-resolution policy and providing a link to the policy does not provide adequate notice to bind employees to mandatory arbitration of workplace discrimination disputes.

FACTS: The president of General Dynamics (D), Gerard DeMuro, sent an e-mail to all employees announcing the implementation of the new dispute-resolution policy. DeMuro's message stated that arbitration would be the last in a four-step approach to handling legal issues arising out of workplace disputes. It did not mention the policy's potential effect on employees' rights to have workplace disputes heard in court, that agreement to arbitrate would become binding upon continued employment, or that the workplace disputes covered by the new policy included federal statutory claims. The e-mail said the policy would become effective the next day and urged employees to review "enclosed materials carefully." The materials referred to were two Web links at the bottom of the text of the e-mail. One was to a brochure on how the policy worked and, on its second page, said employees who continued their employment would be "covered" by it, it applied to employment discrimination and harassment claims, and it would be the exclusive means for resolving workplace disputes. The second link was to a dispute-resolution handbook, which included the full text of the policy and some related materials. Roderick Campbell (P) was fired for absenteeism and tardiness, and he sued in state court under the Americans with Disabilities Act (ADA) and Massachusetts General Laws, charging that his attendance problems were the result of his sleep apnea and that the company failed to accommodate his condition. General Dynamics (D) removed the case to the U.S. District Court for the District of Massachusetts, which denied the company's motion to compel arbitration, declaring that "a mass e-mail message, without more, fails to constitute the minimal level of notice required" to form a binding agreement to arbitrate ADA claims.

ISSUE: Does a mass e-mail to employees announcing a new dispute-resolution policy and providing a link to the policy provide adequate notice to bind employees to mandatory arbitration of workplace-discrimination disputes?

HOLDING AND DECISION: (Seyla, J.) No. A mass e-mail to employees announcing a new dispute-resolution policy and providing a link to the policy does not provide adequate notice to bind employees to mandatory arbitration of workplace-discrimination disputes. The company could compel arbitration only if it can show that the mandatory arbitration provision is part of a valid contract under the Federal Arbitration Act (FAA) and a court finds that the enforcement of the arbitration provision would be appropriate. The "appropriateness" depends on whether an employer's communication, measured under an objective standard, provided "some minimal level of notice" that continued employment would amount to a waiver of an employee's right to pursue discrimination claims in court. The e-mail here did not satisfy that burden, so General Dynamics (D) could not compel Campbell (P) to arbitrate his disability discrimination claims under the ADA and Massachusetts law. The company had no history of communicating significant personnel matters to employees via e-mail, the e-mail required no affirmative response by employees, it did not explicitly state that the new policy contained an arbitration agreement or indicate that the new dispute-resolution procedure was mandatory, and there was nothing to suggest that reissuance of the company's personnel handbook would have contractual significance. A tracking log was set up to monitor whether employees opened the e-mail, but no steps were taken to record whether they went to the links to review the brochure or handbook. The record showed that Campbell (P) had opened the e-mail, but he denied ever reading or seeing the brochure, handbook, or policy. District Court was right.

▶ *ANALYSIS*

By way of dicta in the full version of the case, the court added that an e-mail, "properly couched," can be an appropriate medium for forming an arbitration agreement. For example, an e-mail that spells out the agreement to arbitrate in a straightforward manner would pass muster. This is especially so, the court stated, given that the Electronic Signatures in Global and National Commerce Act (E-Sign Act), 15 U.S.C. §§ 7001-7031, expressly prohibits any interpretation of the FAA's "written provision" rule

Continued on next page.

that would bar giving legal effect to agreements solely because they are in an electronic form.

■═■

Quicknotes

AMERICANS WITH DISABILITIES ACT (42 U.S.C. §§ 12101-12213) Enacted in 1990, this federal law prohibits discrimination in employment against Americans with physical or mental disabilities.

■═■

The Hiring Process

Quick Reference Rules of Law

Kotch v. Board of River Port Pilot Commissioners

Job applicant (P) v. State river pilots association (D)

330 U.S. 552 (1947).

NATURE OF CASE: Appeal from denial of finding of employment discrimination.

FACT SUMMARY: After he was denied appointment as a state river pilot, although seemingly qualified, Kotch (P) filed suit against the Board of River Port Pilot Commissioners (D), alleging constitutional violations in the state's method of appointing new state river pilots.

🏛 RULE OF LAW
The practice of nepotism in appointing new state river pilots under applicable state statutes does not violate the Equal Protection Clause of the Fourteenth Amendment.

FACTS: Kotch (P) had at least 15 years' experience in the river, the port, and elsewhere, and possessed all the statutory qualifications to be a river pilot, except for serving a required six-month apprenticeship under Louisiana officer pilots. Despite his experience, he was denied appointment as a state pilot. He then filed suit against the Board of River Port Pilot Commissioners (D) in Louisiana state court, alleging that the incumbent pilots, having unfettered discretion under the law in the selection of apprentices, had selected with occasional exception only the relatives and friends of incumbents. He further contended that the selections were made by electing prospective apprentices into the pilots' association, which the pilots had formed by authority of state law; that since membership was closed to all except those having the favor of the pilots, the result was that only their relatives and friends could become state pilots. The Louisiana Supreme Court held that the pilotage law so administered did not violate the Equal Protection Clause of the Fourteenth Amendment. Kotch (P) appealed.

ISSUE: Does the practice of nepotism in appointing new state river pilots under applicable state statutes violate the Equal Protection Clause of the Fourteenth Amendment?

HOLDING AND DECISION: (Black, J.) No. The practice of nepotism in appointing new state river pilots under applicable state statutes does not violate the Equal Protection Clause of the Fourteenth Amendment. The states have had full power to regulate pilotage of certain kinds of vessels since 1789 when the first Congress decided that then-existing state pilot laws were satisfactory and made federal regulation unnecessary. Louisiana's pilotage system is typical of that which grew up in most seaboard states and in foreign countries. Since 1805, Louisiana pilots have been state officers whose work has been controlled by the state. It is within the framework of this long-standing pilotage regulation system that the practice has apparently existed of permitting pilots if they choose, to select their relatives and friends as the only ones ultimately eligible for appointment as pilots by the governor. The close association in which pilots must work and live in their pilot communities and on the water and the discipline and regulation that is imposed to assure the state competent pilot service after appointment might have prompted the legislature to permit Louisiana pilot officers to select those with whom they would serve. It is not possible to say that the practice is the kind of discrimination that violates the Equal Protection Clause of the Fourteenth Amendment. Affirmed.

DISSENT: (Rutledge, J.) The result of the decision is to approve as constitutional state regulation that makes admission to the ranks of pilots turn finally on consanguinity. That is forbidden by the Fourteenth Amendment's guaranty against denial of the equal protection of the laws.

▶ ANALYSIS

The Court explained that the practice of nepotism in appointing public servants has been a subject of controversy in this country throughout our history. Some states have adopted constitutional amendments or statutes to prohibit it, reflecting state policies to wipe out the practice. But Louisiana and most other states have adopted no such general policy. The Court declared it can only assume that the Louisiana legislature weighed the obvious possibility of evil against whatever useful function a closely knit pilotage system might serve.

Quicknotes

CONSANGUINITY The relatedness of persons based on the existence of common ancestors.

DISCRIMINATION Unequal treatment of individuals without justification.

EQUAL PROTECTION CLAUSE Provision of the Fourteenth Amendment to the U.S. Constitution prohibiting a state from denying any person within its jurisdiction the equal protection of the laws.

NEPOTISM Appointment to positions of friends or relatives by those in public office.

EEOC v. Consolidated Service Systems

Government agency (P) Immigrant-owned company (D)

989 F.2d 233 (7th Cir. 1993).

NATURE OF CASE: Appeal from dismissal of a Title VII action for race discrimination.

FACT SUMMARY: Consolidated Service Systems (D), owned by a Korean immigrant, hired through word-of-mouth recruiting, which resulted in Koreans making up 81 percent of the new employees, although they made up only one percent of the work force in the area.

🏛 RULE OF LAW
The use of word-of-mouth recruiting does not give rise to an inference of intentional discrimination.

FACTS: Hwang, a Korean immigrant, bought Consolidated Services Systems (Consolidated) (D) in 1983. During the next four years, 81 percent of the new employees hired by Consolidated were Korean, although Koreans made up only one percent of the work force in the surrounding area. In order to find new employees, Consolidated (D) placed advertisements in the local newspapers but had failed to find acceptable candidates through that method. As a result, Consolidated (D) relied on word-of-mouth recruiting through its present employees. This method was costless and produced better candidates. The Equal Employment Opportunity Commission (EEOC) (P) filed a Title VII action against Consolidated (D) for race discrimination since their recruiting methods had created a work force that was disproportionately Korean. The district court dismissed the case, and the EEOC (P) appealed.

ISSUE: May the use of word-of-mouth recruiting give rise to an inference of intentional discrimination?

HOLDING AND DECISION: (Posner, J.) No. The use of word-of-mouth recruiting does not give rise to an inference of intentional discrimination. In order to prove discriminatory treatment in Title VII cases, it must be shown that the employer had a discriminatory motive and acted out of that motive. An employer who prefers employees of a certain race is not guilty of discrimination unless it acts on that preference. The use of the most efficient method of recruiting does not give rise to an inference of discrimination even if it corresponds with a racial preference held by the employer. A rule that confines hiring to relatives of existing employees would compel an inference of intentional discrimination, but the use of word-of-mouth recruiting does not rise to that level. Accordingly, since Consolidated (D) used word-of-mouth recruiting because it was the cheapest and most effective way of obtaining new employees rather than for some more insidious reason, an inference of discrimination is improper, even if Consolidated's (D) method had a disproportionate impact. Affirmed.

▶ ANALYSIS

Title VII prohibits employment advertisements that are discriminatory. Thus, a want ad may not seek a "woman" or "man" for a position. In *Hailes v. United Airlines*, 464 F.2d 1006 (5th Cir. 1972), the court ruled that United could not advertise for stewardesses.

Quicknotes

DISCRIMINATION Unequal treatment of individuals without justification.

DISPARATE TREATMENT Unequal treatment of employees or of applicants for employment without justification.

EQUAL EMPLOYMENT OPPORTUNITY COMMISSION (EEOC) Created by Title VII of the Civil Rights Act of 1964, its purpose is to end employment discrimination based on race, color, religion, age, sex, or national origin.

Aramark Facility Services v. Services Employees International Union

Employer (P) v. Union (D)

530 F.3d 817 (9th Cir. 2008).

NATURE OF CASE: Appeal from district court decision that vacated arbitration award.

FACT SUMMARY: After Aramark Facility Services (Aramark) (P) received "no match letters" from the Social Security Administration regarding discrepancies in employee information, Aramark (P) fired 33 union employees for failing to provide proper social security card information.

🏛 RULE OF LAW

In order for an employer to claim it has constructive knowledge of an employee's undocumented status, the employer must at least have positive information that the employee is undocumented.

FACTS: In 2003, the Social Security Administration (SSA) sent a "no match letter" to Aramark Facility Services (Aramark) (P) informing the company that the social security numbers of 3,300 of its employees did not match those in the SSA database. Aramark (P) subsequently sent instructions to 48 Aramark (P) employees at the Staples Center in Los Angeles about the discrepancy in their social security numbers. The instruction demanded that the employees bring in a new social security card or verification that a new card was being processed. Aramark (P) gave the employees three days to comply. Fifteen employees complied, but 33 did not. Aramark (P) fired those 33 employees. The company informed the terminated-employees that it would rehire them if they later completed the required documentation. The Services Employees International Union (SEIU) (D) filed a grievance on the terminated employees' behalf on the grounds there was no just cause to terminate them. The arbiter agreed, finding that there was no "convincing information" that the workers were actually undocumented. Aramark (P) filed suit in federal district court to vacate the award on the grounds the award was in violation of public policy because it forced Aramark (P) to violate federal immigration law by rehiring alleged undocumented workers. The district court agreed and vacated the arbitration award. SEIU (D) appealed to the Ninth Circuit Court of Appeals.

ISSUE: In order for an employer to claim it has constructive knowledge of an employee's undocumented status, must the employer at least have positive information that the employee is undocumented?

HOLDING AND DECISION: (Hall, J.) Yes. In order for an employer to claim it has constructive knowledge of an employee's undocumented status, the employer must at least have positive information that the employee is undocumented. While arbitration awards are typically upheld, courts may vacate awards if they violate public policy. To do so, courts must first find that an explicit, well defined public policy exists and that the award goes against the policy. Here, Aramark's (P) argument rests on a valid public policy based on the Immigration Reform and Control Act of 1986. Under the law, employers are subject to civil and criminal penalties if they knowingly employ undocumented workers. "Knowingly" includes constructive knowledge. The second part of the analysis is crucial, here: if the arbitration award would have forced Aramark (P) to rehire employees when the company had constructive knowledge of their undocumented status. This court has held in other cases that dismissal of an employee for undocumented status is not proper when the employer did not have "positive information" that the employee was actually undocumented. Aramark's (P) two arguments that it had "positive information" are both unavailing. First, in regards to the "match letters," there are many reasons why the SSA sends employers such letters. Name changes, typographical errors and compound last names often result in the generation of "no match letters." The purpose of the "no match letter" is not to discover undocumented employees but to inform the employer that some of their employees are not being properly credited with their social security earnings. Accordingly, the receipt of a "no match letter" is not "positive information" to an employer that an employee is undocumented. Second, the failure of some employees to comply with Aramark's (P) instructions also does not qualify as positive information. The turnaround time was simply too short. Accordingly, the district court improperly found that the arbitrator's award reinstating the employees was against public policy. Reversed.

▶ ANALYSIS

The decision does place a burden on employers to produce some affirmative evidence that an employee is actually undocumented before terminating that employee. While the term "positive information" is vague, this decision provides an example of what it is not. Both the "no match letter" and the employees' reactions were circumstantial evidence only giving rise to a justifiable suspicion of their alleged undocumented status. However, neither constituted positive or actual affirmative evidence of that fact.

■━■

Continued on next page.

Quicknotes

ARBITRATION An alternative resolution process where a dispute is heard and decided by a neutral third party, rather than through legal proceedings.

PUBLIC POLICY Policy administered by the state with respect to the health, safety and morals of its people in accordance with common notions of fairness and decency.

■▬■

Hoffman Plastic Compounds, Inc. v. NLRB

Employer (P) v. Federal agency (D)

535 U.S. 137 (2002).

NATURE OF CASE: Petition to Supreme Court from court of appeal's refusal to review a National Labor Relations Board award of back pay.

FACT SUMMARY: When the National Labor Relations Board (NLRB) (D) awarded Jose Castro, an illegal alien, back pay against his employer, Hoffman Plastics Compounds, Inc. (P), the latter argued that the NLRB (D) had no authority to award back pay to an illegal alien.

🏛 RULE OF LAW

National Labor Relations Board relief by way of back pay to an undocumented alien is foreclosed by federal immigration policy as expressed in the Immigration Reform and Control Act of 1986.

FACTS: The National Labor Relations Board (NLRB) (D) awarded back pay to Jose Castro, an undocumented alien who had never been legally authorized to work in the United States. The NLRB (D) determined that the employer, Hoffman Plastics Compounds, Inc. (Hoffman Plastics) (P), laid off Castro and other employees to rid itself of known union supporters. The NLRB (D) ordered reinstatement and back pay notwithstanding Castro's illegal status. The court of appeals denied Hoffman Plastics' (P) petition for review, and Hoffman Plastics (P) petitioned for review in the Supreme Court.

ISSUE: Is NLRB relief by way of back pay to an undocumented alien foreclosed by federal immigration policy as expressed in the Immigration Reform and Control Act of 1986?

HOLDING AND DECISION: (Rehnquist, C.J.) Yes. NLRB (D) relief by way of back pay to an undocumented alien is foreclosed by federal immigration policy as expressed in the Immigration Reform and Control Act of 1986 (IRCA). Awarding back pay in a case like this not only trivializes the immigration laws, but also condones and encourages future violations. Here, Castro admittedly qualified for the NLRB's (D) award only by remaining inside the United States illegally. Castro could not even mitigate damages, a duty required by case law, without triggering new IRCA violations, either by tendering false documents to employers or by finding employers willing to ignore IRCA and hire illegal workers. Thus, allowing the NLRB (D) to award back pay to illegal aliens would unduly trench upon explicit statutory prohibitions critical to federal immigration policy and would encourage the successful evasion of apprehension by immigration authorities. Far from "accommodating" IRCA, the NLRB's (D) position, recognizing employer misconduct but discounting the misconduct of illegal alien employees, subverts it. Any perceived deficiency in the NLRB's (D) existing remedial arsenal must be addressed by congressional action, not the courts. Reversed.

DISSENT: (Breyer, J.) The NLRB's (D) limited back pay order would not interfere with the implementation of immigration policy. Rather, it realistically helps to deter unlawful activity that both labor laws and immigration laws seek to prevent. Denying the NLRB's (D) power to award back pay increases an employer's incentive to find and to hire illegal alien employees.

▌ ANALYSIS

Lack of NLRB (D) authority to award back pay does not mean an employer who violates federal labor legislation gets off scot-free. In the *Hoffman* case, the NLRB (D) had already imposed other significant unchallenged sanctions against Hoffman Plastics (P), such as, for example, cease and desist orders and notice posting requirements.

■■▶■

Quicknotes

IMMIGRATION REFORM AND CONTROL ACT OF 1986 Law prohibiting employers from hiring undocumented workers. Employers are required to ask all job applicants for documents to confirm they have the legal right to work in the United States.

NATIONAL LABOR RELATIONS BOARD An agency established pursuant to the National Labor Relations Act for the purpose of prohibiting unfair labor practices by employers and unions.

■■▶■

Wardwell v. Board of Education

Teacher (P) v. School board (D)

529 F.2d 625 (6th Cir. 1976).

NATURE OF CASE: Appeal from denial of injunction and invalidation of a residency requirement.

FACT SUMMARY: Wardwell (P) challenged a Board of Education (D) rule requiring him as a newly hired teacher to live within the city school district where he was to teach.

🏛 RULE OF LAW
Where a continuing-employee residency requirement affecting at most the right of intrastate travel is involved, the rational basis test determines its validity.

FACTS: When Wardwell (P) was hired to teach in the Cincinnati schools, as a condition of his employment he agreed to move into the city school district pursuant to a rule that all newly employed teachers must establish residence within the district within 30 days after employment. The rule permitted those already hired to remain or move outside the district. Wardwell (P) lived outside the district but within the state of Ohio. Despite the requirement, he failed to change his residence. Wardwell (P) filed the present action, challenging the residency requirement on equal protection grounds and seeking injunctive relief and attorney fees. The district court denied the request for an injunction and upheld the validity of the rule. Wardwell (P) argued that the Board of Education's (D) residency requirement infringed his constitutionally protected right to travel, and appealed.

ISSUE: Where a continuing employee residency requirement affecting at most the right of intrastate travel is involved, does the rational basis test determine its validity?

HOLDING AND DECISION: (Miller, J.) Yes. Where a continuing employee residency requirement affecting at most the right of intrastate travel is involved, the rational basis test determines its validity. In its cases, it is clear that the Supreme Court was dealing with the validity of durational residency requirements that penalized recent interstate travel. Unlike the right of intrastate travel at issue in the instant case, restrictions on interstate travel require application of the compelling state interest test. There is no support for Wardwell's (P) theory that the right to intrastate travel has been afforded federal constitutional protection. A number of rational bases exist for the residency requirement of the Cincinnati Board of Education (D). Many other courts have recognized the importance of employees being highly committed to the area in which they work and motivated to find solutions for its problems. Such commitment and motivation, it is not unreasonable to suppose, may best be fostered by requiring teachers to

live and pay taxes in the place where they are employed to work. The possession of an Ohio certificate establishes only that a teacher has met certain minimum standards. It does not entitle him to a teaching position with any particular local school board. Local boards are free to impose additional qualifications and conditions of employment or to adopt higher standards. Affirmed.

▶ *ANALYSIS*

The court declared that it did not believe that the residency requirement must fail because it applied only to newly hired teachers employed by the Cincinnati schools. The Supreme Court has pointed out that there is no constitutional requirement that regulations must cover every class to which they might be applied. It has further stated that "if the classification has some 'reasonable basis', it does not offend the Constitution simply because the classification is not made with mathematical nicety or because in practice it results in some inequality." *Dandridge v. Williams*, 397 U.S. 471 (1970).

Quicknotes

EQUAL PROTECTION CLAUSE A constitutional guarantee that no person should be denied the same protection of the laws enjoyed by other persons in like circumstances.

RATIONAL BASIS REVIEW A test employed by the court to determine the validity of a statute in equal protection actions, whereby the court determines whether the challenged statute is rationally related to the achievement of a legitimate state interest.

RIGHT TO TRAVEL Constitutional guaranty affording the privileges and benefits of one state to citizens of another residing therein for the statutory period.

Starbucks Corp. v. Superior Court

Corporation (D) v. Job applicants (P)

Ca. Ct. App., 86 Cal. Rptr. 3d 482 (2008).

NATURE OF CASE: Appeal from trial court decision denying motion for summary judgment.

FACT SUMMARY: A class of job applicants contended that Starbucks Corp.'s (D) application form impermissibly inquired as to whether the job applicants had any prior marijuana convictions more than two years old.

> ## 🏛 RULE OF LAW
> A plaintiff seeking to recover for an alleged illegal question on an employment application regarding prior criminal history must prove he or she qualifies as an aggrieved person with an injury protected by an applicable statute.

FACTS: A putative class of 135,000 job applicants to Starbucks Corp. (D) brought this action against Starbucks (D) based on an alleged illegal question on Starbucks' (D) job application. Specifically, Starbucks (D) asked whether the applicant had been convicted of a crime in the last seven years. In California, statutory law dictates that applicants need not report any convictions for any marijuana related offenses that are more than two years old. On the back of the form, Starbucks (D) included a disclaimer at the end of a 346-word paragraph that California residents must only provide information for marijuana related offenses less than two years old. The class brought this action on the grounds the application is in violation of the statute because page one of the application seeks all convictions for the past seven years and that the page-two disclaimer was buried "within a block of type" at the end of a long paragraph. The trial court denied Starbucks' (D) motion for summary judgment on the grounds there was a triable issue of fact as to the effectiveness of the disclaimer. The lower court also concluded that proof of damages was not an essential element to the plaintiffs' claims. During discovery, two of the lead plaintiffs testified they had read the disclaimer and understood they did not need to report marijuana offenses more than two years old. Also, none of the 135,000 applicants had any prior marijuana related offenses. Starbucks (D) appealed the denial of the motion.

ISSUE: Must a plaintiff seeking to recover for an alleged illegal question on an employment application regarding prior criminal history prove he or she qualifies as an aggrieved person with an injury protected by an applicable statute?

HOLDING AND DECISION: (Ikola, J.) Yes. A plaintiff seeking to recover for an alleged illegal question on an employment application regarding prior criminal history must prove he or she qualifies as an aggrieved person with an injury protected by an applicable statute. As an initial matter, the court has serious reservations about Starbucks' (D) poor placement of the disclaimer regarding California residents. If that information had immediately followed the question on convictions, summary judgment would be appropriate. However, the class action fails for two other reasons. First, two of the plaintiffs testified they had actually read the disclaimer and understood they were under no obligation to report any older marijuana convictions. Second, none of the plaintiffs were aggrieved by the alleged illegal question in any event. To allow the plaintiffs here to move forward without evidence of damages would create a new class of job seekers whose purpose was solely to fill out defective applications in order to pursue litigation. The law does not support such activity. Because there is no issue of fact that the California disclaimer was unambiguous, summary judgment shall be granted to Starbucks (D). Reversed.

▶ ANALYSIS

Essentially, the appeals court here determined the statute limiting disclosure of marijuana offenses did not require that employers be held strictly liable for any violation of that statute. The plaintiffs must still prove actual damages as an element of their case.

■━■

Quicknotes

CLASS ACTION A suit commenced by a representative on behalf of an ascertainable group that is too large to appear in court, who shares a commonality of interests and who will benefit from a successful result.

SUMMARY JUDGMENT Judgment rendered by a court in response to a motion made by one of the parties, claiming that the lack of a question of material fact in respect to an issue warrants disposition of the issue without consideration by the jury.

■━■

Lysak v. Seiler Corp.

Pregnant woman employee (P) v. Company (D)

Mass. Sup. Jud. Ct., 614 N.E.2d 991 (1993).

NATURE OF CASE: Appeal from denial of directed verdict following defense verdict in wrongful termination action.

FACT SUMMARY: During an employment interview, prospective employee Lysak (P) told the president of Seiler Corp. (D) that she had no intention of having any more children, when in fact she was pregnant at the time of the interview.

🏛 RULE OF LAW
An employer may lawfully discharge an employee who makes unsolicited, volunteered, false statements about pregnancy in a job interview.

FACTS: While interviewing for a job at Seiler Corp. (D), Lysak (P) voluntarily told Zammer, Seiler Corp.'s (D) president, that she was career oriented and did not plan to have any more children. One month after she was hired by Seiler Corp. (D), she told Zammer that she was pregnant. Zammer felt personally betrayed by her lie and believed that he could not trust her anymore. He terminated her employment but agreed to use her as an independent contractor. Lysak (P) subsequently brought suit against Seiler Corp. (D) for sex discrimination, admitting that she was pregnant at the time of the interview but denying that she and Zammer had discussed her plans regarding children. The jury found for Seiler Corp. (D), the court rejected Lysak's (P) motion for a directed verdict, and Lysak (P) appealed.

ISSUE: May an employer lawfully discharge an employee who makes unsolicited, volunteered, false statements about pregnancy in a job interview?

HOLDING AND DECISION: (O'Connor, J.) Yes. An employer may lawfully discharge an employee who makes unsolicited, volunteered, false statements about pregnancy in a job interview. In support of her motion for a directed verdict, Lysak (P) relied on *Kraft v. Police Comm'r of Boston*, 571 N.E.2d 380 (1991), which held that an employer may not discharge an employee because of an employee's false responses to the employer's unlawful inquiries. Lysak's (P) reliance on *Kraft* is misplaced. There is no evidence in this case that Zammer asked Lysak (P) whether she was pregnant or if she planned to have more children. Therefore, Seiler Corp. (D) could have properly based an employment decision on an unsolicited misrepresentation by Lysak (P) concerning pregnancy, if the jury found those to be the facts. Affirmed.

▶ ANALYSIS

Conversely, employers may encounter problems when their interviewers make misrepresentations during job interviews. In *Stewart v. Jackson & Nash*, 976 F.2d 86 (2d Cir. 1992), the court found that a law firm that had induced an attorney to leave her job by promising her, falsely, that she would be given certain responsibilities could be held liable for fraudulent inducement. Employers may also find themselves contractually bound by misstatements made by interviewers. See *Weiner v. McGraw-Hill, Inc.*, 443 N.E.2d 441 (N.Y. 1982).

■▬■

Quicknotes

DIRECTED VERDICT A verdict ordered by the court in a jury trial.

DISCRIMINATION Unequal treatment of individuals without justification.

JURY INSTRUCTIONS A communication made by the court to a jury regarding the applicable law involved in a proceeding.

MISREPRESENTATION A statement or conduct by one party to another that constitutes a false representation of fact.

■▬■

Kadlec Medical Center v. Lakeview Anesthesia Associates

Hospital (P) v. Medical practice and hospital (D)

527 F.3d 412 (5th Cir. 2008).

NATURE OF CASE: Appeal from jury decision in favor of plaintiff.

FACT SUMMARY: Kadlec Medical Center (Kadlec) (P) hired an anesthesiologist that the defendants had previously terminated for drug use. Kadlec (P) alleged the defendants, a hospital and a medical practice, affirmatively misrepresented the anesthesiologist's credentials.

🏛 **RULE OF LAW**
Except where an employer chooses to speak about a former employee, an employer has no affirmative legal duty to disclose negative information about the employee.

FACTS: In 2000, Lakeview Anesthesia Associates (LAA) (D) fired Dr. Robert Berry for on the job use of Demerol. As part of his practice, Dr. Berry provided services to Lakeview Medical Regional Health Center (Lakeview Medical) (D). After his termination, Kadlec Medical Center (Kadlec) (P) requested credentialing information about Dr. Berry from both LAA (D) and Lakeview Medical (D). Two other shareholders of LAA (D) wrote letters of recommendation to Kadlec (P) in which they referred to Dr. Berry as an excellent clinician. The letters said nothing about the investigation and subsequent termination of Dr. Berry for drug use. Lakeview Medical (D) provided only a one sentence reply, informing Kadlec (P) only of the dates when Dr. Berry performed services at the hospital. After Dr. Berry began working at Kadlec (P), his drug use continued, leading to an incident where Dr. Berry failed to revive a patient. The patient subsequently slipped into a coma. The family of the patient sued Kadlec (P), which it resolved in an $8,000,000 settlement. Kadlec (P) then brought this suit in diversity alleging that LAA (D) and Lakeview Medical (D) intentionally and negligently misrepresented the credentials of Dr. Berry. A jury decided in favor of Kadlec (P), and LAA (D) and Lakeview Medical (D) appealed to the Fifth Circuit Court of Appeals.

ISSUE: Except where an employer chooses to speak about a former employee, does an employer have an affirmative legal duty to disclose negative information about the employee?

HOLDING AND DECISION: (Reavley, J.) No. Except where an employer chooses to speak about a former employee, an employer has no affirmative legal duty to disclose negative information about the employee. First, to prove intentional misrepresentation, there must be a misrepresentation of a material fact, made with intent to deceive, and reliance with a resulting injury. To establish

intentional misrepresentation, a plaintiff must also prove the defendant had a duty to disclose information. For negligent misrepresentation cases, a plaintiff must prove the defendant has a duty to supply correct information, a breach of that duty based upon an omission or affirmative misrepresentation, and damages. A party may keep silent and violate no duty of law. However, for negligent misrepresentation cases, once a party volunteers information, that information must be correct. Because the letters from the LAA (D) clinicians offered only excellent recommendations of Dr. Berry only two months after his termination, those letters were obviously affirmatively misleading. However, the one line letter from Lakeview Medical (D) did not provide any positive information about Dr. Berry. Accordingly, the hospital did not make any misleading affirmative representations. Kadlec (P) argues this court should recognize a duty to disclose negative information on the part of a private employer. Sitting in diversity, this federal court cannot say that the state of Louisiana would impose an affirmative duty to disclose negative information on employers. Currently, a duty to disclose only exists where there is a special fiduciary or confidential relationship between the parties. The existence of this duty is a question of law. Here, unlike LAA (D) whose clinicians opened themselves up to liability by making false statements, Lakeview Medical (D) did not have a duty to disclose negative information. Kadlec (P) and Lakeview Medical (D) had no fiduciary or contractual relationship. Moreover, employers in Lakeview Medical's (D) position justifiably fear defamation claims if the employer reports negative information about a former employee. Accordingly, the jury decision against Lakeview Medical (D) is reversed outright, and the remainder of the jury verdict against LAA (D) is also vacated. The case is remanded for a determination as to whether the fault percentage amounts and damage assessments against LAA (D) may now change in light of this decision. Reversed and remanded.

▶ **ANALYSIS**

This decision places employers and in particular, health care institutions, in the difficult position of choosing how much to say about past employees. It may actually serve as an incentive to employers to simply not provide any information at all. Regarding a duty to disclose, the reason courts have failed to impose duties to disclose negative information is the difficulty placed on employers to determine what conduct constitutes negative information. Moreover, it is much easier for courts to make judicial

Continued on next page.

decisions when an employer takes some affirmative action or makes a statement regarding the former employee.

■≡■

Quicknotes

FIDUCIARY DUTY A legal obligation to act for the benefit of another, including subordinating one's personal interests to that of the other person.

MISREPRESENTATION A statement or conduct by one party to another that constitutes a false representation of fact.

NEGLIGENT MISREPRESENTATION A misrepresentation that is made pursuant to a business relationship, in violation of an obligation owed, upon which the plaintiff relies to his detriment.

■≡■

Lewis v. Equitable Life Assurance Society

Employees claiming defamation (P) v. Company (D)

Minn. Sup. Ct., 389 N.W.2d 876 (1986).

NATURE OF CASE: Appeal from award of damages for defamation.

FACT SUMMARY: After being discharged for "gross insubordination," Lewis (P) and three others filed suit, alleging self-compelled defamation.

🏛 RULE OF LAW
In an action for defamation, the publication requirement may be satisfied where the plaintiff was compelled to publish a defamatory statement to a third person if it was foreseeable to the defendant that the plaintiff would be so compelled.

FACTS: Lewis (P) and three others were at-will employees of Equitable Life Assurance Society (Equitable) (D). They (P) were discharged for the stated reason of "gross insubordination." When asked for the first time to travel on company business, Lewis (P) was given inadequate instructions regarding company policy relating to travel advances and expenditures. As a result, her report of those items was not as complete as the company required them to be. After making some changes in the report, at Equitable's (D) request, Lewis (P) refused to make further changes and was then terminated for "gross insubordination." She filed suit, claiming breach of her employment contract, and that she was defamed because Equitable (D) knew she would have to repeat the reason for her discharge to prospective employers. Equitable (D) admitted that Lewis's (P) production and performance was at all times satisfactory and even commendable. Management also admitted that the problems could have been avoided had Lewis (P) been given proper guidelines prior to departing for Pittsburgh. In seeking new employment, Lewis (P) was asked to disclose her reasons for leaving the company and to explain her termination. Only one of the four terminated employees found employment while being completely forthright with a prospective employer about her termination by the company. The jury found in favor of Lewis (P), awarding both compensatory and punitive damages. The court of appeals affirmed but remanded on the issue of contract damages for future harm.

ISSUE: In an action for defamation, may the publication requirement be satisfied where the plaintiff was compelled to publish a defamatory statement to a third person if it was foreseeable to the defendant that the plaintiff would be so compelled?

HOLDING AND DECISION: (Amdahl, C.J.) Yes. In an action for defamation, the publication requirement may be satisfied where the plaintiff was compelled to publish a defamatory statement to a third person if it was foreseeable to the defendant that the plaintiff would be so compelled. Generally, there is no publication where a defendant communicates a statement directly to a plaintiff, who then communicates it to a third person. Company management told Lewis (P) that she had engaged in gross insubordination, and Lewis (P) herself informed prospective employers that she had been terminated for gross insubordination. Courts that have considered the question of defamation by means of "self-publication" have recognized a narrow exception to the general rule that communication of a defamatory statement to a third person by the person defamed is not actionable. Compelled self-publication holds the originator of the defamatory statement liable for damages caused by the statement where the originator knows, or should know, of circumstances where the defamed person would be compelled to publish the statement. However, the originator of the statement will not be held liable if the statement is published under circumstances that make it conditionally privileged and if privilege is not abused. A qualified privilege is abused and therefore lost if the plaintiff demonstrates that the defendant acted with actual malice. The jury found the actual malice that negates the company's entitlement to the privilege. Affirmed as to compensatory damages; reversed as to punitive damages.

▶ ANALYSIS

The court acknowledged that recognition of the compelled self-publication doctrine provided a significant new basis for maintaining a cause of action for defamation and should be cautiously applied. According to the court, however, when properly applied, it need not substantially broaden the scope of liability for defamation. The court also recognized the need for a qualified privilege, which seemed to be the only effective means of addressing the concern that an employer would otherwise subject itself to potential liability for defamation every time it stated the reason for discharging an employee.

■═■

Quicknotes

ACTUAL MALICE The issuance of a publication with knowledge of its falsity or with reckless disregard as to its truth.

DEFAMATION An intentional false publication, communicated publicly in either oral or written form, subjecting a person to scorn, hatred or ridicule, or injuring him or her in relation to his or her occupation or business.

Continued on next page.

PUBLICATION The communicating of a defamatory statement to a third party.

QUALIFIED PRIVILEGE Immunity from liability for libelous or slanderous statements communicated in the execution of a political, judicial, social or personal obligation, unless it is demonstrated that the statement was made with actual malice and knowledge of its falsity.

■━━■

Greenawalt v. Indiana Department of Corrections

Employee (P) v. Employer (D)

397 F.3d 587 (7th Cir. 2005).

NATURE OF CASE: Appeal of dismissal of employee's claim for invasion of privacy.

FACT SUMMARY: Kristin Greenawalt (P) was required to take a psychological test, or be fired from her job at the Indiana Department of Corrections (D). After the test, she filed suit for invasion of privacy under the Fourth Amendment.

🏛 RULE OF LAW
Subjecting a public employee to a mandatory psychological test is not a "search" for purposes of the Fourth Amendment of the U.S. Constitution.

FACTS: Kristin Greenawalt (P) worked as a research analyst for the Indiana Department of Corrections (D). She was told after two years on the job that she would have to undergo a psychological examination to keep her job. After submitting to the test, which probed the details of her personal life, Greenawalt (P) filed suit under the Civil Rights Act of 1871 (42 U.S.C. § 1983) against the Indiana Department of Corrections (D) and her superiors. She alleged that the testing was an unreasonable search in violation of the Fourth Amendment. The district court dismissed the claims.

ISSUE: Is subjecting a public employee to a mandatory psychological test a "search" for purposes of the Fourth Amendment of the U.S. Constitution?

HOLDING AND DECISION: (Posner, J.) No. Subjecting a public employee to a mandatory psychological test is not a "search" for purposes of the Fourth Amendment of the U.S. Constitution. The drawing of blood for alcohol testing, the administration of breathalyzer tests, and the taking of urine samples by the state all have been recognized as "searches" subject to the Fourth Amendment. In addition, the Fourth Amendment also is understood to protect privacy rights. Wiretapping is deemed a search, for example, even though there is no physical trespass and all that is taken is thoughts, often concerning private matters, expressed in conversation. Rifling through papers on an employee's desk also constitutes a search. But while the invasion of privacy caused by submitting to the kind of psychological test given to Greenawalt (P) may have been more profound than the invasion caused by any of these types of "searches," the Fourth Amendment search cannot be broadened to include psychological testing, even when the questions are skillfully designed to elicit information that most people would regard as highly private. The principle of these privacy-based cases cannot be applied to a case involving mere questioning. A search warrant could end up being required whenever a government trial lawyer wanted to cross-examine a witness in a sex case or a law enforcement officer wanted to inquire about a witness's sexual history in a rape case. Even questioning in a credit check would be in peril of being deemed a search of the person about whom the questions were asked. Psychological tests resemble lie-detector tests, which, even though they involve placing censors on the body, have been treated as raising Fifth Amendment, rather than Fourth Amendment, concerns. The ultimate objective is not to get physical evidence, but to obtain testimonial evidence. The Fourth Amendment was not drafted, and has not been interpreted, with interrogations in mind. Affirmed.

▶ ANALYSIS

The court suggested that Greenawalt (P), without a viable Fourth Amendment claim, should pursue tort relief in the state courts, suggesting that public employers may be prohibited from administering certain psychological tests in the Seventh Circuit.

■=■

Quicknotes

FIFTH AMENDMENT Provides that no person shall be compelled to serve as a witness against himself, or be subject to trial for the same offense twice, or be deprived of life, liberty, or property without due process of law.

FOURTH AMENDMENT Provides that persons be secure as to their person and private belongings against unreasonable searches and seizures.

■=■

Harrison v. Benchmark Electronics Huntsville, Inc.

Employee (P) v. Employer (D)

593 F.3d 1206 (11th Cir. 2010).

NATURE OF CASE: Appeal from entry of summary judgment for the defendant.

FACT SUMMARY: After applying for a permanent position at Benchmark Electronics Huntsville, Inc. (Benchmark) (D), Harrison (P) tested positive for use of barbiturates, a drug he took to control his epilepsy. Benchmark (D) then decided not to hire Harrison (P).

🏛 RULE OF LAW
A private right of action exists for employees who allege that their employers have engaged in a prohibited medical inquiry in violation of the Americans with Disabilities Act.

FACTS: Harrison (P), a temporary employee posted at Benchmark Electronics Huntsville, Inc. (Benchmark) (D), suffered from epilepsy. To control his disease, he took barbiturates pursuant to a properly obtained prescription. Harrison (P) applied for a permanent position to debug and repair electronic boards. As part of the application, Harrison (P) consented to a drug test which came back positive. Benchmark's (D) human resources department instructed Doug Anthony, Harrison's (P) supervisor, of the positive result. The company had a procedure where a medical review officer would then determine if there was a medically necessary reason for the presence of the drug. In the presence of Anthony, Harrison (P) informed the medical officer over the phone that he took the drug to control his epilepsy. The medical officer subsequently informed human resources that Harrison's (P) test had been cleared and that he could be hired. Anthony then decided not to hire Harrison (P) and informed Aerotek, the placement firm, not to send Harrison (P) back to Benchmark (D) in the future. Aerotek then terminated Harrison (P) because of alleged performance and attitude issues while at Benchmark (D).

ISSUE: Does a private right of action exist for employees who allege that their employers have engaged in a prohibited medical inquiry in violation of the Americans with Disabilities Act?

HOLDING AND DECISION: (Siler, J.) Yes. A private right of action exists for employees who allege that their employers have engaged in a prohibited medical inquiry in violation of the Americans with Disabilities Act (ADA). Covered employers under the ADA may not conduct medical examinations or make inquiries as to an applicant's disability at the pre-offer stage. The relevant section of the ADA prohibiting such inquiries applies to all applicants, and not just qualified individuals with disabilities. Turning to the legislative history, it is clear Congress sought to prevent questioning that would identify an applicant's disability before the applicant had the opportunity to show he or she could perform the duties of the position. Congress was particularly concerned with those applicants who had hidden disabilities, such as epilepsy. Accordingly, non-disabled and disabled applicants alike may bring suit for violations of the prohibition on pre-offer medical inquiries. There is an exemption to this rule for drug tests. However, applicants who take drugs to control a medical condition still have the right not to disclose their medical condition before a conditional offer of employment has been made. In this case, the facts support a denial of Benchmark's (D) motion for summary judgment. A reasonable jury could have inferred that Anthony's presence in the room while Harrison (P) was on the phone with the medical officer was an impermissible attempt by the employer to learn of Harrison's (P) medical condition. Reversed and remanded.

▶ ANALYSIS

Pre-offer inquiries are traps for the unwary. The standard pursuant to Equal Employment Opportunity Commission (EEOC) regulations is that employers may not ask questions "likely to elicit information" about a disability. When there is a positive drug test, employers may ask if the employee has a prescription for the drug, but nothing further.

■=■

Quicknotes

AMERICANS WITH DISABILITIES ACT (ADA) Prohibits discrimination in employment, housing, transportation and other services on the basis of an individual's physical or mental disabilities.

PRIVATE RIGHT OF ACTION A fact or set of facts the occurrence of which entitle a party to seek judicial relief.

■=■

National Treasury Employees Union v. Von Raab

Union (P) v. Government employer (D)

489 U.S. 656 (1989).

NATURE OF CASE: Appeal from decision vacating injunction against employee drug-testing program.

FACT SUMMARY: After Von Raab (D), Commissioner of Customs, announced implementation of a drug-testing program for employees in certain sensitive positions, the National Treasury Employees Union (P) filed suit, alleging that the program violated the Fourth Amendment provision against unreasonable searches.

🏛 RULE OF LAW
Employee drug testing does not violate the Fourth Amendment proscription against unreasonable searches where the government demonstrates a compelling interest in maintaining a drug-free workforce for certain sensitive positions.

FACTS: In May 1986, Von Raab (D), Commissioner of Customs, announced implementation of a drug-testing program. The tests were made a condition of employment for positions entailing direct involvement in drug interdiction, for positions requiring employees to carry firearms, and for positions requiring employees to handle "classified" material. Customs employees who tested positive for drugs and who could offer no satisfactory explanation were subject to dismissal from the Service. National Treasury Employees Union (Union) (P) brought this suit on behalf of current Customs Service employees who sought covered positions, alleging the drug-testing program violated the Fourth Amendment. The district court agreed and enjoined the drug-testing program. The court of appeals vacated the injunction, and the Union (P) appealed.

ISSUE: Does employee drug testing violate the Fourth Amendment proscription against unreasonable searches where the government demonstrates a compelling interest in maintaining a drug-free workforce for certain sensitive positions?

HOLDING AND DECISION: (Kennedy, J.) No. Employee drug testing does not violate the Fourth Amendment proscription against unreasonable searches where the government demonstrates a compelling interest in maintaining a drug-free workforce for certain sensitive positions. It is settled that the Fourth Amendment protects individuals from unreasonable searches conducted by the government, even when the government acts as an employer. In view of this Court's holding in *Skinner v. Railway Labor Executives' Assn.*, 489 U.S. 602 (1989), that urine tests are searches, it follows that the Customs Service's drug-testing program must meet the reasonableness requirement of the Fourth Amendment. The Government (D) has a compelling interest in ensuring that front-line interdiction personnel are physically fit and have unimpeachable integrity and judgment. The public interest demands effective measures to bar drug users from positions directly involving the interdiction of illegal drugs and also demands effective measures to prevent the promotion of drug users to positions that require the incumbent to carry a firearm. Against these valid public interests, the interference with individual liberty that results from requiring these classes of employees to undergo a urine test must be weighed. While reasonable tests designed to elicit this information doubtless infringe on some privacy expectations, these expectations do not outweigh the Government's (D) compelling interests in safety and in the integrity of our borders. Thus, the testing of employees involved in drug interdiction and those required to carry firearms is reasonable under the Fourth Amendment. However, it is not possible, on the present record, to assess the reasonableness of the Government's (D) testing program insofar as it covers employees who are required "to handle classified material," and the case should be remanded to the court of appeals to clarify the scope of this category of employees subject to testing. Affirmed in part; vacated in part; and remanded for further proceedings.

DISSENT: (Marshall, J.) Here, as in *Skinner*, the Court's abandonment of the Fourth Amendment's express requirement that searches of the person rest on probable cause is unprincipled and unjustifiable.

DISSENT: (Scalia, J.) Absent here is the recitation of even a single instance in which any of the speculated horribles actually occurred. Neither frequency of use nor connection to harm is demonstrated or even likely, making the Customs Service's rules a kind of immolation of privacy and human dignity in symbolic opposition to drug use.

▌ANALYSIS

The Court declared that the national interest in self-protection could be irreparably damaged if those charged with safeguarding it were, because of their own drug use, unsympathetic to their mission of interdicting narcotics. It described the Customs Service as the nation's first line of defense against one of the greatest problems affecting the health and welfare of the population in a "veritable national crisis in law enforcement caused by smuggling of illicit narcotics." Dissenting in *Skinner*, Justices Marshall and Brennan pointed out that grave threats to liberty often

Continued on next page.

come in times of urgency, when constitutional rights seem too extravagant to endure.

■═■

Quicknotes

FOURTH AMENDMENT Provides that persons be secure as to their person and private belongings against unreasonable searches and seizures.

LIBERTY INTEREST A right conferred by the Due Process Clauses of the state and federal constitutions.

SEARCH An inspection conducted in order to obtain evidence to be utilized for the prosecution of a crime.

■═■

Malorney v. B & L Motor Freight, Inc.

Victim of assault (P) v. Employer of perpetrator (D)

Ill. App. Ct., 496 N.E.2d 1086 (1986).

NATURE OF CASE: Interlocutory appeal from order denying defense motion for summary judgment in action for damages for negligence.

FACT SUMMARY: After B & L Motor Freight, Inc.'s (B & L) (D) employee sexually attacked her in the sleeping facilities of the truck which he drove for B & L (D), Malorney (P) filed suit against B & L (D) for negligent hiring for not having checked the employee's negative response to a question concerning prior criminal convictions other than traffic violations.

🏛 RULE OF LAW
A vehicle owner has a duty to deny the entrustment of a vehicle to a driver it knows, or by the exercise of reasonable diligence could have known, is unfit for the job.

FACTS: When B & L Motor Freight, Inc. (B & L) (D) hired Edward Harbour as a truck driver and furnished him with a truck with sleeping facilities, it checked his negative response to an inquiry about any vehicular offenses he may have had, but neglected to check his negative response to an inquiry as to other criminal convictions. Harbour, as it happened, had a history of convictions for violent sex-related crimes, and just the year prior to being hired by B & L (D) he had been arrested for aggravated sodomy of two teenage hitchhikers while driving a truck for another employer. After being hired by B & L (D), Harbour picked up Karen Malorney (P), a 17-year-old hitchhiker. In the sleeping compartment of his truck, he repeatedly raped and sexually assaulted her, threatened to kill her, and viciously beat her. After Harbour released her, Malorney (P) notified police. Harbour was arrested, tried, convicted, and sentenced to 50 years with no parole. Malorney (P) charged B & L (D) with recklessness and willful and wanton misconduct in negligently hiring Harbour as an over-the-road driver without adequately checking his background before providing a vehicle with a sleeping compartment. She sought compensatory and punitive damages from B & L (D). In filing its motion for summary judgment, B & L (D) contended that it had no duty to verify Harbour's negative response to the question regarding criminal convictions because it was not reasonably foreseeable that he would use the truck to pick up and sexually assault a hitchhiker, and that to impose such a duty would be against public policy by placing too great a burden on employers. The trial court denied B & L's (D) motion for summary judgment, and B & L (D) filed an interlocutory appeal.

ISSUE: Does a vehicle owner have a duty to deny the entrustment of a vehicle to a driver it knows, or by the exercise of reasonable diligence could have known, is unfit for the job?

HOLDING AND DECISION: (Murray, J.) Yes. A vehicle owner has a duty to deny the entrustment of a vehicle to a driver it knows, or by the exercise of reasonable diligence could have known, is unfit for the job. B & L (D) correctly argued that the existence of a duty is a question of law to be determined by the court, rather than by the fact finder. However, once a duty has been found, the question of whether the duty was properly performed is a fact question to be decided by the trier of fact, whether court or jury. Under prior holdings, it is not essential that one should have foreseen the precise injury that resulted from the act or omission. It is clear that B & L (D) had a duty to entrust its truck to a competent employee fit to drive an over-the-road truck equipped with a sleeping compartment. Thus, the issue of whether B & L (D) breached its duty to hire a competent driver who was to be entrusted with one of their over-the-road trucks now becomes one of fact. Based on the circumstances of this case, it is apparent that reasonable persons could arrive at different conclusions as to whether B & L (D) used due care in the performance of this duty when it employed Harbour. Questions of negligence, due care, and proximate cause are questions of fact to be determined by the fact finder. The order denying summary judgment for B & L (D) was properly denied. Affirmed and remanded.

▶ ANALYSIS

There are two types of negligent hiring cases—an injury of a third party by an employee, as in the instant case, or an injury by an employee of a co-employee. Because in many states access to information about criminal convictions (or other contacts with the criminal justice system) is restricted, and thus not easily available to prospective or current employers, employers may not be able to learn the true criminal history of a prospective employee. If the employer uses due diligence in its check on an applicant's past under applicable legal restrictions, it should be able to satisfy the burden. An additional problem today is the reluctance of prior employers to divulge an employee's arrest or criminal record for fear of liability for defamation or invasion of privacy.

Continued on next page.

Quicknotes

DUE CARE The degree of care that can be expected from a reasonably prudent person under similar circumstances; synonymous with ordinary care.

DUTY An obligation owed by one individual to another.

FORESEEABILITY A reasonable expectation that an act or omission would result in injury.

NEGLIGENT ENTRUSTMENT The negligent lending of a dangerous instrument to a person whom the lender knows, or has reason to know, will utilize it so as to pose an unreasonable risk of injury to others.

■═■

Discrimination

Quick Reference Rules of Law

McDonnell Douglas Corp. v. Green

Former employer (D) v. Laid-off employee (P)

411 U.S. 792 (1973).

NATURE OF CASE: Appeal from remand of action under Title VII of the Civil Rights Act of 1964.

FACT SUMMARY: Green (P), a former employee of McDonnell Douglas Corp. (D), was denied re-employment based on his participation in illegal protests of McDonnell Douglas's (D) discriminatory employment practices.

⚖ RULE OF LAW
If a prima facie case of racial discrimination is rebutted by the defendant, the complainant must then show that the reason given for rejection was a pretext for discrimination.

FACTS: Green (P), a black man, had been employed by McDonnell Douglas Corp. (D) as a mechanic for eight years prior to being laid off during a reduction of McDonnell Douglas's (D) workforce. In protest of this layoff and McDonnell Douglas's (D) discriminatory hiring practices, Green (P) participated in illegal demonstrations against McDonnell Douglas (D), for which he was arrested and fined. When McDonnell Douglas (D) began to solicit applicants for Green's (P) previous position, Green (P) applied but was rejected because of his activities against the company. The district court rejected Green's (P) Title VII claim, stating that nothing in the Act prevented an employer from refusing to rehire a person who undertook illegal actions against them. The Eighth Circuit affirmed that unlawful protests were not protected by Title VII but remanded for trial on Green's (P) claims relating to discriminatory hiring practices. McDonnell Douglas (D) appealed, and the Supreme Court granted review.

ISSUE: If a prima facie case of racial discrimination is rebutted by the defendant, must the complainant then show that the reason given for rejection of the complainant was a pretext for discrimination?

HOLDING AND DECISION: (Powell, J.) Yes. If a prima facie case of racial discrimination is rebutted by the defendant, the complainant must then show that the reason given for rejection of complainant was a pretext for discrimination. The purpose of Title VII is to eliminate employment procedures that have a discriminatory effect. The Act does not require an employer to rehire an employee who has undertaken illegal activities against the company. However, the employee should be given the opportunity to show that the apparently legitimate reason for rejecting the applicant was merely an excuse for discrimination. Here, Green (P) must be permitted to show that the policy of not hiring applicants who have participated in illegal activities against McDonnell Douglas (D) was either a pretext or exercised discriminatorily. Affirmed.

▶ ANALYSIS

To establish a prima facie case of racial discrimination, a complainant must show that (1) he is a member of a racial minority; (2) he was a qualified applicant for the position the employer was filling; (3) he was not chosen in spite of his qualifications; and (4) the position remained open after his rejection. The burden then shifts to the employer to articulate some legitimate nondiscriminatory reason for the employer's rejection. The burden then shifts a third time, pursuant to *Green*, to the complainant to demonstrate, if possible, that the employer's presumptively valid reason was in fact a cover-up for a racially discriminatory decision.

◼▬◼

Quicknotes

DISCRIMINATION Unequal treatment of a class of persons.

DISCRIMINATORY IMPACT The effect of an action that affects one group of persons more significantly than another; insufficient to prove discriminatory intent on its own.

DISPARATE TREATMENT Unequal treatment of employees or of applicants for employment without justification.

◼▬◼

Price Waterhouse v. Hopkins

Female claiming sex discrimination (P) v. Company (D)

490 U.S. 228 (1989).

NATURE OF CASE: Appeal from award of back-pay and other monetary relief for sex discrimination.

FACT SUMMARY: After her candidacy for partnership was held for reconsideration the following year and the partners later refused to re-propose her for partnership, Hopkins (P) sued Price Waterhouse (D) under Title VII, charging sex discrimination.

🏛 RULE OF LAW
When an employee proves that her gender played a motivating part in an employment decision, her employer may avoid a finding of liability only by proving by a preponderance of the evidence that it would have made the same decision had it not taken her gender into account.

FACTS: Hopkins (P) was a senior manager in an office of Price Waterhouse (D) when she was proposed for partnership in 1982. Her candidacy was held for reconsideration the following year. There were some complaints about Hopkins's (P) interpersonal skills, but there were also signs that some of the partners reacted negatively to her personality because she was a woman. In order to improve her chances for partnership, Hopkins (P) was told she should walk more femininely, talk more femininely, dress more femininely, wear makeup, have her hair styled, and wear jewelry. When the partners in her office later refused to re-propose her for partnership, Hopkins (P) filed suit against Price Waterhouse (D) under Title VII of the Civil Rights Act of 1964, charging that the firm had discriminated against her on the basis of sex. The district court held that Price Waterhouse (D) unlawfully discriminated against Hopkins (P) on the basis of sex by consciously giving credence and effect to partners' comments that resulted from sex stereotyping. It further held that Price Waterhouse (D) failed to show by clear and convincing evidence that it would have placed Hopkins's (P) candidacy on hold even absent this discrimination. Price Waterhouse (D) appealed.

ISSUE: When an employee proves that her gender played a motivating part in an employment decision, may her employer avoid a finding of liability only by proving by a preponderance of the evidence that it would have made the same decision had it not taken her gender into account?

HOLDING AND DECISION: (Brennan, J.) Yes. When an employee proves that her gender played a motivating part in an employment decision, her employer may avoid a finding of liability only by proving by a preponderance of the evidence that it would have made the same

decision had it not taken her gender into account. In passing Title VII, Congress announced that sex, race, religion, and national origin are not relevant to the selection, evaluation, or compensation of employees. Title VII thus eliminates certain bases for distinguishing among employees while otherwise preserving employers' freedom of choice. This balance between employee rights and employer prerogatives turns out to be decisive in the instant case. In the specific context of sex stereotyping, an employer who acts on the basis of a belief that a woman cannot be aggressive, or that she must not be, has acted on the basis of gender. An employer who objects to aggressiveness in women but whose positions require this trait places women in an intolerable and impermissible catch-22: out of a job if they behave aggressively and out of a job if they don't. Title VII lifts women out of this bind. The courts below held that an employer who has allowed a discriminatory impulse to play a motivating part in an employment decision must prove by clear and convincing evidence that it would have made the same decision in the absence of discrimination. The better rule is that the employer must make this showing by a preponderance of the evidence. Reversed and remanded for further proceedings.

CONCURRENCE: (O'Connor, J.) What is required is what Ann Hopkins (P) showed here: direct evidence that decision-makers placed substantial negative reliance on an illegitimate criterion in reaching their decision.

DISSENT: (Kennedy, J.) Hopkins (P) failed to meet the requisite standard of proof after a full trial, and the case should be remanded for entry of judgment in favor of Price Waterhouse (D).

▶ ANALYSIS

Hopkins (P) resigned before filing her action for an order making her a partner, plus an award of backpay and other monetary relief. The district court ruled that she was entitled to monetary relief, but not to an order making her a partner because she failed to prove she was constructively discharged. On remand, the district court determined that Price Waterhouse (D) had failed to carry its burden of demonstrating that Hopkins (P) would not have been offered a partnership absent the gender stereotyping surrounding its consideration of her. The court required Price Waterhouse (D) to offer Hopkins (P) a partnership effective July 1, 1990, with compensation and benefits retroactive to July 1, 1983. However, because the court felt she had not pursued with sufficient diligence equivalent work

Continued on next page.

during those years, it awarded backpay of only $371,175. *Hopkins v. Price Waterhouse*, 737 F. Supp. 1202 (D.D.C. 1990).

■══■

Quicknotes

CLEAR AND CONVINCING PROOF   An evidentiary standard requiring a demonstration that the fact sought to be proven is reasonably certain.

PREPONDERANCE OF EVIDENCE   A standard of proof requiring the trier of fact to determine whether the fact sought to be established is more probable than not.

TITLE VII OF THE CIVIL RIGHTS ACT OF 1964   Prohibits employment discrimination based on sex. Disparate-treatment cases focus on intent rather than effects.

■══■

Preston v. Wisconsin Health Fund

Employee (P) v. Employer (D)

397 F.3d 539 (7th Cir. 2005).

NATURE OF CASE: Appeal of district court grant of summary judgment for the employer.

FACT SUMMARY: Jay Preston (P) was fired and replaced by a female coworker with substantially less experience than he. He sued his employer, alleging sex discrimination.

RULE OF LAW

When no reason is given why men might be expected to discriminate against men, the plaintiff must present some evidence beyond the bare fact that a woman got a job that a man wanted to get or keep, in order to raise a triable issue of discrimination.

FACTS: The Wisconsin Health Fund (Fund) (D) provides health services through clinics it owns and by paying for treatment obtained elsewhere by participants. The Fund (D) had been in financial trouble for years. Jay Preston (P), the longtime director of the dental clinic and an M.B.A. as well as a dentist, presented Bruce Trojak, who was the Fund's (D) chief executive office (CEO), with a business plan setting forth his ideas for turning around the dental clinic. Trojak nevertheless fired Preston and replaced him with Linda Hamilton, who Preston (P) alleged had no apparent credentials for the job other than being a dentist. Preston (P) sued the Fund (D), Trojak, and Hamilton, alleging sex discrimination under Title VII of the 1964 Civil Rights Act and that Trojak and Hamilton had conspired to destroy his contractual relationship with the Fund (D) in violation of the state's law against tortious interference with a contract. Preston (P) claimed that Trojak and Hamilton were having an affair, and there was evidence that they frequently dined together and sometimes after dinner would go to his apartment. Trojak and Hamilton claimed that the trips to his apartment were just to discuss the future of the dental clinic. But Hamilton admitted that she told Trojak about her desire for the dental director position during those meetings. The trial court granted summary judgment for the Fund (D), dismissing Preston's (P) claims, and he appealed, arguing that he had presented enough evidence to get to the jury on both claims.

ISSUE: When no reason is given why men might be expected to discriminate against men, must the plaintiff present some evidence beyond the bare fact that a woman got a job that a man wanted to get or keep, in order to raise a triable issue of discrimination?

HOLDING AND DECISION: (Posner, J.) Yes. When no reason is given why men might be expected to discriminate against men, the plaintiff must present some

evidence beyond the bare fact that a woman got a job that a man wanted to get or keep, in order to raise a triable issue of discrimination. Preston's (P) sex discrimination claim failed because his primary allegation—that Trojak fired him and gave Hamilton his job because the two were romantically involved—only described favoritism, not bias based on sex. That is, the favoritism shown Hamilton was not based on a belief that women are better workers than men. Also, the favoritism shown Hamilton would likely not affect the workplace, because the disadvantaged competitor could have been a man or a woman. Preston's (P) additional allegations that Trojak gave large raises to several women and that there was talk in the office about "Bruce and his harem" did not save his claim, because he failed to provide any details that would enable a jury to link the raises to the recipients' sex. Affirmed.

ANALYSIS

Keep in mind that Title VII is not a catchall for all unfair employment decisions. Title VII applies only to those unfair employment decisions that are based on discrimination covered by the statute. In addition, courts are mindful, generally, that most employment is at-will, a status that often weighs against a finding of discrimination in all but the most egregious cases.

■=■

Quicknotes

TORTIOUS INTERFERENCE WITH CONTRACTUAL RELATIONSHIP An intentional tort whereby a defendant intentionally elicits the breach of a valid contract resulting in damages.

■=■

Back v. Hastings on Hudson Union Free School District

Employee (P) v. Employer (D)

365 F.3d 107 (2d Cir. 2004).

NATURE OF CASE: Appeal of dismissal of sex bias case.

FACT SUMMARY: A teacher brought sex discrimination claims against her former supervisors at an elementary school, alleging that the reason she was denied tenure was because she is a young mother.

RULE OF LAW
(1) Stereotypes related to motherhood and employment can constitute sex discrimination under the principles of equal protection.
(2) This type of bias can be shown without comparative evidence concerning fathers.

FACTS: Elana Back (P) was hired as school psychologist on a three-year tenure track. Her responsibilities included counseling and performing psychological evaluations of students, assisting teachers with students who acted out in class, and working with parents on issues related to their children. For two years, she received outstanding evaluations from her two immediate superiors and was repeatedly assured that she would receive tenure. After she returned from maternity leave during her second year, however, circumstances changed substantially. One of her immediate supervisors allegedly told Back (P) for the first time on January 8, 2001, that she might not support her for tenure, citing what Back (P) characterized as minor errors in a report. On April 30, 2001, her supervisors stated for the second time concerns about her ability to balance work and family and told her they would recommend that she not be granted tenure. They suggested that perhaps "another year to assess the child-care situation" was in order. Through her attorney, Back (P) complained to John Russell, the superintendent, about her supervisors' behavior, and they subsequently filed their first negative evaluation of Back (P)—including alleged complaints by parents—and recommended to Russell that she not be granted tenure. Russell investigated, found the complaint meritless, and recommended that Back (P) be denied tenure. A union grievance committee agreed with the "no tenure" recommendation, and Back (P) was notified that her probationary period would be terminated. Back (P) sued the school district (D), Russell, and her two immediate supervisors for sex-based violation of her equal-protection rights and gender discrimination under state law.

ISSUE:
(1) Can stereotypes related to motherhood and employment constitute sex discrimination under the principles of equal protection?

(2) Can this type of bias be shown without comparative evidence concerning fathers?

HOLDING AND DECISION: (Calabresi, J.)
(1) Yes. Stereotypes related to motherhood and employment can constitute sex discrimination under the principles of equal protection. Back's (P) argument that the stereotyped comments about work and motherhood allegedly made to her constitute unlawful discrimination is supported by the Supreme Court's decision in *Price Waterhouse v. Hopkins*, 490 U.S. 228 (1989), which held that the supposition that a woman is unqualified for a position because she does not conform to a gender stereotype is wrong. It takes no special training to discern stereotyping in the view that a woman cannot "be a good mother" and have a job that requires long hours, or in the statement that a mother who received tenure "would not show the same level of commitment she had shown because she had little ones at home."

(2) Yes. This type of bias can be shown without comparative evidence concerning fathers. The defendants' argument that this case requires comparative evidence regarding the treatment of fathers, because this is a case not just based on gender discrimination, but on gender plus parenthood discrimination, is rejected. The stereotyped statements alleged by Back (P) may constitute direct evidence and alone are sufficient to meet her prima facie burden, and together with evidence of her strong work performance are enough to support a finding of pretext. And since Russell relied on Back's immediate supervisors' final, negative evaluation of Back (P) and their recommendations that she not be granted tenure, a jury could find proximate cause. Affirmed in part, reversed in part, and remanded.

▶ ANALYSIS

The court made clear that this was not a "sex plus" case: "The Equal Protection Clause forbids sex discrimination no matter how it is labeled. The relevant issue is not whether a claim is characterized as 'sex plus' or 'gender plus,' but rather, whether the plaintiff provides evidence of purposefully sex-discriminatory acts." But it also made clear that "sex plus" discrimination is actionable under the Civil Rights Act of 1871: "Although we have never explicitly said as much, 'sex plus' discrimination is certainly actionable in a [Civil Rights Act of 1871 (42 U.S.C. § 1983)] case."

Continued on next page.

Quicknotes

EQUAL PROTECTION CLAUSE A constitutional provision that each person be guaranteed the same protection of the laws enjoyed by other persons in like circumstances.

GENDER DISCRIMINATION Unequal treatment of individuals without justification on the basis of their sex.

■━■

Griggs v. Duke Power Co.

Employees claiming discrimination (P) v. Power company (D)

401 U.S. 424 (1971).

NATURE OF CASE: Appeal from decision upholding employment-testing requirements.

FACT SUMMARY: Griggs (P) and others challenged the hiring requirements and testing practices of Duke Power Co. (D) as violative of the Civil Rights Act of 1964, alleging that they rendered a disproportionate number of blacks ineligible for hiring or promotion.

🏛 RULE OF LAW
Practices, procedures, or tests neutral on their face, and even neutral in terms of intent, cannot be maintained if they operate to freeze the status quo of prior discriminatory employment practices.

FACTS: Duke Power Co. (Duke) (D) had a policy of requiring a high-school education for initial assignment to any department except labor, the only department employing blacks. When Duke (D) abandoned its policy of restricting blacks to the labor department in 1965, completion of high school also was made a prerequisite to transfer from labor to any other department. Starting on the date on which Title VII of the Civil Rights Act of 1964 (Act) became effective, Duke (D) made it necessary for new employees to register satisfactory scores on two professionally prepared aptitude tests, as well as to have a high-school education, for placement in any department other than labor. In September 1965, Duke (D) began to permit incumbent employees who lacked a high-school education to qualify for transfer from labor or coal handling to an "inside" job by passing two tests, general intelligence and comprehension. The court of appeals (1) held that, in the absence of a discriminatory purpose, use of such requirements was permitted by the Act and (2) rejected the claim that the requirements' effect of rendering ineligible a markedly disproportionate number of blacks was unlawful under Title VII unless shown to be job related.

ISSUE: Can practices, procedures, or tests neutral on their face, and even neutral in terms of intent, be maintained if they operate to freeze the status quo of prior discriminatory employment practices?

HOLDING AND DECISION: (Burger, C.J.) No. Practices, procedures, or tests neutral on their face, and even neutral in terms of intent, cannot be maintained if they operate to freeze the status quo of prior discriminatory employment practices. In this case, whites did far better on Duke's (D) alternative requirements than blacks. This consequence would appear to be directly traceable to race. Basic intelligence must have the means of articulation to manifest itself fairly in a testing process. Because they are

blacks, Griggs (P) and the others have long received inferior education in segregated schools and this Court has expressly recognized these differences. The objective of Congress in the enactment of Title VII was to achieve equality of employment opportunities and remove barriers that have operated to favor an identifiable group of white employees over other employees. Congress did not intend by Title VII, however, to guarantee a job to every person regardless of qualifications. What Congress required is the removal of artificial, arbitrary, and unnecessary employment barriers that operate invidiously to discriminate on the basis of racial or other impermissible classification. The Act proscribes not only overt discrimination but also practices that are fair in form, but discriminatory in operation. If an employment practice that operates to exclude blacks cannot be shown to be related to job performance, the practice is prohibited. On the record in this case, the high-school completion requirement and the general-intelligence test were adopted, as the court of appeals noted, without meaningful study of their relationship to job-performance ability. While the Act does not preclude the use of testing or measuring procedures, Congress has forbidden giving them controlling force unless they are demonstrably a reasonable measure of job performance. Reversed.

▶ ANALYSIS

The Court explained that the requisite scores used for both initial hiring and transfer approximated the national median for high-school graduates. Thus, the test standards were more stringent than the high-school requirement, since they would screen out approximately half of all high-school graduates. Moreover, 1960 census statistics show that in North Carolina while 34 percent of white males had completed high school, only 12 percent of black males had done so. Similarly, with respect to standardized tests, the Equal Employment Opportunity Commission (EEOC) in one case found that use of a battery of tests, including the Wonderlic and Bennett tests used by Duke (D) in the instant case, resulted in 58 percent of whites, as compared with only 6 percent of blacks, passing the tests.

■ ══ ■

Quicknotes

CIVIL RIGHTS ACT OF 1964 TITLE VII Prohibits employment and discrimination based on race, color, religion, sex or

Continued on next page.

national origin. It applies to all government employers and to all private employers with 15 or more employees.

DISCRIMINATION Unequal treatment of individuals without justification.

INVIDIOUS Arbitrary, without justification.

NEUTRAL Disinterested; not displaying a tendency to favor a particular position.

OVERT Openly.

Wards Cove Packing Co. v. Atonio

Cannery (D) v. Employees claiming racial discrimination (P)

490 U.S. 642 (1989).

NATURE OF CASE: Appeal from finding that employer's employment practices have a disparate impact on minorities.

FACT SUMMARY: Atonio (P) and others employed at the Wards Cove Packing Co. (Wards Cove) (D) cannery filed a class-action suit against Wards Cove (D), alleging that its hiring/promotion practices were responsible for the racial stratification of the work force, denying them and other nonwhites, on the basis of race, employment as noncannery workers.

🏛 RULE OF LAW
Statistical evidence comparing an employer's practice of hiring nonwhite workers in one position to a low percentage of such workers in other positions does not establish a prima facie case of disparate impact of employer's policies in violation of Title VII of the Civil Rights Act of 1964.

FACTS: Wards Cove Packing Co. (Wards Cove) (D), which operated a salmon cannery in a remote area during the salmon runs each year, hired employees and transported them to the cannery. Cannery jobs were nonskilled positions filled primarily by nonwhites, while noncannery jobs were skilled positions filled predominantly by white workers. Virtually all of the noncannery jobs paid more than cannery positions. The predominantly white noncannery workers and the predominantly nonwhite cannery employees lived in separate dormitories and ate in separate mess halls. Atonio (P) filed a class-action suit against Wards Cove (D), alleging that a variety of Wards Cove's (D) hiring/promotion practices were responsible for the racial stratification of the work force, denying him and other nonwhites employment as noncannery workers on the basis of race. Atonio (P) also complained of the racially segregated housing and dining facilities. The court of appeals held that Atonio (P) had made out a prima facie case of disparate impact, relying solely on statistics showing a high percentage of nonwhite workers in the cannery jobs and a low percentage of such workers in the noncannery positions. This appeal followed.

ISSUE: Does statistical evidence comparing an employer's practice of hiring nonwhite workers in one position to a low percentage of such workers in other positions establish a prima facie case of disparate impact of employer's policies in violation of Title VII?

HOLDING AND DECISION: (White, J.) No. Statistical evidence comparing an employer's practice of hiring nonwhite workers in one position to a low percentage of such workers in other positions does not establish a prima facie case of disparate impact of employer's policies in violation of Title VII. However, if an absence of minorities holding skilled positions is due to a lack of qualified nonwhite applicants, an employer's employment practices cannot be said to have had a disparate impact on nonwhites. There can be no doubt that the comparison misconceived the role of statistics in employment-discrimination cases. The proper comparison is between the racial composition of the jobs at issue and the racial composition of the qualified population in the relevant labor market. Such a comparison generally forms the proper basis for the initial inquiry in a disparate-impact case. With respect to the skilled noncannery jobs at issue here, the cannery work force in no way reflected the pool of qualified job applicants or the qualified population in the labor force. Measuring alleged discrimination in the selection of accountants, managers, boat captains, electricians, doctors, and engineers comprising the skilled noncannery positions by comparing the number of nonwhites occupying these jobs to the number of nonwhites filling cannery worker positions is nonsensical. On remand, the courts below must require, as part of Atonio's (P) prima facie case, a demonstration that specific elements of the Wards Cove (D) hiring process had a significantly disparate impact on nonwhites. Meeting that burden of proof with respect to any of Wards Cove's (D) employment practices, the case will shift to any business justification Wards Cove (D) offers for its use of these practices. The court must consider the justifications Wards Cove (D) offers for its use of these practices, and also the availability of alternate practices to achieve the same business ends with less racial impact. Reversed and remanded.

DISSENT: (Stevens, J.) This Court has unanimously held that Title VII of the Civil Rights Act of 1964 prohibits employment practices that have discriminatory effects as well as those that are intended to discriminate. The Court's opinion rejects a long-standing rule of law and underestimates the probative value of evidence of a racially stratified work force.

DISSENT: (Blackmun, J.) The majority's opinion essentially immunizes this industry's discriminatory practices from attack under a Title VII disparate-impact analysis.

▶ ANALYSIS

In this case, the trial court had dismissed for lack of jurisdiction, and the court of appeals affirmed in part,

Continued on next page.

reversed in part, and remanded. On remand, the judgment was for Wards Cove (D), and the court of appeals again affirmed. The court of appeals, in a rehearing en banc, then reversed and remanded solely on the basis of the statistics Atonio (P) presented. According to the Court here, *Griggs v. Duke Power Co.*, 401 U.S. 424 (1971), construed Title VII to proscribe not only overt discrimination but also practices that were facially neutral. Under this basis for liability, known as the "disparate impact" theory, a facially neutral employment practice may be deemed violative of Title VII without evidence of the employer's subjective intent to discriminate as required in "disparate treatment" cases like *Price Waterhouse v. Hopkins*, 490 U.S. 228 (1989).

■══■

Quicknotes

DISCRIMINATORY IMPACT The effect of an action that affects one group of persons more significantly than another; insufficient to prove discriminatory intent on its own.

DISCRIMINATORY PURPOSE Intent to discriminate; must be shown to establish an Equal Protection violation.

DISPARATE TREATMENT Unequal treatment of employees or of applicants for employment without justification.

PRIMA FACIE CASE An action where the plaintiff introduces sufficient evidence to submit the issue to the judge or jury for determination.

■══■

Wilson v. Southwest Airlines Co.

Male job applicants (P) v. Airline (D)

517 F. Supp. 292 (N.D. Tex. 1981).

NATURE OF CASE: Class-action suit challenging an employer's hiring practice as a violation of Title VII of the Civil Rights Act of 1964.

FACT SUMMARY: This class-action suit was filed against Southwest Airlines Co. (Southwest) (D) by Wilson (P) and other male job applicants as a result of Southwest's (D) open refusal to hire males as flight attendants or ticket agents.

> 🏛 **RULE OF LAW**
> Customer preference gives rise to a bona fide occupational qualification (BFOQ) for the sex of an employee only where it is reasonably necessary for the essence or primary function of that business.

FACTS: Wilson (P) and the class of male job applicants he represented challenged Southwest Airlines Company's (Southwest) (D) open refusal to hire males for flight-attendant or ticket-agent positions as a violation of Title VII of the Civil Rights Act of 1964. Southwest (D) conceded that its refusal to hire males was intentional, but contended that the BFOQ exception to Title VII's ban on sex discrimination justified its hiring only females for the public-contact positions in question. Southwest (D) reasoned it could discriminate against males because its attractive female flight attendants and ticket agents personified the airline's "sexy" image promoted by its advertising campaign and fulfilled its public promise to take passengers "skyward with love." Southwest (D) also claimed that maintenance of its females-only hiring policy was crucial to its continued financial success.

ISSUE: Does customer preference give rise to a bona fide occupational qualification for the sex of an employee only where it is reasonably necessary for the essence or primary function of that business?

HOLDING AND DECISION: (Higginbotham, J.) Yes. Customer preference gives rise to a bona fide occupational qualification (BFOQ) for the sex of an employee only where it is reasonably necessary for the essence or primary function of that business. The EEOC has steadfastly adhered to its position that a BFOQ for sex occurs only where it is necessary for the purpose of authenticity or genuineness, e.g., an actor or actress. This court's prior decisions have given rise to a two-step BFOQ test: (1) does the particular job under consideration require that the worker be of one sex only; and, if so, (2) is that requirement reasonably necessary to the "essence" of the employer's business. Applying the first-level test for a BFOQ, with its legal gloss, to Southwest's (D) particular operations results in the conclusion that being female is not a qualification required to perform successfully the jobs of flight attendant and ticket agent with Southwest (D). Accordingly, Southwest's (D) ability to perform its primary business function, the transportation of passengers, would not be jeopardized by hiring males.

⟩ ANALYSIS

The court was aware of only one decision, *Fernandez v. Wynn Oil Co.*, 20 FEP Cases 1162 (C.D. Cal. 1979), where sex was held to be a BFOQ for an occupation not providing primarily sex-oriented services. In *Fernandez*, the court approved restricting the job of international marketing director to males because the position primarily involved attracting and transacting business with Latin American and Southeast Asian customers who would not feel comfortable doing business with a woman. However, *Fernandez* was reversed in 1981.

■■■

Quicknotes

BONA FIDE OCCUPATIONAL QUALIFICATION A statutory exception to the prohibition on discrimination in employment if the individual's sex, religion or national origin is a necessary qualification for the operation of the business.

■■■

Ferrill v. Parker Group, Inc.

Former employee (P) v. Employer (D)

168 F.3d 468 (11th Cir. 1999).

NATURE OF CASE: Appeal from a summary judgment award for plaintiff in an employment-discrimination suit.

FACT SUMMARY: When Ferrill (P), a black woman, was assigned by The Parker Group, Inc. (D) to make "race-matched" calls to other blacks, she sued her employer for racial discrimination on the basis of her job assignment.

🏛 RULE OF LAW
A defendant who acts with no racial animus but makes job assignments on the basis of race can be held liable for intentional discrimination under § 1981 of the Civil Rights Act of 1991.

FACTS: The Parker Group, Inc. (TPG) (D), a telephone-marketing corporation performing work for a political campaign, hired Shirley Ferrill (P), a black woman, to make "get-out-the-vote" calls for various political candidates preceding the November 1994 election. She was assigned to "race-matched" calls in which she used a "black script" to her callers, as opposed to a "white script" which white TPG employees used for their calls to white voters. Also, the black callers were physically separated from the white callers. She was laid off after the election. Ferrill (P) subsequently filed a lawsuit against TPG (D) under § 1981 of the Civil Rights Act of 1991, alleging race discrimination in her job assignment. The district court granted Ferrill's (P) motion for summary judgment on her unlawful job assignment claim, and TPG (D) appealed.

ISSUE: Can a defendant who acts with no racial animus but makes job assignments on the basis of race be held liable for intentional discrimination under § 1981 of the Civil Rights Act of 1991?

HOLDING AND DECISION: (Alaimo, J.) Yes. A defendant who acts with no racial animus but makes job assignments on the basis of race can be held liable for intentional discrimination under § 1981 of the Civil Rights Act of 1991. Discrimination in employment on the basis of protected traits such as sex, religion, national origin, or race, may be permissible under certain circumstances. For example, it may be permissible where race is a bona fide occupational qualification reasonably necessary to the normal operation of a particular business or enterprise. Also, where the use of race in job assignments is part of an authorized affirmative-action program, there is no discrimination. Here, however, Ferrill's (P) assignment to call African-Americans was not affirmative action nor benign discrimination needed to correct racial imbalance. Rather, it was based on a racial stereotype that blacks would respond to blacks, and on the premise that Ferrill's (P) race was directly related to her ability to do the job. Here, TPG (D) admitted that its assignments of "get-out-the-vote" calls and scripts were made on the basis of race and that TPG (D) employees were in fact physically segregated on the basis of race. TPG's (D) admission is direct evidence of disparate treatment on the basis of race and sustains Ferrill's (P) prima facie case. Because TPG (D) did not present a First Amendment argument in the district court, this court will not consider its argument on appeal that their practice of using race-matched calling is political speech protected by the First and Fourteenth Amendments. Specifically, TPG (D) argues that its clients, political candidates, should be able to choose the particular mode of political expression, namely, race-matched get-out-the-vote calling. Affirmed in part and reversed in part.

▶ ANALYSIS

The *Ferrill* court noted that racial animus and intent to discriminate are not synonymous. So long as discrimination is shown, racial animus is not required to exist to sustain a § 1981 claim.

■=■

Quicknotes

BENIGN DISCRIMINATION Government action which favors particular minorities and which is subject to a strict scrutiny standard.

DISCRIMINATORY IMPACT The effect of an action that affects one group of persons more significantly than another; insufficient to prove discriminatory intent on its own.

DISPARATE TREATMENT Unequal treatment of employees or of applicants for employment without justification.

■=■

Staub v. Proctor Hospital

Employee (P) v. Employer (D)

560 F.3d 647 (7th Cir. 2009), *cert. granted*, ___ U.S. ___, 130 S. Ct. 2089 (2010).

NATURE OF CASE: Appeal from jury verdict in favor of the plaintiff.

FACT SUMMARY: The head of Proctor Hospital's (D) human resources department terminated Staub (P) after conducting her own investigation of his job performance. Staub (P) alleged his direct supervisor discriminated against him because Staub (P) was a member of the Army Reserves.

🏛 **RULE OF LAW**
Where a decisionmaker conducts his or her own independent investigation into an employee's job performance and does not rely upon one source of information, the employer shall not be liable for the discriminatory animus of other employees.

FACTS: Staub (P), an Army Reservist, worked at Proctor Hospital (Proctor) (D) as an angiography technologist in the Diagnostic Imaging Department of the hospital. His Army Reserve duties consisted of one weekend a month and two weeks of training during the summer. Prior to 2000, Staub (P) did not have to work weekend shifts. Then, in 2000, Staub's (P) new supervisor, Janice Mulally, began placing him on weekend shifts. Mulally openly mocked Staub's (P) Army Reserve duties; once referring to them as "bullshit." Another supervisor, Korenchuk, called Staub's (P) duties a "waste of taxpayers' money." Staub (P) did also have a history of attitude problems. During his ten years at the hospital, many nurses complained about his behavior, including two who resigned rather than continue working with him. In January of 2004, Staub (P) allegedly failed to assist a different section of the Imaging Department and received a written warning that he must inform his supervisors of his whereabouts if he left the imaging diagnostics area. On the day of termination, Staub (P) went to lunch and left a message for his supervisor as to his location. Upon his return, his supervisor stated he did not know where Staub (P) had gone. His supervisor escorted Staub (P) to the office of the head of human resources, Ms. Buck. After conducting her own investigation and review of Staub's (P) employment history, Ms. Buck terminated Staub (P) at that time. Staub (P) brought this suit pursuant to the Uniformed Services Employment and Reemployment Rights Act on the grounds his termination was because of his association with the military. A jury agreed and awarded Staub (P) $57,000 in damages. Proctor (D) appealed.

ISSUE: Where a decisionmaker conducts his or her own independent investigation into an employee's job performance and does not rely upon one source of information, shall the employer be liable for the discriminatory animus of other employees?

HOLDING AND DECISION: (Evans, J.) No. Where a decisionmaker conducts his or her own independent investigation into an employee's job performance and does not rely upon one source of information, the employer shall not be liable for the discriminatory animus of other employees. Employers typically are not held liable for the discriminatory animus of their nondecisionmaking employees, unless the decisionmaker acts solely upon the recommendation of a discriminatory employee without any further investigation. Here, the critical fact is that Staub (P) admitted at trial that Ms. Buck, Proctor's (D) decisionmaker, did not terminate him because of any military based animus. Instead, the facts show Ms. Buck conducted her own investigation and made her decision based upon Staub's (P) entire tenure with Proctor (D), including the frequent complaints about his attitude and poor treatment of other hospital staff. Reversed.

▶ *ANALYSIS*

Employers obviously cannot base their personnel decisions solely upon the discriminatory actions or opinions of low level employees. However, there will be times when employers will conduct perfunctory investigations simply to comply with the holding of this case. Aggrieved employees in this situation should examine carefully the steps the decisionmaker takes as part of his or her investigation and the specific grounds for the alleged adverse action.

■■■

Quicknotes

ANIMUS Intention, will.

DISCRIMINATORY PURPOSE Intent to discriminate.

■■■

Yanowitz v. L'Oreal USA, Inc.

Employee (P) v. Employer (D)

Cal. Sup. Ct., 116 P.3d 1123 (2005).

NATURE OF CASE: Appeal by employer of state court of appeals revival of employee's retaliation claim.

FACT SUMMARY: Elysa Yanowitz (P) objected to her supervisor's order that she fire a sales associate who was "not good looking enough" and hire someone "hot," but did not explicitly complain about his behavior.

> ## 🏛 RULE OF LAW
> An employee who opposed but did not explicitly complain about a supervisor's perceived sexist behavior may proceed with a claim of retaliation under California state law.

FACTS: Elysa Yanowitz (P) started working for L'Oreal USA, Inc. (L'Oreal) (D) in 1981. She had a history of consistently good job reviews. She claimed that, while touring a store with Jack Wiswall, the general manager of her division, he told her that a female sales associate in the store was "not good looking enough" and should be fired. He told Yanowitz (P) to "get me somebody hot." On a later visit to the store, he reiterated his instruction that the sales associate should be fired and told her, "God damn it, get me one that looks like that," after they passed a woman he described as "a young attractive blonde girl, very sexy." Yanowitz (P) ignored those and later calls to fire the sales associate, repeatedly asking Wiswall for an "adequate justi-fication." Before long, Wiswall and her immediate boss began a pattern of retaliation against her, which included soliciting negative feedback about her from the employees she supervised, unwarranted negative performance evalua-tions, "humiliating" and unjustified criticism of her in front of subordinates, and denial of needed resources and assistance. That court granted summary judgment to L'Oreal (D), but the appeals court reversed, holding that she engaged in a protected activity under state law when she refused Wiswall's order to fire the sales associate for not meeting his standards for sexual attractiveness, and her treatment for doing so could be found to constitute adverse employment action under the "deterrence test."

ISSUE: May an employee who opposed but did not explicitly complain about a supervisor's perceived sexist behavior proceed with a claim of retaliation under California state law?

HOLDING AND DECISION: (George, C.J.) Yes. An employee who opposed but did not explicitly complain about a supervisor's perceived sexist behavior may proceed with a claim of retaliation under California state law. An employee's refusal to follow a supervisor's order that she reasonably believes to be discriminatory constitutes

protected activity under California's Fair Employment and Housing Act (FEHA), and an employer may not retal-iate against an employee on the basis of such conduct when the employer, in light of all the circumstances, knows that the employee believes the order to be discriminatory, even when the employee does not explicitly state to her supervisor or employer that she believes the order to be discriminatory. The test for determining whether the treat-ment an employee experiences constitutes an adverse-employment action under the meaning of FEHA is the "materiality" test, which looks at whether the terms and conditions of the employee's job have been materially af-fected. The broader "deterrence" test that the California Court of Appeals had adopted in reviving Yanowitz's (P) retaliation claim is rejected. And in determining whether an employee has been subjected to treatment that materi-ally affects the terms and conditions of employment, it is appropriate to consider the totality of the circumstances and to apply the "continuing violation" doctrine. Because Yanowitz's (P) evidence still raised a jury question on the issue of adverse action, Yanowitz (P) can go forward with her claim.

DISSENT: (Chin, J.) The court should have backed the trial court's grant of summary judgment for the employer because this case presents the question whether a person can be a whistleblower without blowing the whistle. At least in this case, where the personnel order was not clearly unlawful, the answer should be "no." The whole point behind giving whistleblowers special protection is to en-courage them to speak out to try to prevent employment discrimination before it takes place or to expose it after it occurs. It makes no sense to give this special protection to someone, like Yanowitz (P), who did nothing (until she filed a lawsuit) to communicate to her employer that she opposed what she believed to be a discriminatory act.

▌ *ANALYSIS*

The court rejected federal law limiting the "continuing violations" doctrine to harassment claims. The court's ra-tionale for applying the "continuing violations" doctrine to this case was to give effect to the state statute at issue: "Contrary to L'Oreal's (D) assertion that it is improper to consider collectively the alleged retaliatory acts, there is no requirement that an employer's retaliatory acts constitute one swift blow, rather than a series of subtle, yet damag-ing, injuries," the court said. "Enforcing a requirement that each act separately constitute an adverse employment

Continued on next page.

action would subvert the purpose and intent of the statute." Despite the appropriate rationale, the rejection of federal law limitations could prompt an appeal of the case to federal court.

∎══∎

Quicknotes

CONTINUING VIOLATION RULE Rule recognizing behavior persistently repeated at intervals—enduring behavior, not ended with a single act—used to determine when the statute of limitations begins to run on claims stating a continual pattern of unacceptable behavior on which relief can be granted.

∎══∎

Crawford v. Metropolitan Government of Nashville

Employee (P) v. Employer (D)

129 S. Ct. 846 (2009).

NATURE OF CASE: Appeal from granting of summary judgment to the defendant.

FACT SUMMARY: During an internal investigation of sexual harassment by another employee, Crawford (P) provided information of alleged sexual harassment in response to questioning from the investigator. Crawford was later terminated.

RULE OF LAW
Just like an affirmative employee-filed complaint, an employee's response to questions from an employer about alleged unlawful employment practices qualifies as conduct covered by the antiretaliation provisions of Title VII.

FACTS: In 2002, Metropolitan Government of Nashville (Metropolitan) (D) began an investigation into allegations of sexual harassment of employee Gene Hughes. A human resources officer asked Crawford (P), who did not make the initial complaint, if she had witnessed any conduct by Hughes that would qualify as sexual harassment. Crawford (P) described several instances of such behavior to the investigator, but did not file any separate complaint. Metropolitan (D) subsequently terminated Crawford (P), allegedly for embezzlement. Crawford (P) brought this suit on the grounds Metropolitan (D) retaliated against her for the information she provided against Hughes during the investigation. The federal district court and the court of appeals both held that summary judgment for Metropolitan (D) was appropriate because Crawford (P) had never made an affirmative claim herself to oppose the alleged unlawful employment actions of her employer. Crawford (P) appealed to the Supreme Court.

ISSUE: Just like an affirmative employee-filed complaint, does an employee's response to questions from an employer about alleged unlawful employment practices qualify as conduct covered by the antiretaliation provisions of Title VII?

HOLDING AND DECISION: (Souter, J.) Yes. Just like an affirmative employee-filed complaint, an employee's response to questions from an employer about alleged unlawful employment practices qualifies as conduct covered by the antiretaliation provisions of Title VII. Under Title VII, it is unlawful for an employer to discriminate against an employee because that employee has "opposed" any unlawful employment practice of the employer (the opposition clause) or because the employee made a charge or testified as part of an internal investigation pursuant to a filed complaint with the Equal Employment Opportunity Commission (EEOC) (the participation clause). The investigation here was not pursuant to a filed EEOC claim so the participation clause is not at issue. Accordingly, Crawford's (P) retaliation claim may move forward only if her response to questions in an internal investigation constitute actions to oppose an unlawful employment practice. The term "oppose" is undefined in the statute, but it means to resist or to contend against. Here, Crawford's (P) statements are covered by the opposition clause. Her answers to the investigator qualify as "resistant" to her employer. To oppose goes far beyond active or affirmative opposition and Crawford's (P) statements qualify as such. Accordingly, Crawford (P) has stated a valid retaliation claim and summary judgment should not have been granted to Metropolitan (D). Reversed and remanded.

ANALYSIS

Crawford continues the recent trend of the Supreme Court to expand the availability of retaliation claims for employees. This decision is practical. It would not make sense to allow claims for retaliation when an employee makes some affirmative complaint, but disallow them if the employee provides the same information in response to a question from a supervisor.

Quicknotes

RETALIATORY DISCHARGE The firing of an employee in retaliation for an act committed against the employer's interests.

SUMMARY JUDGMENT Judgment rendered by a court in response to a motion made by one of the parties, claiming that the lack of a question of material fact in respect to an issue warrants disposition of the issue without consideration by the jury.

Burlington Northern & Santa Fe Railway Co. v. White

Employer (D) v. Employee (P)

548 U.S. 53 (2006).

NATURE OF CASE: Appeal of judgment for employee in retaliation case.

FACT SUMMARY: Sheila White (P) was transferred and suspended, but then awarded backpay by her employer to cover the suspension period. A jury awarded her damages in her employment discrimination trial. On appeal, Burlington Northern & Santa Fe Railway Co. (D) argued that she didn't suffer an adverse employment action, so that she didn't have the right to sue under Title VII of the 1964 Civil Rights Act.

🏛 RULE OF LAW
The definition of retaliation under Title VII of the 1964 Civil Rights Act includes acts that are "materially adverse" to a reasonable employee, including transfers or suspensions that do not result in a loss of pay, benefits, or privileges.

FACTS: Sheila White (P) was the only woman working in the Maintenance of Way Department of the Burlington Northern Santa Fe Railroad's (Burlington Northern) (D) Tennessee facility. After she complained of harassment by her supervisor, White was transferred from her position as a forklift operator to less desirable duties as a track laborer, though her job classification remained the same. She was subsequently suspended for 37 days without pay, but was eventually reinstated and given full backpay. White (P) filed suit in federal court. A jury rejected her claims of sex discrimination but found that she had been retaliated against for complaining about sex discrimination, in violation of Title VII of the 1964 Civil Rights Act. The jury awarded her $43,000 in damages. On appeal, Burlington Northern (D) argued that White (P) had not suffered "adverse employment action" and therefore could not bring the suit, because she had not been fired, demoted, denied a promotion, or denied wages. The Sixth Circuit Court of Appeals disagreed, finding that the suspension without pay—even if backpay was eventually awarded—was an adverse employment action, as was the change of responsibilities within the same job category.

ISSUE: Does the definition of retaliation under Title VII of the 1964 Civil Rights Act include acts that are "materially adverse" to a reasonable employee, including transfers or suspensions that do not result in a loss of pay, benefits, or privileges?

HOLDING AND DECISION: (Breyer, J.) Yes. The definition of retaliation under Title VII of the 1964 Civil Rights Act includes acts that are "materially adverse" to a reasonable employee, including transfers or suspensions

that do not result in a loss of pay, benefits, or privileges. Congressional intent and the language of the statutes indicate that while the substantive discrimination provision of Title VII is designed to prevent injury to individuals based on status, such as gender, the antiretaliation provision seeks to prevent harm based on conduct, such as the reporting by an employee that she has been harassed. The retaliation provision of Title VII covers those, and only those, employer actions that would be "materially adverse" to a reasonable employee or job applicant. In other words, the employer's actions must be harmful to the point that they could dissuade a reasonable worker from making, or supporting, a charge of discrimination. In this case, White's (P) suspension and transfer were "materially adverse," in that it could dissuade a reasonable worker from making or supporting a charge of discrimination, and therefore constitute retaliatory discrimination that violates Title VII. Affirmed.

▶ ANALYSIS

The holding in this case resolved a circuit split. Pay special attention to the court's distinction between substantive discrimination and retaliatory discrimination. Under the court's ruling, discrimination has to occur in the workplace to be actionable under Title VII, but retaliation doesn't. That is, Title VII proscribes retaliatory actions that occur outside the workplace. The justices wrote that retaliation provision is not limited just to the "terms, conditions, and benefits" of employment because employers can chill dissent and the reporting of discrimination in other ways. Although preventing discrimination can be achieved by prohibiting employment-related discrimination, it is not as simple to discourage retaliation, according to the justices. The Court wrote that a provision limited to employment-related actions would not "deter the many forms that effective retaliation can take." Thus, "such a limited construction would fail to fully achieve the antiretaliation provision's 'primary purpose,' namely, '[m]aintaining unfettered access to statutory remedial mechanisms.'"

■═■

Quicknotes

RETALIATION The infliction of injury or penalty upon another in return for an injury or harm caused by that party.

■═■

Ricci v. DeStefano

Applicants for promotion (P) v. Employer (D)

129 S. Ct. 2658 (2009).

NATURE OF CASE: Appeal from granting of summary judgment to the defendant.

FACT SUMMARY: After the fire department of the City of New Haven, Connecticut (City), administered a written test for promotions for vacant lieutenant and captain positions, only white and Hispanic employees were eligible for promotion. Fearing a lawsuit from the black applicants, the City decided not to certify the test results and to not promote the white and Hispanic applicants.

RULE OF LAW
Under Title VII of the Civil Rights Act of 1964, a public employer may engage in intentional discrimination to remedy an unintentional disparate impact only when the employer can show a strong basis in evidence that it will be subject to disparate impact liability if it fails to take the discriminatory action.

FACTS: In 2003, City of New Haven, Connecticut (City) (D) administered written tests for firefighters seeking promotion to the ranks of lieutenant and captain. The written test accounted for 60 percent of the applicant's score, with an oral interview accounting for the other 40 percent. The City (D) hired an outside vendor to design the tests. The evidence in the record established that the City (D) included broad participation from different ethnicities to develop tests that were neutral and fair. For the lieutenant's test 34 candidates passed—25 white, 6 black, and 3 Hispanics. All ten of the top scorers were white. There were eight vacancies. For the captain's test 22 candidates passed—16 white, 3 black, and 3 Hispanic. Seven whites and 2 Hispanics were eligible for promotion. The City (D) then voted not to certify the results. Seventeen white firefighters and one Hispanic (P) (firefighters) brought this suit on the grounds the City's (D) action constituted prohibited disparate treatment under Title VII of the Civil Rights Act of 1964. The City (D) responded that it took its action because the test appeared to violate the disparate impact requirements of Title VII. The federal district court granted summary judgment to the City (D) and the circuit court of appeals affirmed. The firefighters (P) appealed to the Supreme Court.

ISSUE: Under Title VII of the Civil Rights Act of 1964 may a public employer engage in intentional discrimination to remedy an unintentional disparate impact only when the employer can show a strong basis in evidence that it will be subject to disparate impact liability if it fails to take the discriminatory action?

HOLDING AND DECISION: (Kennedy, J.) Yes. Under Title VII of the Civil Rights Act of 1964, a public employer may engage in intentional discrimination to remedy an unintentional disparate impact only when the employer can show a strong basis in evidence that it will be subject to disparate impact liability if it fails to take the discriminatory action. The firefighters (P) do not dispute that the City (D) was likely to be faced with a prima facie showing of a disparate impact claim because of the test results. However, a prima facie claim does constitute a strong basis in evidence that the City (D) would have been liable under a disparate impact theory. The City (D) would only be liable if the test itself was not job related and consistent with the business necessity of the fire department. Here, the record established the test design phase was a fair and open process. Under this Court's precedent, the City (D) could not fail to promote the successful applicants based solely on the test results. Additional evidence regarding an improper test or some other evidence would be needed to support the strong basis in evidence standard that the City (D) would likely face disparate impact liability. Summary judgment should enter for the firefighters (P). Reversed and remanded.

CONCURRENCE: (Scalia, J.) The Court properly decided this issue by relying solely on the Title VII disparate treatment provisions, without the need for any constitutional analysis. However, the day will come when the Court will have to resolve the obvious conflict between the disparate impact provisions of Title VII and the Constitution's guarantee of equal protection.

DISSENT: (Ginsburg, J.) Context matters. Sixty percent of the population of New Haven, Connecticut, is minorities and the City's (D) decision to not certify the test results are a legal effort to combat prior discrimination. Congress specifically sought to protect such voluntary efforts by public employers to avoid disparate impact situations such as this. In addition, the majority ignores evidence that there were multiple flaws in the various tests employed by the City (D).

ANALYSIS

The future of Title VII's disparate impact jurisprudence will likely depend upon the makeup of the Supreme Court. The conservative justices plus Justice Kennedy believe that the disparate impact requirements are in conflict with the constitutional guarantees of equal protection. In

Continued on next page.

keeping with Justice Roberts's goal of crafting narrowly tailored opinions, the majority avoided a resolution of the constitutional issue in this case.

■■■■

Quicknotes

EQUAL PROTECTION CLAUSE A constitutional provision that each person be guaranteed the same protection of the laws enjoyed by other persons in like circumstances.

TITLE VII Prohibits unlawful discrimination against individuals based on race or sex.

■■■■

Reed v. Great Lakes Cos.

Employee (P) v. Employer (D)

330 F.3d 931 (7th Cir. 2003).

NATURE OF CASE: Appeal of summary judgment in favor of employer.

FACT SUMMARY: Melvin Reed (P) sued his employer for religious discrimination and failure to accommodate his religion. The trial court granted summary judgment in favor of the employer.

🏛 RULE OF LAW
Summary judgment in favor of an employer is proper where an employee alleging religious discrimination and failure-to-accommodate claims fails to identify his religion or otherwise provide any guidance for determining what accommodation might be necessary.

FACTS: Melvin Reed (P) was the executive housekeeper of the newly opened Milwaukee Holiday Inn, which was operated by Great Lakes Companies. (D). The Gideons provided newly opened hotels owned by Great Lakes (D) with a free copy of the Bible for each of its hotel rooms, and customarily met with hotel representatives when supplying the Bibles. Reed (P) and his manager attended a meeting with the Gideons, but Reed (P) walked out of the meeting when it unexpectedly included Bible reading and prayer. After a confrontation with his manager about his behavior, he was fired for insubordination. Reed (P) sued Great Lakes (D), alleging intentional religious bias and failure to accommodate his religion in violation of Title VII of the 1964 Civil Rights Act. The district court granted summary judgment to Great Lakes (D), finding that Reed (P) had failed to support his claims and imposed sanctions against Reed (P) and his lawyer because of Reed's (P) 15-year pattern of filing employment discrimination cases. Reed (P) appealed.

ISSUE: Is summary judgment in favor of an employer proper where an employee alleging religious discrimination and failure-to-accommodate claims fails to identify his religion or otherwise provide any guidance for determining what accommodation might be necessary?

HOLDING AND DECISION: (Posner, J.) Yes. Summary judgment in favor of an employer is proper where an employee alleging religious discrimination and failure-to-accommodate claims fails to identify his religion or otherwise provide any guidance for determining what accommodation might be necessary. Title VII of the 1964 Civil Rights Act prohibits discrimination against an employee based on the employee's religion, and even extends to an employee's "antipathy to religion." So, even if Reed (P) were an atheist, Title VII would provide protection if

he in fact suffered discrimination as a result of his beliefs. In this case, however, Reed (P) never identified what his beliefs were or what measures Great Lakes (D) should take to accommodate his beliefs, and there is therefore no indication that he was fired because of his religious beliefs. There is evidence, however, that he was fired because of his abrupt departure from the meeting with the Gideons and for insubordination. But while the summary judgment is affirmed, the order of sanctions is reversed and remanded because Reed's (P) sanctions were appropriate only if his intentional discrimination claim could be characterized as frivolous, and it was unclear whether the trial judge had properly considered that question. Affirmed in part, vacated in part, and remanded.

CONCURRENCE IN PART AND DISSENT IN PART: (Ripple, J) Reed (P) has proven neither intentional discrimination based on religion nor failure to accommodate his religion. His allegations, however, are not frivolous, and accordingly that part of the judgment of the district court that imposes sanctions should be reversed.

▶ ANALYSIS

This case illustrates the difficult task of distinguishing between asking for an accommodation to a religious belief and the right to disobey a superior's orders. As the court states: "There is a line, indistinct but important, between an employee who seeks an accommodation to his religious faith and an employee who asserts as Reed (P) did an unqualified right to disobey orders that he deems inconsistent with his faith though he refuses to indicate at what points that faith intersects the requirements of his job."

■■■

Quicknotes

DISCRIMINATION Unequal treatment of a class of persons.

■■■

Fragante v. City & County of Honolulu

Job applicant claiming discrimination (P) v. Government employer (D)

888 F.2d 591 (9th Cir. 1989), *cert. denied*, 494 U.S. 1081 (1990).

NATURE OF CASE: Appeal from dismissal of a Title VII (of the 1964 Civil Rights Act) action for national origin discrimination.

FACT SUMMARY: Fragante (P) contended that he was discriminated against on the basis of national origin when he was not hired by the Honolulu's Division of Motor Vehicles and Licensing (D) because of his heavy accent.

⚖ RULE OF LAW
Employment decisions may be predicated on an individual's accent when it materially interferes with job performance.

FACTS: Fragante (P), an immigrant from the Philippines, applied for a clerk's job at the Honolulu's Division of Motor Vehicles and Licensing (DMV) (D) in 1981. The job involved orally providing information to the public. Fragante (P) had the highest score on the written test given to applicants and was chosen to be interviewed by the DMV (D). The interviewers had difficulty understanding Fragante (P) because of his pronounced accent and determined that Fragante (P) would have difficulties communicating with the public. After the Honolulu DMV (D) hired two other applicants who had scored lower, Fragante (P) filed a Title VII action, asserting that he had been discriminated against on the basis of his national origin. The district court dismissed the suit, and Fragante (P) appealed.

ISSUE: May employment decisions be predicated on an individual's accent when it materially interferes with job performance?

HOLDING AND DECISION: (Trott, J.) Yes. Employment decisions may be predicated on an individual's accent when it materially interferes with job performance. Title VII of the 1964 Civil Rights Act prohibits employment discrimination on the basis of national origin. The employer may defend a Title VII action by articulating a legitimate, nondiscriminatory reason for the decision. Although accent and national origin are inextricably intertwined in many cases, there is nothing improper about an employer making an honest assessment of the oral communications skills of a job candidate. An employer may base a decision on the effect of an accent regarding the necessary qualifications for a position. The evidence shows that Fragante (P) was not hired by the Honolulu DMV (D) because of his perceived inability to communicate effectively. Fragante (P) has not shown that there was any discriminatory motive or intent. Therefore, the dismissal was proper. Affirmed.

▶ *ANALYSIS*

Both the court and Fragante's (P) appellate lawyer, Professor Mari Matsuda, noted the discrepancies in the DMV's (D) interview of Fragante (P). Matsuda argued that the interview was cursory, the interviewers failed to identify any specific incidences of misunderstanding, and they did not have any instruction in speech assessment. The decision merely noted that the "process may not have been perfect."

Quicknotes

BONA FIDE OCCUPATIONAL QUALIFICATION A statutory exception to the prohibition on discrimination in employment if the individual's sex, religion or national origin is a necessary qualification for the operation of the business.

DISCRIMINATION Unequal treatment of individuals without justification.

Smith v. City of Jackson

Employees (P) v. Public employer (D)

544 U.S. 228 (2005).

NATURE OF CASE: Appeal of judgment for employer in age discrimination claim.

FACT SUMMARY: A police department employee (P) in Jackson, Mississippi argued that the department's policy of giving officers with five or fewer years of tenure with the department bigger raises than those with more than five years of tenure violated the Age Discrimination in Employment Act (ADEA).

🏛 RULE OF LAW
A disparate-impact claim may be made under the Age Discrimination in Employment Act of 1967.

FACTS: Azel Smith and group of other police department employees over the age of 40 (P) sued the police department (D) and the city of Jackson, Mississippi (City) (D), alleging that the department salary plan violated the Age Discrimination in Employment Act (ADEA) by giving officers with five or fewer years of tenure with the department larger raises than those with more than five years of tenure. The group made a disparate-impact claim under the ADEA, arguing the department and city unintentionally engaged in age discrimination. The District Court and the U.S. Court of Appeals for the Fifth Circuit ruled that disparate-impact claims could not be made under the ADEA.

ISSUE: Can a disparate-impact claim be made under the Age Discrimination in Employment Act of 1967?

HOLDING AND DECISION: (Stevens, J.) Yes. A disparate-impact claim may be made under the Age Discrimination in Employment Act of 1967 (ADEA). But even though ADEA authorized recovery in disparate-impact cases, Smith (P) and his co-plaintiffs in this case failed to set forth a valid claim. Disparate-impact claims brought under Title VII of the 1964 Civil Rights Act were first authorized in *Griggs v. Duke Power*, 401 U.S. 424 (1971), and the ADEA authorized disparate-impact claims in cases similar to *Griggs*, because the language of Title VII and ADEA is virtually identical. However, ADEA is narrower than Title VII and allowed an otherwise prohibited action where the discrimination was based on reasonable factors other than age. The employees (P) in this case failed to identify any specific practice within the pay plan that had an adverse impact on older workers. Further, the City's (D) plan was based on reasonable factors other than age. Affirmed.

▶ ANALYSIS

Unlike disparate-treatment claims, disparate-impact claims do not require a showing of discriminatory intent. They focus instead on whether employer policies and practices adversely affect one or more protected groups. As a result of this case, older workers may recover against employers if they can show that a practice or policy has a disparate impact on them, even though the practice or policy may have been adopted with no discriminatory intent or motivation.

Quicknotes

DISCRIMINATORY PURPOSE Intent to discriminate; must be shown to establish an Equal Protection violation.

DISPARATE IMPACT Unequal treatment of employees or of applicants for employment due to practices that appear neutral, but are not.

DISPARATE TREATMENT Unequal treatment of employees or of applicants for employment without justification.

Sutton v. United Air Lines, Inc.

Applicants (P) v. Employer (D)

527 U.S. 471 (1999).

NATURE OF CASE: Suit alleging disability discrimination in violation of the Americans with Disabilities Act.

FACT SUMMARY: Petitioners, twin sisters who both suffered from severe myopia, brought suit against United Air Lines (United) (D) alleging that United's (D) failure to offer them pilot positions constituted unlawful disability discrimination in violation of the Americans with Disabilities Act.

🏛 RULE OF LAW
In determining whether an individual is substantially limited with respect to a major life activity under the disabled definition of the Americans with Disabilities Act, such disability must be determined taking into consideration any corrective measures.

FACTS: Petitioners, twin sisters who both suffered from severe myopia, applied to United Air Lines (D) for employment as commercial airline pilots. During their interviews they were told that a mistake had been made in inviting them to interview since they did not meet the minimum vision requirement. Their interviews were terminated and neither was offered a position. Petitioners filed suit alleging United Air Lines (United) (D) discriminated against them on account of their disability in violation of the Americans with Disabilities Act (ADA). The district court dismissed for failure to state a claim. Since they could fully correct their visual impairments, they were not actually substantially limited in any major life activity and therefore were not disabled under the ADA. The court of appeals affirmed.

ISSUE: In determining whether an individual is substantially limited with respect to a major life activity under the disabled definition of the ADA, must such disability be determined taking into consideration any corrective measures?

HOLDING AND DECISION: (O'Connor, J.) Yes. In determining whether an individual is substantially limited with respect to a major life activity under the disabled definition of the ADA, such disability must be determined taking into consideration any corrective measures. The ADA prohibits discrimination against qualified individuals with disabilities. "Disability" is defined as (1) a physical or mental impairment substantially limiting one or more major life activities; (2) a record of such impairment; or (3) being regarded as having such impairment. The first issue is whether the petitioners stated a claim under the definition of disability; that is, whether they have alleged that they possess a physical impairment that substantially limits them in one or more major life activities. Since petitioners claim that with corrective measures they are not actually disabled, it must be determined whether disability is to be determined with reference to corrective measures. Petitioners argued that whether impairment is substantially limiting should be determined without regard to corrective measures. United (D) argued that impairment does not substantially limit a major life activity if it is corrected and that the Equal Employment Opportunity Commission (EEOC) guidelines conflict with the plain meaning of the ADA. United (D) is correct. Taking the ADA as a whole, corrective measures must be considered in determining whether a person is substantially limited with respect to a major life activity, and thus "disabled," under the ADA. Three provisions of the ADA support this conclusion. First, the term "disability" is defined as a physical or mental impairment that substantially limits one or more major life activities of the individual. This requires that the person presently be substantially limited with respect to the activity, and not potentially or hypothetically limited. Where the person is able to take corrective measures to mitigate the impairment, it cannot be said to substantially limit a major life activity. Second, a determination of whether a person suffers from a disability must be made on an individual basis. The EEOC guidelines stating that the person be evaluated in his uncorrected state runs directly contrary to this individual inquiry. Last, findings enacted as part of the ADA indicate that Congress did not intend to include within the statute's scope all those persons whose uncorrected conditions would constitute disabilities. Since a disability must be determined with respect to corrective measures, the petitioners failed to state a claim that they are substantially limited in a major life activity. Affirmed.

▶ ANALYSIS

The authority to promulgate rules under the ADA is divided among three different agencies: the EEOC, attorney general, and the secretary of transportation. However, no agency was delegated the authority to promulgate regulations implementing the ADA's general provisions, including the definition of the term "disability." The EEOC, however, did promulgate such regulation and thereby exceeded its authority.

■≡■

Continued on next page.

Quicknotes

AMERICANS WITH DISABILITIES ACT Enacted in 1990, the federal law prohibits discrimination in employment, housing, transportation and other services on the basis of an individual's physical or mental disabilities.

EEOC v. Schneider National, Inc.

Government agency (P) v. Employer (D)

481 F.3d 507 (7th Cir. 2007).

NATURE OF CASE: Appeal of summary judgment for the employer.

FACT SUMMARY: A truck driver with an excellent driving record was fired when his employer discovered he had a condition that causes his blood pressure to suddenly drop and cause fainting spells. The Equal Employment Opportunity Commission (P) filed a lawsuit on the driver's behalf. Even though the condition is treatable, and the risk of a fainting spell is small, the lower court granted summary judgment in favor of the employer, holding that the employer did not violate the Americans with Disabilities Act by having standards for drivers that were higher than most other companies.

🏛 RULE OF LAW
An employer does not violate the Americans with Disabilities Act (ADA) if it fires an employee because of a physical condition, but does not regard him as disabled within the meaning of the ADA.

FACTS: Jerome Hoefner was a valued employee of Schneider National, Inc. (Schneider) (D) with an excellent driving record. Schneider (D) nevertheless fired Hoefner from his truck-driving job after he experienced a fainting spell while off work and was diagnosed with neurocardiogenic syncope, a nervous system disorder that can cause a sudden drop in blood pressure. Department of Transportation (DOT) standards do not bar individuals with neurocardiogenic syncope from driving on public highways a truck with a gross vehicular weight of more than 26,000 pounds or a vehicle used to transport hazardous materials or at least 16 passengers. Despite this, and despite that the condition is treatable with medication, Schneider (D) was skittish about allowing employees diagnosed with neurocardiogenic syncope to drive trucks. Two years earlier, a Schneider (D) driver who had recently been diagnosed with the condition drove his truck off a bridge and was killed. Even though investigators were unable to determine whether the condition caused the accident, Schneider (D) instituted a policy barring any driver with neurocardiogenic syncope. Schneider (D) encouraged Hoefner to apply for a nondriving job with the company, but he found another driving job with a different company. Since receiving his diagnosis, he repeatedly has been cleared to drive by doctors and has received a renewal of his DOT medical certificate. The U.S. District Court for the Eastern District of Wisconsin granted summary judgment to Schneider (D) on Equal Employment Opportunity Commission's (EEOC's) (P) claim that Schneider (D) regarded Hoefner as having an impairment that substantially limits

the major life activity of working. The court found that Schneider (D) only viewed Hoefner as unable to work as a truck driver for that company, not that he was unable to drive trucks generally.

ISSUE: Does an employer violate the ADA if it fires an employee because of a physical condition, but does not regard him as disabled within the meaning of the ADA?

HOLDING AND DECISION: (Posner, J.) No. An employer does not violate the ADA if it fires an employee because of a physical condition, but does not regard him as disabled within the meaning of the ADA. Schneider (D) did not have a mistaken understanding of neurocardiogenic syncope. Rather, the company (D) was simply unwilling to risk a possible repetition of the accident that resulted in the death of another driver with the condition. The risk of that occurring is not zero, because Hoefner could forget to take his medication and the drug he takes is not totally efficacious. The risk of danger to the driver may be small, but Schneider (D) is entitled to determine how much risk is too great. In addition, the liability implications for Schneider (D) could be high. If there was an accident, victims' lawyers would "wave" the previous accident in front of the jury. The decision to avoid risk is a decision irrelevant to liability under the ADA, even if that company's degree of risk aversion was unique in its industry. Finally, there is no evidence that Schneider (D) considers neurocardiogenic syncope to impair any life activity other than driving a truck for Schneider, and perhaps for some other truck companies like Schneider (D) that have safety standards higher than the minimum required by the federal government. Affirmed.

▌ ANALYSIS

The court's holding incorporates a fair reading of *Sutton v. United Air Lines, Inc.*, 527 U.S. 471 (1999), but the discussion of risk aversion may have undesirable repercussions. Judge Posner seems to be saying that an employer who inflicts an adverse employment action on an employee on the basis of an irrational fear does not run afoul of the ADA if the employer really believes it is acting rationally. Taken to the extreme, that reasoning allows a school system to fire a kindergarten teacher with diabetes that is medically treated, on the small risk that she could have a seizure in class, if that small chance scares the employer. To conclude that the ADA has nothing to say about such a decision seems to undercut its purpose.

■=■

Continued on next page.

Quicknotes

AMERICANS WITH DISABILITIES ACT Enacted in 1990, the federal law prohibits discrimination in employment, housing, transportation and other services on the basis of an individual's physical or mental disabilities.

■▬■

Lyons v. Legal Aid Society

Employee (P) v. Employer (D)

68 F.3d 1512 (2d Cir. 1995).

NATURE OF CASE: Appeal from granting of motion to dismiss to defendant.

FACT SUMMARY: After Lyons (P) was struck and injured by an automobile, she petitioned her employer to pay for a parking space adjacent to her place of work in lower Manhattan. Her employer denied her request.

🏛 RULE OF LAW
An employer's duty to provide a qualified disabled employee with a reasonable accommodation includes assistance with the employee's ability to get to work.

FACTS: Lyons (P), a staff attorney with the Legal Aid Society (Legal Aid) (D) in lower Manhattan, was struck by an automobile in 1989 and suffered serious injuries. She was on disability for four years. When she returned to work, she could only walk by using different walking devices, including canes and walkers. She wore a brace on her left knee and could not stand for long periods of time. When she returned to work, rather than take public transportation from her home in New Jersey, Lyons (P) asked Legal Aid (D) to pay for a parking spot near the building. Legal Aid (D) denied her request. Lyons (P) spends $300 to $520 per month on parking. The district court granted Legal Aid's (D) motion to dismiss on the grounds the request was not reasonable. Lyons (P) appealed to the Second Circuit Court of Appeals.

ISSUE: Does an employer's duty to provide a qualified disabled employee with a reasonable accommodation include assistance with the employee's ability to get to work?

HOLDING AND DECISION: (Kearse, J.) Yes. An employer's duty to provide a qualified disabled employee with a reasonable accommodation includes assistance with the employee's ability to get to work. Under both the Americans with Disabilities Act and its predecessor, the Rehabilitation Act, a plaintiff must allege the following to state a claim for failure to provide a reasonable accommodation: (1) the employer is subject to the federal statutes; (2) the plaintiff has a disability covered by the statutes; (3) the plaintiff can perform his or her essential job functions with or without a reasonable accommodation; and (4) the employer had notice of the disability and failed to provide the accommodation. Lyons (P) has adequately pled the first, second and fourth elements. The only issue is whether the parking request is reasonable. Legal Aid (D) argues it does not provide parking benefits to its other employees. This is outside the face of the complaint and cannot support dismissal of the complaint at this stage of the litigation. Congress envisioned that getting to work was an essential aspect of a job and employers should assist in that endeavor. Accordingly, Lyons (P) has stated a claim for failure to provide a reasonable accommodation and the motion to dismiss should not have been granted. In discovery, Legal Aid (D) shall have the opportunity to present evidence regarding its geographic location, its financial resources, and whether such evidence amounts to an undue burden placed upon it. Reversed.

▶ ANALYSIS

In employment cases, trial judges are most vulnerable when granting motions to dismiss. The issue at the motion to dismiss stage is not whether Lyons (P) actually needed the parking spot or whether Legal Aid (D) had the resources to provide the parking. The motion to dismiss standard is simply whether the complaint has adequately pled the essential elements of the claim. Here, the court's decision held, as a matter of law, that reasonable accommodations may include transportation related benefits to the disabled employee. Questions of fact regarding the reasonableness of the request would be resolved through discovery and possibly at trial.

■=■

Quicknotes

AMERICANS WITH DISABILITIES ACT Enacted in 1990, the federal law prohibits discrimination in employment, housing, transportation and other services on the basis of an individual's physical or mental disabilities.

REHABILITATION ACT, 29 U.S.C. § 794, SECTION 504 Prohibits discrimination on the basis of disability.

■=■

Shahar v. Bowers

Lesbian attorney/employee (P) v. State attorney general (D)

114 F.3d 1097 (11th Cir. 1997) (en banc), *cert. denied*, 522 U.S. 1049 (1998).

NATURE OF CASE: Appeal of summary judgment for the defense in action for damages and injunction alleging violations of federal constitutional rights.

FACT SUMMARY: The Attorney General of the State of Georgia (D), upon learning that Shahar (P), a female attorney who had accepted an offer to work in the Attorney General's (D) office, had "married" another woman, withdrew the job offer.

> ## 🏛 RULE OF LAW
> A government employer's concerns regarding public perception of a former employee's exercise of associational rights may be weighed against those rights in determining whether the termination of the employment relationship was lawful.

FACTS: In 1990, Bowers (D), the Attorney General of the State of Georgia, offered Robin Shahar (P) the position of staff attorney in the Georgia Department of Law upon her graduation from law school, and Shahar (P) accepted. Meanwhile, Shahar (P), a woman, was making plans for her wedding to another woman. Shahar's (P) rabbi performed the ceremony in a "Jewish, lesbian-feminist, outdoor wedding" in a public park in June 1991. Also in June 1991, Shahar (P) informed Deputy Attorney General Coleman that she was getting married and taking a trip to Greece and would not begin work with the department until September. Although she did not tell Coleman she was marrying another woman, other department employees knew of this fact and eventually the issue came to the attention of Attorney General Bowers (D) and his senior aides. In July 1991, Bowers (D) withdrew Shahar's (P) job offer, stating in a letter to Shahar (P) that "inaction on my part would constitute tacit approval of this purported marriage and jeopardize the proper functioning of this office." Seeking damages and injunctive relief, Shahar (P) sued Bowers (D), claiming violations of her constitutional rights to free exercise of speech and freedom of association, as well as her rights to equal protection and substantive due process. The district court granted Bowers's (D) motion for summary judgment, and Shahar (P) appealed.

ISSUE: May a government employer consider public perception of an employee's associations in deciding whether to continue the employment relationship?

HOLDING AND DECISION: (Edmondson, J) Yes. A government employer's concerns regarding public perception of a former employee's exercise of associational rights may be weighed against those rights in determining whether the termination of the employment relationship

was lawful. In this case, the relative value of Shahar's (P) associational rights must be balanced against the disruption and other harm feared by Bowers (D), as in the free-exercise case of *Pickering v. Board of Education*, 391 U.S. 563 (1968). Bowers's (D) concerns about his office engaging in litigation with which Shahar's (P) personal interests conflicted are reasonable. Same-sex marriage is not sanctioned by Georgia law; in fact, Bowers (D) had recently won a battle in the U.S. Supreme Court to uphold the constitutionality of Georgia's law against homosexual sodomy. Bowers (D) was entitled to consider public perception of Shahar's (P) conduct, and to consider any affect her conduct might have on his ability to enforce Georgia's laws. For example, Bowers (D) alleges that her conduct could confuse the public about the Law Department's stand on same-sex marriage. These judgments are within the Attorney General's (D) role as head of the Law Department. The revocation of the job offer was neither unreasonable nor unconstitutional. Affirmed.

DISSENT: (Barkett, J.) The majority discounts Shahar's (P) interests, recognizing neither that her claims that her relationship with her partner is largely private, nor that she has engaged in no illegal conduct. The Attorney General (D) has an evidentiary burden to offer credible predictions of harm or disruption based on more than mere speculation.

▶ ANALYSIS

This case involved government employment and thus Shahar (P) was able to invoke, albeit unsuccessfully, the protections of the First Amendment. Had her employer been in the private sector, the First Amendment would not apply. Title VII of the Civil Rights Act of 1964, the civil rights statute that protects individuals against sex discrimination by private employers, has been held not to apply to cases involving sexual orientation.

■═■

Quicknotes

EQUAL PROTECTION CLAUSE A constitutional guarantee that no person should be denied the same protection of the laws enjoyed by other persons in like circumstances.

FIRST AMENDMENT The First Amendment to the United States Constitution prohibiting Congress from enacting any law respecting an establishment of religion, prohibiting the free exercise of religion, abridging freedom of

Continued on next page.

speech or the press, the right of peaceful assembly and the right to petition for a redress of grievances.

FREEDOM OF ASSOCIATION The right to peaceably assemble.

SUBSTANTIVE DUE PROCESS A constitutional safeguard limiting the power of the state, irrespective of how fair its procedures may be; substantive limits placed on the power of the state.

■═■

Wages and Hours

Quick Reference Rules of Law

Lochner v. New York

Employer (D) v. State (P)

198 U.S. 45 (1905).

NATURE OF CASE: Appeal from conviction for labor law violations.

FACT SUMMARY: Lochner (D), an employer, challenged a New York law that limited the hours that bakers could work to ten per day and sixty per week.

🏛 RULE OF LAW
The right of a person to freely contract and work may not be proscribed by a state law that does not safeguard the public health.

FACTS: In 1897, New York passed a labor law that made it a violation for bakeries to allow or require workers to work more than ten hours a day and sixty hours a week. The statute provided for no exceptions to these rules. Lochner (D) was found guilty of violating the law and appealed the conviction, claiming that the statute interfered with the right of contract and was therefore unconstitutional under the Fourteenth Amendment.

ISSUE: May states regulate the number of hours that employees may work?

HOLDING AND DECISION: (Peckham, J.) No. The right of a person to freely contract and work may not be proscribed by a state law that does not safeguard the public health. The Fourteenth Amendment prohibits states from depriving persons of life, liberty, or property without due process of law. The right to purchase or sell labor is part of the liberty protected under the Fourteenth Amendment. States do have the right to pass laws that relate to the safety, health, and general welfare of the public. Thus, the police powers of the state may prevent certain contracts between parties. However, if the law is an unreasonable, unnecessary, and arbitrary interference with the right of an individual to freely contract and work, the law is invalid. There is no reasonable ground for interfering with the right of bakery employees to work the hours that they choose. A limitation on these hours does not involve the safety or welfare of the public. All other professions involve health to some small degree, and there is no basis for distinguishing bakery workers. Thus, the New York law is an unreasonable restraint on the right of bakery employees to work. Reversed.

DISSENT: (Harlan, J.) The law must be taken as expressing the belief of the people of New York that labor in excess of 60 hours per week by bakery employees may endanger the health of those workers. This determination should be left for the legislatures and not the courts.

▶ ANALYSIS

This decision marked a high point in judicial activism by the Supreme Court. Over 30 years later, the Court essentially overruled this case when it determined that states could regulate economic matters such as these as long as there was a reasonable relation between the law and a legitimate goal. While the majority appears to use this same standard, they actually pay no deference whatsoever to the legislature's factual findings.

Quicknotes

FOURTEENTH AMENDMENT No state shall deny to any person within its jurisdiction the equal protection of the laws.

POLICE POWERS The power of a state or local government to regulate private conduct for the health, safety and welfare of the general public.

Donovan v. DialAmerica Marketing, Inc.

Secretary of Labor (P) v. Marketing company (D)

757 F.2d. 1376 (3d Cir.), *cert. denied*, 474 U.S. 919 (1985).

NATURE OF CASE: Appeal from defense judgment in action to enforce the Fair Labor Standards Act.

FACT SUMMARY: Because DialAmerica Marketing, Inc. (D) was paying less than minimum wage to two groups of its workers, whom it considered independent contractors, Donovan (P), Secretary of Labor, filed suit, alleging violation of the Fair Labor Standard Act minimum-wage requirement for employees.

🏛 RULE OF LAW
A worker may be determined to be an employee based on the degree of the employer's control; the worker's opportunity for profit or loss; his investment in equipment or materials; whether his service requires a special skill; the permanence of the working relationship; and whether his service is an integral part of the alleged employer's business.

FACTS: DialAmerica Marketing, Inc. (DialAmerica) (D) was a telephone-marketing firm operating in 20 states. The question arose as to whether two groups of workers for DialAmerica (D) were employees or independent contractors. One group researched telephone numbers for DialAmerica (D) in their homes, while the other group also distributed telephone-research work to other home researchers. Donovan (P), Secretary of Labor, brought an action under the Fair Labor Standards Act (FLSA), alleging that DialAmerica (D) had failed to comply with the minimum-wage and record-keeping provisions of the FLSA. The district court ruled that both groups of workers were independent contractors, not employees subject to the provisions of the FLSA.

ISSUE: May a worker be determined to be an employee based on the degree of the employer's control; the worker's opportunity for profit or loss; his investment in equipment or materials; whether his service requires a special skill; the permanence of the working relationship; and whether his service is an integral part of the alleged employer's business?

HOLDING AND DECISION: (Becker, J.) Yes. A worker may be determined to be an employee based on the degree of the employer's control; the worker's opportunity for profit or loss; his investment in equipment or materials; whether his service requires a special skill; the permanence of the working relationship; and whether his service is an integral part of the alleged employer's business. Also to be considered are the circumstances of the whole activity and whether, as a matter of economic reality, the workers are dependent upon the business to which they render service.

The district court stated that, for the most part, the investment of these workers was not great, the opportunity for profit and loss was small, and the skills required were few. Of the six factors and general consideration used as the basis for determining "employee" status, only one factor weighed in favor of the conclusion that the home researchers were not "employees." And that factor, the right-to-control factor, was overemphasized by the district court because homeworkers by their very nature are generally subject to little supervision and control by an alleged employer. Upon application of the factors to the distributors, however, the district court was correct in finding they were independent contractors not subject to the minimum-wage protection of the FLSA for their work in delivering cards to and from other home researchers. They were subject to minimal oversight or control over their distribution activities. Moreover, they faced a real opportunity for either a profit or loss in their operations, depending on the amount of their investment and their skills in management. Finally, their work as distributors was not an integral part of DialAmerica's (D) business. The district court erred in concluding that the home researchers were not employees of DialAmerica (D), but the court did not err in its conclusion that the distributors were independent contractors rather than employees.

▶ ANALYSIS

In discussing new work arrangements and the flexible workplace, the authors of the casebook state that despite the potential pitfalls, homework is a growing phenomenon, especially among women with children and older workers. In 1988, according to the authors, 25 million people were doing all or part of their job-related work at home, with an estimate of as many as 40 million homeworkers by the year 2000. In the instant case, the home researchers were generally women, some of whom had small children.

■⚡▬

Quicknotes

EMPLOYEE An individual who performs work at the direction of another pursuant to an express or implied agreement between the parties and in exchange for compensation.

FAIR LABOR STANDARDS ACT Enacted in 1938, the statute establishes a minimum wage applicable to all employees of covered employers and provides for mandatory overtime payment for covered employees who work more

Continued on next page.

than 40 hours a week. Executive, administrative and professional employees paid on a salary basis are exempt from the statute.

INDEPENDENT CONTRACTOR A party undertaking a partic-ular assignment for another who retains control over the manner in which it is executed.

■■■

In re Novartis Wage & Hour Litigation

Employees (P) v. Employer (D)

611 F.3d 141 (2d Cir. 2010).

NATURE OF CASE: Appeal from granting of summary judgment to the defendant.

FACT SUMMARY: A class of sales representatives for Novartis (P) demanded overtime pay for hours worked in excess of 40 hours per week. Novartis (D) denied payment on the ground the sales representatives were exempt from coverage of the Fair Labor Standards Act of 1938.

🏛 RULE OF LAW
Under the regulations promulgated under the Fair Labor Standards Act, an employee who merely promotes a product that will eventually be sold by another person does not make a sale and therefore is not an outside salesman exempt from protection of the statute.

FACTS: Novartis (D), a pharmaceutical company, employs sales representatives to promote its prescription drugs to physicians. The plaintiffs are a class of 2,500 sales representatives who worked for Novartis (D) from 2000 to 2007. In this action, the sales representatives (P) claim that under the Fair Labor Standards Act (FLSA), Novartis (D) must compensate them with overtime pay for hours worked in excess of 40 hours per week. Novartis (D) claims the sales representatives qualify as "outside salesman," one of the classes of employees who are exempt from protection of FLSA. The sales representatives (P) do not sell Novartis (D) products. Instead, they conduct five- to ten-minute meetings with physicians in their geographic area promoting the products. Novartis (D) provides training to the sales representatives on how to make the best presentation. Novartis (D) sets standards for number of physician visits, which products to market, and the overall marketing message. The sales representatives (P) have no input on those decisions. The sales representatives (P) receive bonuses depending on the number of Novartis (D) products sold in the sales representatives' geographic area. The sales representatives (P) are expected to work from 8 AM to 5 PM every day, but often work longer hours meeting with clients or attending mandatory dinner programs. The U.S. District Court for the Southern District of New York granted summary judgment to Novartis (D) on the ground the sales representatives (P) were "outside salesmen" exempt from FLSA. The sales representatives (P) appealed.

ISSUE: Under the regulations promulgated under the Fair Labor Standards Act, does an employee who merely promotes a product that will eventually be sold by another person make a sale and is therefore an outside salesman exempt from protection of the statute?

HOLDING AND DECISION: (Kearse, J.) No. Under the regulations promulgated under the Fair Labor Standards Act, an employee who merely promotes a product that will eventually be sold by another person does not make a sale and therefore is not an outside salesman exempt from protection of the statute. To qualify as an outside salesman, the employee must actually make the sale. Under the regulations, promotional activity designed simply to stimulate sales that will be made by another person does not qualify as exempt outside sales work. That is the case here. The sales representatives' (P) meetings with the physicians are something less than a sale. There is no transfer of ownership of any product between the sales representatives (P) and the physicians. The physicians simply recommend the Novartis (D) products to their patients who in turn purchase the drugs from their local pharmacy. Separately, the sales representatives also do not qualify as administrative employees exempt from the statute. To qualify as an administrative employee, the employee must earn $455 per week, perform office or non-manual work, and exercise discretion and independent judgment. Novartis (D) contends the sales representatives determine how to engage physicians based on past history. However, the record is clear Novartis (D) leaves the sales representatives (P) with little ability to deviate from the core marketing messages and the decisions as to which products to market. Accordingly, the sales representatives (P) do not function with enough independence required to classify them as exempt administrative employees. Vacated and reversed.

▶ ANALYSIS

As the text notes, there is currently a split between several of the federal circuit courts on whether pharmaceutical sales representatives are exempt from Fair Labor Standards Act protection. For example, the Third Circuit recently held that the administrative exemption covered a pharmaceutical sales representative who had to make an independent strategic plan to maximize her sales.

■═■

Quicknotes

FAIR LABOR STANDARDS ACT Enacted in 1938, the statute establishes a minimum wage applicable to all employees of covered employers and provides for mandatory overtime payment for covered employees who work more than 40 hours a week. Executive, administrative and professional employees paid on a salary basis are exempt from the statute.

■═■

IBP, Inc. v. Alvarez

Employer (D) v. Employees (P)

546 U.S. 21 (2005).

NATURE OF CASE: Appeal of federal court judgment for employees.

FACT SUMMARY: Meat-packing plant employees (P) argued they were entitled to be paid for time walking from the locker room, where they put on safety gear, to the plant floor, and then back to the locker room at the end of the day. The U.S. Court of Appeals for the Ninth Circuit ruled in favor of the employees (P).

🏛 RULE OF LAW

Time spent on the walk between the locker room, where employees are required to dress in protective and safety gear, and floor of the plant, where work is performed, should be compensated under the Fair Labor Standards Act.

FACTS: [This case represents two consolidated cases, *IBP, Inc. v. Alvarez*, 39 F.3d 894 (9th Cir. 2003), and *Tum v. Barber Foods Inc.*, 360 F.3d 274 (1st Cir. 2004). The facts in *Tum* are similar to those in *IBP*.] IBP (D) produces beef, pork and related products. It employs approximately 178 workers (P) in the slaughter division and 800 line workers (P) in the processing division at its Pasco, Washington, plant. All workers (P) must wear outer garments, hardhats, hairnets, earplugs, gloves, sleeves, aprons, leggings, and boots. Those who use knives must also wear protective equipment for their hands, arms, torsos, and legs, including chain-link metal aprons and vests. Their equipment is stored in company locker rooms. Pay was based on time spent cutting and bagging meat, and originally began with the first piece of meat, and ended with the last piece of meat. Since 1998, the company has paid for four minutes of clothes-changing time. IBP employees (P) filed a class action to recover compensation for preproduction and postproduction work, including time spent donning and doffing protective gear and walking between the locker rooms and the production floor before and after their assigned shifts. The Court of Appeals for the Ninth Circuit rejected IBP's (D) argument that walking between the locker rooms and the production areas is excluded from Fair Labor Standards Act coverage by the Portal-to-Portal Act, and held that the workers (P) had to be paid from the moment they began putting on safety gear required for their jobs until they took off the gear. But in the companion case, the Court of Appeals for the First Circuit reached the opposite conclusion. The Supreme Court granted certiorari to resolve the circuit split.

ISSUE: Should time spent on the walk between the locker room, where employees are required to dress in protective and safety gear, and floor of the plant, where work is performed, be compensated under the Fair Labor Standards Act?

HOLDING AND DECISION: (Stevens, J.) Yes. Time spent on the walk between the locker room, where employees are required to dress in protective and safety gear, and floor of the plant, where work is performed, should be compensated under the Fair Labor Standards Act. Any activity that is "integral and indispensable" to a "principal activity" of the workplace is itself a "principal activity" under § 4(a) of the Portal-to-Portal Act (Act), and donning and doffing the protective gear is therefore a principal activity under the Act. The locker rooms where the special safety gear is donned and doffed are the relevant "place of performance" of the principal activity that the employee (P) was employed to perform within the meaning of § 4(a)(1). Walking to that place before starting work is excluded from Fair Labor Standards Act coverage, but the statutory text does not exclude walking from that place to another area within the plant immediately after the workday has begun. The employers' (D) argument that a footnote in the original Portal-to-Portal Act implementing regulations—which said that paying employees to change clothes "does not necessarily mean" they are compensated for walking to their workstation—meant compensation for walking was foreclosed, is rejected. But while the walking time before reaching the plant floor was compensable, that does not mean that travel time before the start of the actual workday would be compensable.

▌ ANALYSIS

Congress passed the Portal-to-Portal Act of 1947, in order to make such activities as walking from the time clock to the plant noncompensable. Eight years after the enactment of the Portal-to-Portal Act and the Labor Department's interpretative regulations, the Supreme Court explained only that the term "principal activity or activities" as used in the Act embraces all activities that are "an integral and indispensable part of the principal activities," including the donning and doffing of specialized protective gear "before or after the regular work shift, on or off the production line." *Steiner v. Mitchell*, 350 U.S. 247, 256 (1956). The *IBP* case expands the "continuous workday" deemed compensable under the Portal-to-Portal Act to include all time spent after donning safety equipment and before taking it off, including the time walking to and from the locker rooms, but not so far as to include the time waiting to perform the first "principal work activity" as compensable.

■═■

Continued on next page.

Quicknotes

FAIR LABOR STANDARDS ACT   Enacted in 1938, this statute establishes a minimum wage applicable to all employees of covered employers and provides for mandatory over-time payment for covered employees who work more than 40 hours a week. Executive, administrative and professional employees paid on a salary basis are exempt from the statute.

■≡■

Wernsing v. Department of Human Services

Employee (P) v. Employer (D)

427 F.3d 466 (7th Cir. 2005).

NATURE OF CASE: Appeal of judgment for employer.

FACT SUMMARY: Jenny Wernsing's (P) starting salary at the Department of Human Services (DHS) (D) was $1,261 less than the starting salary of a male coworker, who was hired at the same time as Wernsing (P). DHS (D) based starting salaries in part on the salary history of the individual applicant, and Wernsing's (P) last salary was less than the male coworker's.

🏛 RULE OF LAW

An employer that bases pay scale on each employee's wage history does not violate the Equal Pay Act even if the practice results in different pay for two employees doing the same job.

FACTS: The Department of Human Services (DHS) (D) hired Jenny Wernsing (P) in 1998 as an internal security investigator. The salary range for the job was $2,478 to $4,466 per month. Wernsing's (P) starting salary was the bottom of the pay scale, but it was 30 percent more than her salary of $1,925 a month in her previous position. Charles Bingaman, who was hired by DHS at the same time as Wernsing (P), started at $3,739 a month, which was 10 percent more than his prior salary. Wernsing (P) also identified four other men in her job classification who had higher salaries than she did. Wernsing (P) sued DHS (D) under the Equal Pay Act, which prohibits employers from discriminating "between employees on the basis of sex by paying wages to employees . . . at a rate less than the rate at which he pays wages to employees of the opposite sex . . . for equal work on jobs the performance of which requires equal skill, effort, and responsibility, and which are performed under similar working conditions" (29 U.S.C. § 206(d)(1)). However, Section 206(d)(1)(iv) permits a pay "differential based on any other factor other than sex." The district court ruled in favor of DHS (D), holding that prior wages is a factor other than sex and that determining an employee's starting pay based in part on prior wages does not violate the Equal Pay Act.

ISSUE: Does an employer that bases pay scale on each employee's wage history violate the Equal Pay Act if the practice results in different pay for two employees doing the same job?

HOLDING AND DECISION: (Easterbrook, J.) No. An employer that bases pay scale on each employee's wage history does not violate the Equal Pay Act even if the practice results in different pay for two employees doing the same job. The Seventh Circuit's long-standing position

that employers do not have to show an acceptable business reason for taking prior salary into account when setting an employee's starting pay still stands. The Equal Pay Act does not authorize courts to set their own standards of "acceptable" business practices.

▶ ANALYSIS

The judge in this case made much of the fact that the Seventh Circuit would not deviate from a position on the issue that it has held since 1987. Note, however, that the circuit courts are split four to two in favor of requiring an acceptable business reason.

Quicknotes

EQUAL PAY ACT 29 U.S.C. § 206 Passed in 1963 as an amendment to the Fair Labor Standards Act, it prohibits sex-based wage discrimination and requires equal pay for equal work.

AFSCME v. Washington

Unions (P) v. State (D)

578 F. Supp. 846 (W.D. Wash. 1983).

NATURE OF CASE: Class action to enjoin sex discrimination in employment.

FACT SUMMARY: When Washington's (D) new governor eliminated a budget appropriation made by the prior governor to help eliminate salary discrepancies based on sex, two unions (P) representing state employees in jobs held primarily by women filed a class-action suit, alleging violation of Title VII of the Civil Rights Act of 1964.

RULE OF LAW
A state's historical failure to pay workers their full evaluated worth in predominately female jobs demonstrates a pattern of sex discrimination in violation of Title VII of the Civil Rights Act of 1964.

FACTS: When a study conducted for the state of Washington (D) by an independent consulting firm showed a 20 percent disparity between pay for women's job classes and men's job classes, the governor included an appropriation in the budget to begin eliminating the wage discrimination in state employment. However, when the new governor took office a month later, in 1977, he removed the appropriation from the budget, even though there was a budget surplus. The state legislature then endorsed continuing study of the wage differentials. Two unions (P) filed this class-action suit against the state of Washington (D) for discriminating on the basis of sex in its salary structure. The district judge ruled that the state (D) was guilty of intentionally discriminating against employees in predominately female job classifications. Washington (D) argued that injunctive relief should not be formulated and enforced because of: (1) the tremendous costs involved; (2) lack of revenue due to the depressed economy; (3) prior state revenue commitments; (4) the state constitution's balanced-budget requirement; (5) disruption in the state's work force and the state's compensation scheme; (6) the state's prior initiation of a remedy to eliminate the sex discrimination by 1993; and (7) the Tenth Amendment to the U.S. Constitution.

ISSUE: Does a state's historical failure to pay workers their full evaluated worth in predominately female jobs demonstrate a pattern of sex discrimination in violation of Title VII of the Civil Rights Act of 1964?

HOLDING AND DECISION: (Tanner, J.) Yes. A state's historical failure to pay workers their full evaluated worth in predominately female jobs demonstrates a pattern of sex discrimination in violation of Title VII of the Civil Rights Act of 1964. Washington's (D) arguments fail for

the following reasons: (1) Title VII does not contain a cost-justification defense comparable to the affirmative defense available in a price-discrimination suit; (2) Washington's (D) shortage of revenue, prior revenue commitments, and constitutionally mandated balanced-budget defenses cannot withstand the evidence produced at trial (it was uncontroverted that at the time the state had a surplus budget, was aware of the disparity which is the subject of this lawsuit, and did not consider the acknowledged discrimination enough of a priority to divert the surplus to the victims of the discrimination); (3) any disruption full implementation of the proposed injunctive relief would effect is a direct result of the discrimination Washington (D) created and has maintained; and (4) the belated May 1983 appropriation did not purport to eliminate discrimination. Were this court to adopt the May 1983 legislation as the injunctive remedy herein, it would be endorsing a compensation plan that works a grave injustice to the victims of discrimination. Injunctive orders couched in terms of "with all deliberate speed" result in nonaction. This court sees no credible distinction between endorsing a remedy to be phased in over a ten-year period and an injunction ordering compliance "with all due speed." Washington's (D) preoccupation with its budget constraints pales when compared with the invidiousness of the impact of pervasive, intentional, ongoing discrimination upon the women affected. The state (D) is adhering to a practice of sex discrimination in violation of the terms of Title VII with full knowledge of, and indifference to, its effect up the plaintiffs.

ANALYSIS

In the court's own words, "the bad faith of Washington's (D) action is patent and cannot be overcome at this late date with arguments that sound in equity." The court went on to say that there was little doubt that had Washington (D) produced evidence that the unlawful discrimination was other than in "bad faith," case precedents would have persuaded the court that backpay would not have been an appropriate remedy. The devastating cost to a defendant who did not act in bad faith would, then and only then, become relevant. The court declared, however, that the record in this case did not favor a finding that Washington (D) acted in good faith when it paid female workers less than their evaluated worth.

Continued on next page.

Quicknotes

GOOD FAITH An honest intention to abstain from any unconscientious advantage of another.

TITLE VII OF THE CIVIL RIGHTS ACT OF 1964 Prohibits discrimination in employment, education and other services based on sex. 42 U.S.C. § 2000E-2(a).

AFSCME v. Washington

Unions (P) v. State (D)

770 F.2d 1401 (9th Cir. 1985).

NATURE OF CASE: Appeal from judgment finding Title VII sex-discrimination violations in class-action suit.

FACT SUMMARY: Fifteen thousand state employees represented by the American Federation of State, County, and Municipal Employees (AFSCME) (P) contended that Washington (D) violated Title VII of the Civil Rights Act of 1964 by compensating employees in predominately female jobs at lower rates than employees in dissimilar, male-dominated jobs of comparable worth.

🏛 RULE OF LAW
Job-evaluation studies and comparable-worth statistics alone are not sufficient to establish the inference of discriminatory motive required by disparate-treatment theory.

FACTS: In 1974, the state of Washington (D) commissioned a study by a management consultant to determine whether a wage disparity existed between state jobs held predominately by women and those held predominately by men. The consultant found a wage disparity of about 20 percent. In 1983, the state (D) enacted legislation providing a compensation scheme based on comparable worth. The AFSCME (P) subsequently contended that the state (D) should have immediately adopted and implemented a comparable-worth compensation based on the results of the study. It sued under Title VII, alleging disparate treatment and arguing that discriminatory motive may be inferred from the study. The study reflected a historical pattern of lower wages for women, and the state (D) perpetuated that disparity by setting wages in its new compensation scheme according to market rates. The district court found in favor of AFSCME (P), and the state (D) appealed.

ISSUE: Are job-evaluation studies and comparable-worth statistics alone sufficient to establish the inference of discriminatory motive required by disparate-treatment theory?

HOLDING AND DECISION: (Kennedy, J.) No. Job-evaluation studies and the comparable-worth statistics alone are not sufficient to establish the inference of discriminatory motive required by disparate-treatment theory. Discriminatory intent must be linked to culpability. But the free market system is merely one factor, and not an insidious one, that influences wage rates. Therefore, AFSCME's (P) attempt to infer a discriminatory motive from the state's (D) participation in the market system must be rejected. While statistical studies may be given some weight in establishing discriminatory motive, they must be cor-

roborated by independent evidence. AFSCME (P) has not presented sufficient independent evidence here to support an inference of discriminatory motive. It has therefore failed to establish a violation of Title VII under a disparate-treatment theory. Reversed.

▶ ANALYSIS

The above case illustrates the unfavorable reception that the controversial "comparable-worth" theory generally receives from courts. The theory holds that men, women, and minorities should be paid equally for jobs that are of comparable value to the employer, even if the jobs themselves are not substantially equal. Courts are reluctant, however, to rely on or interfere with discriminatory labor markets, given that Congress has not indicated any support for comparable-worth claims.

■■■

Quicknotes

DISPARATE TREATMENT Unequal treatment of employees or of applicants for employment without justification.

MOTIVE Reason or other impetus inciting one to action.

■■■

Health Benefits

Quick Reference Rules of Law

Salley v. E.I. DuPont de Nemours & Co.

Employee (P) v. Employer (D)

966 F.2d 1011 (5th Cir. 1992).

NATURE OF CASE: Appeal of an award of damages for failure to make payments under the Employee Retirement Income Security Act (ERISA).

FACT SUMMARY: The administrators of DuPont's (D) ERISA plan refused to pay for Salley's (P) psychiatric care although the doctor indicated that it was medically necessary.

🏛 RULE OF LAW

ERISA administrators can abuse their discretion by failing to obtain the necessary information on which to base a payment decision.

FACTS: Jack Salley was a retired E.I. DuPont de Nemours & Co. (DuPont) (D) employee who participated in its hospital medical-surgical coverage policy, which was regulated under ERISA. Preferred Health Care (Preferred), the administrators, administered the individual cases under the plan, and Dupont (D) reimbursed all medically necessary costs. Danielle Salley (P), Jack's daughter, was also covered under the plan and required in-patient psychiatric care at DePaul Northshore Hospital. Salley (P) had been a patient there under the care of Dr. Blundell twice but had reverted back to her previous behavior each time she was released. When Salley (P) was hospitalized for a third time, Blundell found improvement but was concerned about the possibility of another regression. Blundell contacted Preferred about finding Salley (P) less restrictive treatment. However, the administrator instructed Blundell that it was terminating the payments for the treatments since they were no longer medically necessary. Salley (P) remained at DePaul for several months and then filed suit to recover the costs. The district court ruled for Salley (P), and DuPont (D) appealed.

ISSUE: Can ERISA administrators abuse their discretion by failing to obtain the necessary information on which to base a payment decision?

HOLDING AND DECISION: (Williams, J.) Yes. ERISA administrators can abuse their discretion by failing to obtain the necessary information on which to base a payment decision. Under ERISA, the denial of benefits should be reviewed under a de novo standard unless the benefit plan gives an administrator discretionary authority to determine eligibility. If there is discretion, courts must determine whether there was abuse of discretion by the administrator. If the administrator relies solely on the recommendations of the employee's physician and does not undertake an independent inquiry, the administrator must follow all of the physician's advice. Here, Preferred based its decision to deny benefits to Salley (P) on Blundell's diagnosis. However, Blundell's full recommendation was that Salley (P) would require alternative treatment if hospitalization was terminated. Thus, Preferred, acting for DuPont (D), abused its discretion in determining payments when it failed to fully follow the advice of the only physician to treat Salley (P). Affirmed.

▶ ANALYSIS

The decision noted that the district court may have erred in applying the "treating physician presumption." Under this presumption, deference must be paid to the testimony of the treating doctor unless there is substantial contradictory evidence. The court noted that this presumption should not apply under ERISA, but that the district court could properly find the treating physician more credible as a witness.

━■━■

Quicknotes

ABUSE OF DISCRETION A determination by an appellate court that a lower court's decision was based on an error of law.

DE NOVO The review of a lower court decision by an appellate court, which is hearing the case as if it had not been previously heard and as if no judgment had been rendered.

EMPLOYEE RETIREMENT INCOME SECURITY ACT OF 1974 Federal law of employee benefits which establishes minimum standards to protect employees from breach of benefit promises made by employers.

EMPLOYEE RETIREMENT INCOME SECURITY ACT OF 1974 Section 510 of 29 U.S.C. § 1140 states that it is unlawful to discharge, fine, suspend, expel, discipline, or discriminate against a participant or beneficiary for the purpose of interfering with the attainment of any right to which such participant may become entitled under the plan.

━■━■

Phelps v. Field Real Estate Co.

Employee with HIV (P) v. Real estate company (D)

991 F.2d 645 (10th Cir. 1993).

NATURE OF CASE: Appeal from judgment in an action for violations of the Employee Retirement Income Security Act (ERISA).

FACT SUMMARY: Phelps (P) alleged that he was terminated by Field Real Estate Co. (D) because he had Acquired Immunodeficiency Syndrome (AIDS).

🏛 RULE OF LAW
ERISA prohibits the termination of employees in order to interfere with their benefits under an employee-benefit plan.

FACTS: In 1985, Phelps (P) began working for Field Real Estate Co. (Field) (D) as a vice president of the commercial real estate division. In 1986, Phelps (P) learned that he was HIV positive but did not disclose his condition. Through 1987, Phelps (P) received average evaluations at Field (D). In 1988, Phelps's (P) supervisor Poole was informed by an anonymous note that Phelps (P) had a fatal disease. However, Phelps (P) reassured Poole, with a doctor's letter, that he was capable of doing the job. In 1989, Phelps (P) received an evaluation that described the performance of his division as poor, although Phelps (P) disputed the reasons for the decline in performance. Months later, Poole informed Phelps (P) that he was being terminated due to the poor performance of the division and company reorganization. Phelps (P) filed suit under § 510 of ERISA, alleging that he was fired because he had AIDS. The district court ruled for Field (D), and Phelps (P) appealed.

ISSUE: Does ERISA prohibit the termination of employees in order to interfere with their benefits under an employee-benefit plan?

HOLDING AND DECISION: (Brown, J.) Yes. ERISA prohibits the termination of employees in order to interfere with their benefits under an employee benefit plan. Section 510 of ERISA provides that it is unlawful to discharge an employee who is a participant of an employee-benefit plan for the purpose of interfering with his rights under the plan. This requires that the plaintiff prove by preponderance of the evidence that the employer's decision to terminate was motivated by intent to interfere with benefits. Phelps (P) failed to present any evidence that Poole or anyone at Field (D) was aware of the effect of an AIDS patient on the employee-benefit plan. Thus, even though Poole was aware that Phelps (P) had AIDS, there was no evidence that it was the motivating factor for the termination decision. The district court determined that the poor performance of Phelps's (P) division, rather than the desire to save the costs of health care, was the primary reason for Phelps's (P) discharge. Accordingly, there was no violation of § 510. Affirmed.

▶ ANALYSIS

Generally the type of evidence that a terminated employee must show in order to prove a violation of § 510 includes discharge shortly after notifying the employer of a disease, failure to follow usual termination procedures, and an incentive to avoid high medical costs. See *Folz v. Marriott Corp.*, 594 F. Supp. 1007 (W.D. Mo. 1994). Employers are also prohibited from discharging employees for exercising their rights under ERISA.

■■■

Quicknotes

EMPLOYMENT-AT-WILL The rule an employment relationship is subject to termination at any time, or for any cause, by an employee or an employer in the absence of a specific agreement otherwise.

EMPLOYEE RETIREMENT INCOME SECURITY ACT OF 1974 Section 510 of 29 U.S.C. § 1140 states that it is unlawful to discharge, fine, suspend, expel, discipline, or discriminate against a participant or beneficiary for the purpose of interfering with the attainment of any right to which such participant may become entitled under the plan.

TERMINATION OF EMPLOYMENT Cessation of a relationship between two parties whereby an individual performs work at the direction of another in exchange for compensation.

■■■

McDowell v. Krawchison

Employee (P) v. Former employer (D)

125 F.3d 954 (6th Cir. 1997).

NATURE OF CASE: Appeal from summary judgment in favor of plaintiffs for failure to provide health insurance benefits.

FACT SUMMARY: McDowell (P) brought suit against his former employer, Krawchison (D), for failure to provide adequate notice to him and his wife regarding their rights to continued medical coverage under the Comprehensive Omnibus Budget Reconciliation Act (COBRA).

🏛 RULE OF LAW
A covered spouse is a qualified beneficiary under COBRA, thereby requiring entitlement to notice of his or her rights.

FACTS: Krawchison (D) held an ownership interest in several chiropractic clinics throughout the Midwest. McDowell (P) accepted an offer from Krawchison (D) to work at one such clinic. Subsequently, Krawchison (D) sold the clinic, and McDowell (P) was terminated. McDowell's (P) wife, Sidovar (P), suffered from breast cancer and McDowell (P) wished to continue their health insurance. Anderson, the new owner, assured McDowell (P) that his insurance benefits would continue. McDowell (P) signed a release, waiving all claims against the chiropractic center and Krawchison (D). The following year, McDowell (P) and his wife (P) discovered that they had been terminated from their insurance coverage. They filed suit, claiming violations of COBRA. The court granted summary judgment for McDowell (P), and Krawchison (D) appealed.

ISSUE: Is a covered spouse a qualified beneficiary under COBRA, thereby requiring entitlement to notice of his or her rights?

HOLDING AND DECISION: (Moore, J.) Yes. A covered spouse is a qualified beneficiary under COBRA, thereby requiring entitlement to notice of his or her rights. COBRA requires a plan administrator to notify any qualified beneficiary of his or her right to continue to receive health insurance coverage for a maximum of 18 months after specified events. If a plan administrator fails to provide such notice, it may be required to provide coverage to the beneficiary. Here, both McDowell (P) and Sidovar (P) were qualified beneficiaries entitled to notice. COBRA is silent as to the proper contents of the required notice. However, the provided notice must be adequate to permit the beneficiary to decide whether to elect continued coverage within 60 days of the qualifying event. As a spouse of a qualified beneficiary, Sidovar (P) was entitled to notice of her own rights under COBRA. A qualified beneficiary spouse has COBRA rights independent of his or her spouse and may make a different election regarding the terms and scope of his or her coverage. The provisions of COBRA are consistent with this conclusion. Section 1165(2) entitles each separate qualified beneficiary to select his or her type of coverage. Section 1163(c) specifically excludes from the notice requirement dependent children residing with the qualified beneficiary. Section 1166(c) deems notification to a qualified spouse sufficient notice as to other beneficiaries currently residing with that spouse. Collectively these sections suggest that the qualified beneficiary is entitled to independent treatment under COBRA and that the statute in fact depends upon the independent notification so as to inform any dependents. Moreover, had Congress intended to exclude a spouse from the notice requirement it would have expressly provided for that treatment. Nor did McDowell's (P) release form affect Sidovar's (P) rights to notice. As previously stated, a spouse of a qualified employee has independent rights under COBRA. Assuming McDowell's (P) waiver was effective, it did not effectuate a waiver of Sidovar's (P) rights. Here, the plan administrator failed to provide Sidovar (P) with adequate notice of her right to continued medical coverage in violation of COBRA. Affirmed, reversed for other defendant, and remanded.

▸ ANALYSIS

Generally, the plan administrator bears the burden of demonstrating that adequate notice was given following the "qualifying event." Termination of employment for reasons other than gross misconduct, or a reduction in hours of employment resulting in coverage loss, constitutes a qualifying event for purposes of COBRA. The circumstances constituting a qualifying event also include if the covered employee dies or obtains Medicare coverage, divorce or legal separation, if a child no longer qualifies as a covered dependent, or if the employer files for bankruptcy.

■≡■

Quicknotes

BENEFICIARY A third party who is the recipient of the benefit of a transaction undertaken by another.

COMPREHENSIVE OMNIBUS BUDGET RECONCILIATION ACT Amended ERISA in 1986. 29 U.S.C. §§ 1162-1167 Requires a plan administrator notify any qualified beneficiary of his right to continue health-insurance coverage after termination of employment.

NOTICE Communication of information to a person by an authorized person or an otherwise proper source.

WAIVER The intentional or voluntary forfeiture of a recognized right.

■≡■

New York State Conference of Blue Cross & Blue Shield Plans v. Travelers Insurance Co.

State (D) v. Private insurers (P)

514 U.S. 645 (1995).

NATURE OF CASE: State's appeal of federal appeals court judgment in favor of private insurers.

FACT SUMMARY: A New York (D) state law imposed a surcharge on hospital bills to offset costs of treating indigent patients. The insurance industry (P) rebelled.

🏛 RULE OF LAW
For a state benefits law that imposes surcharges on hospital bills in order to compensate hospitals for care to indigent patients to be preempted by Employee Retirement Income Security Act (ERISA), it must have a sufficient "connection" with ERISA-covered plans.

FACTS: The State of New York (D) passed a law that imposes surcharges on hospital bills. To compensate hospitals for care provided to indigent patients, the law adds surcharges to the bills of patients covered by commercial insurers (P) and self-insured plans, and imposes surcharges on health maintenance organizations (P) if they do not enroll a sufficient number of Medicaid recipients. Surcharges do not apply to bills paid by Medicaid or by the state's Blue Cross & Blue Shield plans, which must accept all enrollees and use community rating to set their premiums. Several insurers (P) and trade associations (P) banded together to challenge the surcharge law, arguing that it was preempted by ERISA. Two lower courts said the surcharge law triggered ERISA's preemption clause.

ISSUE: For a state benefits law that imposes surcharges on hospital bills in order to compensate hospitals for care to indigent patients to be preempted by ERISA, must it have a sufficient "connection" with ERISA-covered plans?

HOLDING AND DECISION: (Souter, J.) Yes. For a state benefits law that imposes surcharges on hospital bills in order to compensate hospitals for care to indigent patients to be preempted by ERISA, it must have a sufficient "connection" with ERISA-covered plans. An example of a sufficient connection is a law that sets requirements for benefit structures or plan administration. The New York law has an indirect impact by creating rate variations, but leaves plan administrators free to choose the best coverage for their own purposes. The state law need not have direct economic effects in order to trigger preemption, however; indirect economic effects of a state law could become severe enough to constitute a mandate on ERISA plans, which would trigger preemption. Reversed and remanded.

▶ ANALYSIS

This decision gave states the option to impose extra fees on health care bills, which necessarily allowed more state regulation of employer-sponsored health plans.

■=■

Quicknotes

EMPLOYEE RETIREMENT INCOME SECURITY ACT OF 1974 Section 510 of 29 U.S.C. § 1140 states that it is unlawful to discharge, fine, suspend, expel, discipline, or discriminate against a participant or beneficiary for the purpose of interfering with the attainment of any right to which such participant may become entitled under the plan.

■=■

Kentucky Association of Health Plans, Inc. v. Miller

HMOs (P) v. Kentucky Department of Insurance (D)

538 U.S. 329 (2003).

NATURE OF CASE: Supreme Court review of state law compliance with the Employee Retirement Income Security Act (ERISA).

FACT SUMMARY: Seven health-maintenance organizations (HMOs) (P), along with the Kentucky Association of Health Plans Inc. (P), a nonprofit association designed to promote the interests of HMOs, filed a lawsuit in 1997 against the Kentucky Department of Insurance (D), alleging that the state's any-willing-provider statute was invalid because it was preempted by ERISA.

> ## 🏛 RULE OF LAW
> State "any-willing-provider" laws, which give health maintenance organization subscribers options in the selection of their physicians, are not preempted by the Employee Retirement Income Security Act.

FACTS: Kentucky's legislature enacted the Kentucky Health Care Reform Act, which included an "any-willing-provider" provision. The provision stated that "health-care benefit plans shall not discriminate against any provider who is located within the geographic coverage area of the health benefit plan and is willing to meet the terms and conditions for participation established by the health-benefit plan." Seven health-maintenance organizations (HMOs) (P), along with the Kentucky Association of Health Plans Inc. (P) a nonprofit association designed to promote the interests of HMOs, filed a lawsuit in 1997 against George Nichols III (D), the commissioner of the Kentucky Department of Insurance (D), alleging that the any-willing-provider statute was invalid because it was preempted by ERISA.

ISSUE: Are state "any-willing-provider" laws, which give health maintenance organization subscribers options in the selection of their physicians, preempted by the Employee Retirement Income Security Act?

HOLDING AND DECISION: (Scalia, J.) No. State "any-willing-provider" laws, which give health maintenance organization subscribers options in the selection of their physicians, are not preempted by ERISA. The HMOs' argument that the Kentucky law was not saved from ERISA preemption because the law regulated not only the insurance industry, but also medical providers, is rejected. The Kentucky law does not impose any prohibitions or requirements on health-care providers. The fact that regulations directed toward certain entities will almost always disable other entities from doing, with the regulated entities, what the regulations forbid does not place such regulation outside the scope of ERISA's savings clause. For a state law to "regulate insurance," the law must meet two requirements: it must be specifically directed toward the insurance business, and it must "substantially affect" the risk pooling arrangement between the insurer and the insured. Kentucky's law satisfies each of these requirements. Affirmed.

▶ ANALYSIS

In this case, the Court explicitly made a "clean break" from its own McCarran-Ferguson factors, which federal courts have used to determine whether a state law regulates the business of insurance within the meaning of ERISA. Under the McCarran-Ferguson Act, a practice constitutes the "business of insurance" if the practice transfers or spreads policyholders' risks, plays an integral part in the policy relationship between the insurer and the insured, and is limited to entities within the insurance industry. According to Scalia: "We believe that our use of the McCarran-Ferguson case law in the ERISA context has misdirected attention, failed to provide clear guidance to lower federal courts, and, as this case demonstrates, added little to the relevant analysis." He added that the court's ERISA preemption rulings using the McCarran-Ferguson factors "raise more questions than they answer and provide wide opportunities for divergent outcomes."

Quicknotes

EMPLOYEE RETIREMENT INCOME SECURITY ACT OF 1974 Section 510 of 29 U.S.C. § 1140 states that it is unlawful to discharge, fine, suspend, expel, discipline, or discriminate against a participant or beneficiary for the purpose of interfering with the attainment of any right to which such participant may become entitled under the plan.

Ragsdale v. Wolverine World Wide, Inc.

Employee (P) v. Employer (D)

535 U.S. 81 (2002).

NATURE OF CASE: Appeal from grant of defense motion for summary judgment in suit for statutory employee benefits.

FACT SUMMARY: When Wolverine World Wide, Inc. (D) failed to provide Tracy Ragsdale (P), an employee, with individualized notice that her medical absence would count as leave under the Family and Medical Leave Act of 1993, she sued Wolverine (D) for violation of the Act.

RULE OF LAW
The Labor Department regulation requiring individual employee notification when an absence will count as leave under the Family and Medical Leave Act of 1993 is invalid as exceeding the powers of the Secretary of Labor.

FACTS: Tracy Ragsdale (P), an employee of Wolverine World Wide, Inc. (Wolverine) (D), was diagnosed with cancer. Though unable to work during her treatment period, she was eligible for seven months of unpaid sick leave under Wolverine's (D) leave plan. She requested and received a one-month leave of absence and a 30-day extension at the end of each of the seven months that followed. Wolverine (D) granted the requests, and Ragsdale (P) missed 30 consecutive weeks of work. Wolverine (D) maintained her health benefits and paid her premiums during this period. Wolverine (D) did not notify her, however, that 12 weeks of the absence would count as her leave under the Family and Medical Leave Act of 1993 (FMLA). The Secretary of Labor had promulgated a regulation under the FMLA that employers must provide this type of notice to employees. Ragsdale (P) brought suit in federal district court against Wolverine (D) under the FMLA, arguing that because Wolverine (D) was in technical violation of this Labor Department notice regulation, she was entitled to more leave. The district court granted summary judgment to Wolverine (D), and the court of appeals agreed. Ragsdale (P) appealed.

ISSUE: Is the Labor Department regulation requiring individual employee notification when an absence will count as leave under the Family and Medical Leave Act of 1993 invalid as exceeding the powers of the Secretary of Labor?

HOLDING AND DECISION: (Kennedy, J.) Yes. The Labor Department regulation requiring individual employee notification when an absence will count as leave under the Family and Medical Leave Act of 1993 is invalid as exceeding the powers of the Secretary of Labor. The challenged regulation is invalid because it alters the FMLA's cause of action in a fundamental way: It relieves employees of the burden of proving any real impairment of their rights and resulting prejudice. Here, for example, the regulation permitted Ragsdale (P) to bring suit under the FMLA despite her inability to show that Wolverine's (D) actions restrained her exercise of FMLA rights. The regulation transformed Wolverine's (D) failure to give notice—along with its refusal to grant her more than 30 weeks of leave—into an actionable statutory violation. This regulatory "sleight of hand" would entitle Ragsdale (P) to reinstatement and back-pay, even though reinstatement could not be said to be appropriate in these circumstances and Ragsdale (P) lost no compensation by reason of Wolverine's (D) failure to designate her absence as FMLA leave. By mandating these results absent a showing of consequential harm, the regulation, "worked an end run" around important limitations of the statute's remedial scheme. The Secretary of Labor's penalty is disproportionate and inconsistent with Congress's intent as reflected in the statutory scheme. Affirmed.

DISSENT: (O'Connor, J) The Secretary of Labor has reasonably determined that individualized notice is necessary to implement FMLA's provisions. Employees need to be made aware of their rights under FMLA. The regulation requiring individualized notice provides assurance that employees taking leave are aware of their rights at the very moment such rights become relevant. Individualized notice also facilitates leave planning, allowing employees to organize their health treatments or family obligations around the total amount of leave they will ultimately be provided.

ANALYSIS

As noted in *Ragsdale*, many employers have adopted policies with terms far more generous than the FMLA actually requires. Congress encouraged as much, mandating in the Act's penultimate provision that nothing in the Act should be construed to discourage employers from adopting or retaining leave policies more generous than any policies that comply with the requirements under the Act.

Quicknotes

NOTICE Communication of information to a person by one authorized or by an otherwise proper source.

Lang v. Star Herald

Employee (P) v. Employer (D)

107 F.3d 1308 (8th Cir.), *cert. denied*, 522 U.S. 839 (1997).

NATURE OF CASE: Appeal from grant of defense motion for summary judgment in a gender-discrimination suit.

FACT SUMMARY: Lang (P) claimed that she was terminated by the Star Herald (D) due to her pregnancy.

RULE OF LAW
A prima facie case for employment discrimination requires a plaintiff to show that the employee was subjected to either disparate treatment or disparate impact.

FACTS: Lang (P), an employee of the Star Herald (D), accumulated vacation time and sick leave consistent with the Star Herald's (D) employee benefits policy. Lang (P) informed her supervisor that she was pregnant, but continued to work. Lang (P) experienced some bleeding and was advised by her doctor to rest for two weeks. Lang (P) did not work for one week and was paid based on her accrued vacation and sick-leave time. The supervisor then informed Lang (P) that her sick leave and vacation time had expired and that the Star Herald (D) did not have a short-term disability policy. Lang's (P) doctor recommended that she not resume work. The Star Herald's (D) employment policy permitted employees who exhausted their vacation and sick-leave time to apply for an unpaid leave of absence; however, the employee was not guaranteed re-employment. Lang (P) refused to apply for an unpaid leave of absence and was terminated. Lang (P) commenced suit charging gender discrimination on the basis of her pregnant status. The district court granted the Star Herald's (D) motion for summary judgment. Lang (P) appealed.

ISSUE: Does a prima facie case for employment discrimination require a plaintiff to show that the employee was subjected to either disparate treatment or disparate impact?

HOLDING AND DECISION: (Hansen, J.) Yes. A prima facie case for employment discrimination requires a plaintiff to show that the employee was subjected to either disparate treatment or disparate impact. Title VII of the Civil Rights Act of 1964 prohibits an employer from failing or refusing to hire or terminating any individual or discriminating against the individual in respect to the terms and conditions of his or her employment on the basis of gender. A prima facie case of disparate treatment on the basis of pregnancy requires a demonstration that the particular employee was denied benefits afforded to non-pregnant, female employees. The burden then shifts to the employer to show a nondiscriminatory reason for the

disparate treatment. Since Lang (P) failed to demonstrate that she was treated differently than nonpregnant employees with respect to a leave of absence, the Star Herald (D) did not have to sustain that burden. Lang (P) also contended that she suffered discrimination on the basis of the disparate impact of the Star Herald's (D) unpaid-leave policy. A prima facie case of disparate impact required Lang to prove that the unpaid sick-leave policy was in fact more burdensome in its application to pregnant employees than to nonpregnant employees. This requires the introduction of statistical evidence to demonstrate that the discriminatory practice had the effect of denying benefits to women. Lang (P) failed to present such evidence. Affirmed.

ANALYSIS

Congress enacted the Pregnancy Discrimination Act (PDA) of 1978 in order to clarify that gender discrimination under Title VII included discrimination on the basis of pregnancy. That Act expressly states that discrimination on the basis of gender includes, but is not limited to, discrimination due to pregnancy, childbirth or related medical conditions. Its provisions also expressly provide for the equal treatment of women subject to such conditions and other similarly situated workers for employment purposes, including the receipt of benefits.

■=■

Quicknotes

DISPARATE TREATMENT Unequal treatment of employees or of applicants for employment without justification.

PREGNANCY DISCRIMINATION ACT Enacted in 1978, amends the definitional provision of Title VII to clarify that discrimination on the basis of pregnancy, childbirth, or related medical conditions is sex discrimination under Title VII 42 U.S.C. § 2000.

TITLE VII OF THE CIVIL RIGHTS ACT OF 1964 States that it shall be an unlawful employment practice for an employer to fail or refuse to hire or otherwise discriminate against any individual with respect to his employment because of such individual's race, color, religion, sex, or national origin.

■=■

In re Union Pacific Railroad Employment Practices Litigation

Employees (P) v. Employer (D)

479 F.3d 936 (8th Cir. 2007).

NATURE OF CASE: Appeal from granting of partial summary judgment to the plaintiffs.

FACT SUMMARY: A class of women employees of Union Pacific Railroad (Union Pacific) (P) brought claims under Title VII and the Pregnancy Discrimination Act based upon Union Pacific's (D) failure to provide health insurance coverage for contraception.

🏛 RULE OF LAW
Under Title VII and the Pregnancy Discrimination Act, contraception is not "related to" pregnancy for purposes of the statutes because contraception is a treatment that occurs prior to pregnancy.

FACTS: Union Pacific Railroad (Union Pacific) (D) denies health insurance coverage for contraception, for both women and men. A class of women employees (P) brought suit against Union Pacific on the grounds the policy discriminated against women. According to the plaintiff class, the Pregnancy Discrimination Act (PDA) requires that employers not discriminate against women on any issue "related to" pregnancy. The class (P) argues contraception is related to pregnancy, while Union Pacific (D) argues the PDA only demands coverage for medical issues that occur after a woman becomes pregnant. The class (P) also brought a separate claim for disparate treatment under Title VII, alleging that Union Pacific (D) provided more favorable health care to men than it did to women. The federal district court granted partial summary judgment to the class (P). Union Pacific (D) appealed.

ISSUE: Under Title VII and the PDA, is contraception not "related to" pregnancy for purposes of the statutes because contraception is a treatment that occurs prior to pregnancy?

HOLDING AND DECISION: (Gruender, J.) Yes. Under Title VII and the PDA, contraception is not "related to" pregnancy for purposes of the statutes because contraception is a treatment that occurs prior to pregnancy. The PDA covers medical conditions that are related to a woman's pregnancy. This court previously held that infertility treatments were not covered by the PDA because those treatments did not relate to medical issues arising out of or related to pregnancy. Such is the case with contraception. It relates to a treatment that is taken before a woman becomes pregnant. Accordingly, like infertility treatments, the PDA does not require that employers cover insurance payments for contraception because it is not related to pregnancy. Neither the language of the PDA

nor the legislative history of the act supports the contention that Congress sought to cover treatments that are pre-pregnancy. In addition, the class's (P) Title VII disparate treatment claim also fails. To establish a claim for disparate treatment, the class (P) must show that other similarly situated employees were treated more favorably than the class. The district court improperly compared the entire health insurance programs offered to both men and women. The only relevant issue here is contraception. Because Union Pacific (D) denied coverage to both men and women for contraception, there is no violation. Reversed and remanded.

DISSENT: (Bye, J.) The district court correctly took a broad view of Union Pacific's (D) treatment of men and women and properly concluded that its health insurance coverage was discriminatory. For example, its policy denying coverage for vasectomies is clearly discriminatory because only women can become pregnant. A review of the legislative history does support the contention that Congress sought to cover pre- and post-pregnancy related issues. Moreover, the majority incorrectly equates infertility treatment and contraception. The difference is, again, that only women can become pregnant and therefore denial of contraception coverage is discriminatory against women.

▌ ANALYSIS

The PDA itself was a Congressional response to a prior Supreme Court ruling that Title VII excluded claims related to a woman's pregnancy. The Supreme Court has yet to rule on the issue of coverage for contraceptives or other pre-pregnancy treatments.

■■■

Quicknotes

DISPARATE TREATMENT Unequal treatment of employees or of applicants for employment without justification.

TITLE VII Prohibits unlawful discrimination against individuals based on race or sex.

■■■

Braatz v. Labor & Industry Review Commission

Teachers (P) v. State board (D)

Wis. Sup. Ct., 496 N.W.2d 597 (1993).

NATURE OF CASE: Appeal from an administrative decision regarding health insurance under a collective-bargaining agreement.

FACT SUMMARY: Maple School District teachers (P) contended that their health-insurance nonduplication policy discriminated based upon marital status.

🏛 RULE OF LAW
Health-insurance nonduplication policies unlawfully discriminate if they apply only to married employees.

FACTS: Under a collective-bargaining agreement between the Maple Board of Education and the teachers' union (P), a health-insurance plan covered the teachers and their spouses. According to one provision, if a married teacher's spouse was eligible for coverage at his/her place of employment, the couple had to choose between the Maple plan and the other coverage. Married teachers (P) at Maple alleged that this nonduplication policy discriminated against them based upon marital status and violated the Wisconsin Fair Employment Act (WFEA). The Labor and Industry Review Commission (LIRC) (D) disagreed, but a court of appeals reversed.

ISSUE: Do health-insurance nonduplication policies unlawfully discriminate if they apply only to married employees?

HOLDING AND DECISION: (Steinmetz, J.) Yes. Health-insurance nonduplication policies unlawfully discriminate if they apply only to married employees. The WFEA prohibits employers from discriminating against any employee on the basis of marital status. One provision of the WFEA states that the antidiscrimination policy should be liberally construed. Health-insurance benefits are protected by the WFEA's prohibition against marital-status discrimination. The Maple Insurance plan forces an election between coverage only for married employees with duplicate coverage. Single employees who have alternative health-insurance coverage are not forced to choose. Thus, the plan treats employees who are similarly situated differently based upon their marital status. LIRC's (D) decision was incorrect, and the court of appeals is affirmed.

▶ ANALYSIS

The decision rejected LIRC's (D) contention that health-insurance benefits had been impliedly excepted from the purview of the WFEA by the decision in *Phillips v. Wisconsin Personnel Commission*, 482 N.W.2d 121 (Ct. App. 1992). In

that case, state employees were held not entitled to coverage of adult companions even though spouses were covered. The court noted that in *Phillips*, spouses and adult companions were not legal equivalents.

━━■

Quicknotes

━━■

Alaska Civil Liberties Union v. State

Employees (P) v. Employer (D)

Alaska Sup. Ct., 122 P.3d 781 (2005).

NATURE OF CASE: Appeal by public employees of summary judgment in favor of employer.

FACT SUMMARY: The Alaska Civil Liberties Union (P) and nine homosexual couples (P) filed suit against the state of Alaska (D) and municipality of Anchorage (D) in 1999, charging that the state's (D) health-insurance and other employment benefits to the spouses of their employees, which are available only to married couples, violated their right to equal protection under the state constitution.

⚖ RULE OF LAW

Same-sex partners of public workers in Alaska who are in "committed domestic relationships" are entitled to the same employee-provided benefits as those given to spouses of public workers.

FACTS: The Alaska Civil Liberties Union (P) and nine homosexual couples (P) filed suit against the state (D) and municipality of Anchorage (D) in 1999, charging that the state's (D) health-insurance and other employment benefits to the spouses of their employees, which are available only to married couples, violated their right to equal protection under the state constitution. Alaska voters had also adopted in 1998 the Marriage Amendment, providing that to be valid, a marriage may exist only between one man and one woman, thus barring homosexual couples (P) from marrying. Therefore, same-sex partners (P) are absolutely precluded from becoming eligible for the benefits. The superior court granted summary judgment for the state (D).

ISSUE: Are same-sex partners of public workers in Alaska who are in "committed domestic relationships" entitled to the same employee-provided benefits as those given to spouses of public workers?

HOLDING AND DECISION: (Eastaugh, J.) Yes. Same-sex partners of public workers in Alaska who are in "committed domestic relationships" are entitled to the same employee-provided benefits as those given to spouses of public workers. While unmarried opposite-sex couples may be legally denied such benefits, same-sex couples in Alaska have no remedy of qualifying for benefits by marrying, the result of the 1998 constitutional amendment that banned gay marriage. Therefore, denying benefits to same-sex partners is a violation of the state constitution's equal protection clause. Supplemental briefing asked.

▶ **ANALYSIS**

This issue caused a furor at the time it was handed down, with Alaska legislators and the governor at the time sounding off in the media against it. On December 19, 2006, the Alaska Supreme Court upheld new regulations stipulating how benefits for same-sex partners of state employees and retirees will be administered, ending uncertainty over how the state would comply with the court's previous order to have the new benefits in effect by January 1, 2007.

■▬■

Freedom in the Workplace

Quick Reference Rules of Law

Kelley v. Johnson

Police officer (P) v. Police Department commissioner (D)

425 U.S. 238 (1976).

NATURE OF CASE: Appeal from judgment in a civil rights action.

FACT SUMMARY: The Suffolk County Patrolmen's Benevolent Association (P) contended that the Department's (D) hair-grooming regulations violated the officer's right of free expression.

> ## 🏛 RULE OF LAW
> Law enforcement organizations may regulate the personal appearance of its officers.

FACTS: The Suffolk County Police Department (Department) (D) promulgated a regulation that established hair-grooming standards applicable to male members of the police force. The regulations prescribed the style and length of hair, beards, and mustaches. The Suffolk County Patrolmen's Benevolent Association (SCPBA) (P) filed an action under the Civil Rights Act of 1871 claiming that the regulations infringed on the officer's right to free expression. The court of appeals ruled in favor of the SCPBA (P), and the Department (D) appealed.

ISSUE: May law enforcement organizations place hair-grooming standards on its officers?

HOLDING AND DECISION: (Rehnquist, J.) Yes. Law enforcement organizations may regulate the personal appearance of its officers. The Fourteenth Amendment protects persons from deprivation of liberty by the states. Generally, liberty has been construed to refer to individuals' freedom of choice regarding basic matters of procreation, marriage, and family life. It is not necessary to determine whether liberty should encompass matters of personal appearance because a standard is used for police employees of the state. The state has a duty to keep the peace and may place special demands upon the police force in order to meet this duty. Choice of organization, dress, and equipment for law enforcement personnel is a decision that is entitled to a presumption of validity. Therefore, the Department (D) must only demonstrate a rational connection between its grooming regulation and the promotion of safety. The desire to make police officers readily recognizable is a sufficiently rational justification. Accordingly, the court of appeals is reversed.

DISSENT: (Marshall, J.) The right in one's personal appearance is inextricably intertwined with the right of every individual to control his own person and to be let alone. Furthermore, hair-grooming regulations have no rational connection with the stated goals of the Department (D).

▶ ANALYSIS

Justice Marshall's dissent also pointed out that the majority's conclusion that grooming regulations would support esprit de corps (morale) on the force was betrayed by the very fact that the union was challenging the regulation. Other hair-length cases have been brought on a Title VII sex discrimination basis but have been equally unsuccessful. See *Fagan v. National Cash Register Co.*, 481 F.2d 1115 (D.C. Cir. 1973).

━━■

Quicknotes

CIVIL RIGHTS ACT OF 1871, 42 U.S.C. § 1983 Enforces basic personal rights guaranteed by the constitution.

FIRST AMENDMENT Prohibits Congress from enacting any law respecting an establishment of religion, prohibiting the free exercise of religion, abridging freedom of speech or the press, the right of peaceful assembly and the right to petition for a redress of grievances.

FOURTEENTH AMENDMENT No state shall deny to any person within its jurisdiction the equal protection of the laws.

RATIONAL BASIS REVIEW A test employed by the court to determine the validity of a statute in equal protection actions, whereby the court determines whether the challenged statute is rationally related to the achievement of a legitimate state interest.

━━■

Jespersen v. Harrah's Operating Co., Inc.

Employee (P) v. Employer (D)

444 F.3d 1104 (9th Cir. 2006) (en banc).

NATURE OF CASE: Appeal of dismissal of employee's sex-discrimination claim.

FACT SUMMARY: Darlene Jespersen (P) argued that the new makeup policy at the Harrah's Casino (Harrah's) (D) in Reno, Nevada, where she worked for 20 years, discriminates against women by subjecting them to job terms to which men are not subjected and requiring them to conform to gender stereotypes as a condition of employment. She brought suit against Harrah's (D) charging unequal burdens and sex stereotyping.

> ⚖ **RULE OF LAW**
> Company dress codes that are not motivated by gender stereotypes and that do not cause burdens to fall unequally on men or women, do not constitute sex discrimination, and therefore do not violate Title VII of the 1964 Civil Rights Act.

FACTS: Harrah's Operating Co., Inc. (Harrah's) (D) had maintained a company policy that encouraged female bartenders to wear makeup throughout Darlene Jespersen's (P) 20-year tenure with the company. But it did not enforce the rule until 2000. That year, as a part of a new "Beverage Department Image Transformation" program implemented at 20 of its locations, including Reno, Nevada, Harrah's (D) adopted a "Personal Best" program, which set new grooming and appearance standards. Under the program, male and female servers are required to wear black pants, a white shirt, a black vest, and a black bow tie. In addition, male servers are prohibited from wearing makeup, and must wear their hair above the collar, while female servers are required to wear makeup, and must "tease, curl, or style" their hair. The program's stated purpose is to ensure that beverage servers are "appealing to the eye," "firm and body toned," and "comfortable with maintaining this look while wearing the specified uniform." Jespersen (P) had no problem with the gender-neutral uniform requirements, but she did have a problem with the makeup rule. She did not wear it on or off the job, she said, and wearing it would conflict with her self-image. The trial court granted summary judgment to Harrah's (D). A split panel of the U.S. Court of Appeals affirmed on slightly different grounds (392 F.3d 1076 [9th Cir. 2004]).

ISSUE: Do company dress codes that are not motivated by gender stereotypes, and that do not cause burdens to fall unequally on men or women, constitute sex discrimination, and therefore violate Title VII of the 1964 Civil Rights Act?

HOLDING AND DECISION: (Schroeder, C.J.) No. Company dress codes that are not motivated by gender stereotypes and that do not cause burdens to fall unequally on men or women, do not constitute sex discrimination, and therefore do not violate Title VII of the 1964 Civil Rights Act. In this case, there was no evidence showing that complying with the "Personal Best" standards caused burdens to fall unequally on men or women, and there was no evidence to suggest Harrah's (D) motivation was to stereotype the women bartenders. Jespersen (P) relied solely on evidence that she had been a good bartender, and that she had personal objections to complying with the policy, in order to support her argument that Harrah's (D) "sells" and "exploits" its women employees. That is insufficient to survive summary judgment under Title VII of the 1964 Civil Rights Act. But the panel majority's holding that *Price Waterhouse v. Hopkins*, 490 U.S. 228 (1989), excluded grooming and appearance standards from the reach of the sex-stereotyping theory except where they amount to sexual harassment for failure to conform to commonly held gender stereotypes is incorrect. Such a claim is viable outside of the harassment context, but Jespersen (P) did not come forward with enough proof to allow a jury to find in her favor. Affirmed.

DISSENT: (Kozinski, J.) Jespersen's evidence also is sufficient to establish that she was subjected to an unequal burden because of her sex.

▌ *ANALYSIS*

The court leaves open the possibility of a successful sex-stereotyping claim. The opinion states that had she put forth sufficient evidence, Jespersen might succeed on such a claim, since the *Price Waterhouse* precedent did not exclude grooming and appearance standards, as the panel majority held.

■≡■

Quicknotes

DISCRIMINATION Unequal treatment of a class of persons.

■≡■

Pennsylvania State Police v. Suders

Public employer (D) v. Employee (P)

542 U.S. 129 (2004).

NATURE OF CASE: Appeal of appeals-court judgment in favor of employee.

FACT SUMMARY: Nancy Drew Suders (P) was a communications officer at a state police barracks. She filed a sexual harassment and constructive discharge lawsuit under Title VII of the 1964 Civil Rights Act against three supervisors and the barracks. The district court ruled in favor of the police (D), and the U.S. Court of Appeals for the Third Circuit reversed and remanded.

> 🏛 **RULE OF LAW**
> Title VII of the 1964 Civil Rights Act encompasses employer liability for a constructive discharge where a plaintiff can show it was reasonable to resign because of unendurable working conditions.

FACTS: Nancy Drew Suders (P) worked as a communications officer at a Pennsylvania police barracks (D). She claimed that three supervisors (D) subjected her to continuous sexual harassment by repeatedly talking about sex with animals, grabbing their genitals, and making other comments and gestures. In June 1998, one of the supervisors (D) accused her of taking a missing accident file home with her. After the incident, Suders (P) said she approached an equal employment opportunity officer and told her she "might need some help." The officer gave Suders (P) her telephone number, but neither woman followed up on the conversation. In August 1998, Suders (P) again contacted the barrack's Equal Employment Opportunity (EEO) officer, saying that she was being harassed and was afraid. The officer told Suders (P) to file a complaint but did not tell her how to obtain the necessary form. Two days later, Suders's (P) supervisors (D) arrested her for theft and she resigned from the force. The arrest came about after Suders (P) discovered exams she had taken to satisfy a state-police job requirement hidden in the women's locker room. Her supervisors (D) had told her she failed the exams, but when she found them in the drawer, she concluded that the exams had never been graded. She took them because she considered the tests to be her property. When the supervisors (D) discovered the tests were missing, they dusted the drawer with a theft-detection powder that turns hands blue when touched. When Suders (P) attempted to return the tests, her hands turned blue. The supervisors (D) apprehended her, handcuffed her, photographed her, and brought her to an interrogation room and gave her *Miranda* rights. Suders (P) resigned, and the theft charges were never brought against her. Suders (P) sued, arguing that she was subjected to sexual harassment and constructively discharged in

violation of Title VII of the 1964 Civil Rights Act. The district court granted the State's (D) motion for summary judgment, finding that although Suders (P) established an actionable hostile environment, the employer (D) effectively defended itself by asserting the *Ellerth/Faragher* defense, [*Burlington Industries, Inc. v. Ellerth*, 524 U.S. 742 (1998) and *Faragher v. Boca Raton*, 524 U.S. 775 (1998) respectively] and showing that Suders (P) never gave the employer (D) the chance to respond to her complaints. The U.S. Court of Appeals for the Third Circuit reversed and remanded the case, finding that Suders (P) demonstrated that the supervisors (D) had engaged in a pervasive pattern of sexual harassment. It also held that a constructive discharge, when proved, constitutes a tangible job action that precludes the employer from asserting the *Ellerth/Faragher* defense.

ISSUE: Does Title VII of the 1964 Civil Rights Act encompass employer liability for a constructive discharge where a plaintiff can show it was reasonable to resign because of unendurable working conditions?

HOLDING AND DECISION: (Ginsburg, J.) Yes. Title VII of the 1964 Civil Rights Act encompasses employer liability for a constructive discharge where a plaintiff can show it was reasonable to resign because of unendurable working conditions. The result for plaintiffs asserting constructive discharge is that a prevailing plaintiff is entitled to all the remedies available for a formal discharge. The plaintiff may recover post-resignation damages, including both backpay and, in fitting circumstances, front-pay, as well as the compensatory and punitive damages now provided for Title VII claims generally. To establish constructive discharge, the plaintiff would have to show that the abusive working environment became so intolerable that her resignation qualified as a fitting response. However, under the *Ellerth/Faragher* defense, when no tangible job action has been taken against a plaintiff, an employer can escape liability for a supervisor's sexual harassment by showing that it exercised reasonable care to prevent and promptly correct sexually harassing behavior and that the plaintiff unreasonably failed to take advantage of any preventive or corrective opportunities to avoid harm. Therefore, unless Suders (P) can show the resignation was prompted by an official adverse job action, the employer (D) can avoid vicarious liability for the supervisors' acts by showing that it had in place a complaint system that Suders (P) unreasonably failed to use before quitting. The constructive

Continued on next page.

discharge in and of itself does not count as an official adverse act. Reversed and remanded.

ANALYSIS

By sending Suders's (P) case against the state police back to the U.S. Court of Appeals for the Third Circuit, the Supreme Court recognized for the first time that a constructive discharge claim could give rise to Title VII liability. The ruling overturns the Third Circuit's decision that a constructive discharge, if proven, could establish a tangible job action, thus preventing the employer from asserting the *Ellerth/Faragher* defense.

■==■

Quicknotes

SEXUAL HARASSMENT The practice of subjecting persons to oppressive conduct on account of their gender.

■==■

Harris v. Forklift Systems, Inc.

Employee (P) v. Employer (D)

510 U.S. 17 (1993).

NATURE OF CASE: Appeal from judgment in a Title VII action for gender discrimination.

FACT SUMMARY: Harris (P), a female employee of Forklift Systems, Inc. (Forklift) (D), brought a Title VII sex-discrimination action based upon offensive comments made by Hardy, Forklift's (D) president.

🏛 RULE OF LAW
Sexual harassment is not required to be psychologically injurious in order to constitute an abusive work environment.

FACTS: Teresa Harris (P) worked as a manager at Forklift Systems, Inc. (Forklift) (D) from 1985 until 1987. Throughout her employment, Hardy, the president of Forklift (D), insulted Harris (P) because of her sex and made her the target of unwanted sexual innuendos. In 1987, Harris (P) complained to Hardy about his conduct, and Hardy promised to stop. However, a short time later Hardy made another offensive comment to Harris (P) in front of other employees, and Harris (P) quit. Harris (P) then brought a Title VII action, claiming that Hardy's conduct had created an abusive work environment because of her sex. The trial court held that Hardy's conduct did not create an abusive environment since it was not so severe as to be expected to seriously affect Harris's (P) psychological well-being. The court of appeals affirmed, and Harris (P) appealed.

ISSUE: Does sexual harassment have to be psychologically injurious in order to constitute an abusive work environment?

HOLDING AND DECISION: (O'Connor, J.) No. Sexual harassment is not required to be psychologically injurious in order to constitute an abusive work environment. Title VII makes it unlawful to discriminate against an employee on the basis of sex. Congress intended to prohibit all disparate treatment of men and women in employment practices, including the work environment. Thus, Title VII is violated when a workplace is permeated with discriminatory intimidation and ridicule that is sufficiently pervasive to alter the condition of the victim's working environment. Mere offensive comments are not sufficient to affect the conditions of employment. Objectively and subjectively harassing conduct that is so severe and pervasive as to create an abusive environment is required. This may be determined by looking at all the circumstances, including the frequency of the conduct, its severity, and whether it interferes with an employee's work performance. Psychological injury to the employee is not required. The district court erred in concluding that the working environment for Harris (P) was not abusive because she did not suffer any psychological injury. Therefore, the judgment is reversed, and the case is remanded.

CONCURRENCE: (Scalia, J.) The standard that the majority opinion states does not provide any clear guidance to trial courts and juries. However, the language of the statute is so vague that no other alternative seems to exist.

CONCURRENCE: (Ginsburg, J.) To show that discriminatory conduct has unreasonably interfered with her work performance, a plaintiff need not prove a tangible decline in productivity but only that harassment made it more difficult to do her job.

▶ ANALYSIS

Prior to this decision, other courts had been urged to adopt a reasonable-woman standard as opposed to a reasonable-person standard for sexual-harassment cases. This decision states that the harassment must be objectively abusive to a reasonable person and also subjectively abusive to the victim. Note that, under some fact patterns, victims of sexual harassment may also be able to sustain complaints for breach of contract, assault, battery, sexual battery, and intentional and negligent infliction of emotional distress.

■■■

Quicknotes

HARASSMENT Conduct directed at a particular person with the intent to inflict emotional distress and with no justification therefor; a criminal prosecution commenced without a reasonable expectation of its resulting in a conviction.

TITLE VII OF THE CIVIL RIGHTS ACT OF 1964 States that it shall be an unlawful employment practice for an employer to fail or refuse to hire or otherwise discriminate against any individual with respect to his employment because of such individual's race, color, religion, sex, or national origin.

■■■

Oncale v. Sundowner Offshore Services, Inc.

Employee (P) v. Employer (D)

523 U.S. 75 (1998).

NATURE OF CASE: Appeal from court of appeal decision rejecting claim of sexual harassment under Title VII.

FACT SUMMARY: Joseph Oncale (P), an employee of Sundowner Offshore Services, Inc. (D), brought suit claiming that he was a victim of sexual harassment by his male coworkers (D) in violation of Title VII of the Civil Rights Act of 1964.

🏛 RULE OF LAW
A plaintiff may maintain an action under Title VII of the Civil Rights Act of 1964 for gender discrimination based on sexual harassment when the harasser and the plaintiff are of the same sex.

FACTS: Joseph Oncale (P) worked for Sundowner Offshore Services, Inc. (Sundowner) (D) on an oil platform in the Gulf of Mexico as part of an eight-man crew. Oncale (P) claimed that he was subjected to sexual and humiliating conduct against him by his other crew members, Lyon (D), Pippen (D) and Johnson (D). Oncale was also assaulted in a sexual manner and threatened with rape. Oncale (P) left his employment and filed a complaint against Sundowner (D), alleging discrimination in his employment on account of his sex in violation of Title VII of the Civil Rights Act of 1964. The district court granted summary judgment in favor of Sundowner (D), and the court of appeals affirmed. Oncale (P) petitioned for certiorari.

ISSUE: May a plaintiff maintain an action under Title VII of the Civil Rights Act of 1964 for gender discrimination based on sexual harassment when the harasser and the plaintiff are of the same sex?

HOLDING AND DECISION: (Scalia, J.) Yes. A plaintiff may maintain an action under Title VII of the Civil Rights Act of 1964 for gender discrimination based on sexual harassment when the harasser and the plaintiff are of the same sex. Title VII prohibits an employer from discriminating against any person regarding the terms and conditions of his or her employment on the basis of gender. The legislature's intent in passing Title VII was not only to preclude discrimination contractually, but also to prevent the unequal treatment of employees in the workplace. Title VII applies equally to both men and women. In the racial context, courts have also held that in determining whether there has been a violation of Title VII, there is no presumption that an employer will not discriminate against persons of his or her own race. Likewise, a claim of discrimination under Title VII is not precluded because the employer and employee are of the same gender. This includes claims of sexual harassment. The determinative

issue in proving a violation of Title VII is whether members of one sex suffer from disadvantageous terms and conditions of employment. Mere offensive sexual comments are not sufficient; rather, the conduct must be sufficiently pervasive that a reasonable person would conclude that the workplace is hostile or abusive. Reversed and remanded.

CONCURRENCE: (Thomas, J.) A claim of sexual harassment requires a plaintiff to satisfy Title VII's requirement that there has been discrimination because of sex.

▶ ANALYSIS

Courts have differed in the appropriate standard to apply in determining cases of sexual harassment. While some courts have followed a "reasonable-woman standard," recognizing that the determinative inquiry is to be made from the victim's perspective, other courts apply a "reasonable-person" standard, requiring the court to ascertain how a reasonable person would react if confronted with similar circumstances. Courts have also held that an action for sexual harassment may be maintained when the work environment is hostile or abusive to members of both sexes.

Quicknotes

REASONABLE PERSON STANDARD The standard of case exercised by one who possesses the intelligence, education, knowledge, attention, and judgment required by society of its members when governing behavior; the standard applies to a person's judgment when determining breach of a duty under the theory of negligence.

SEXUAL HARASSMENT An employment practice subjecting persons to oppressive conduct on account of their gender.

TITLE VII OF THE CIVIL RIGHTS ACT OF 1964 States that it shall be an unlawful employment practice for an employer to fail or refuse to hire or otherwise discriminate against any individual with respect to his employment because of such individual's race, color, religion, sex, or national origin.

Bodewig v. K-Mart, Inc.

Employee (P) v. Former employer (D)

Or. Ct. App., 635 P.2d 657 (1981).

NATURE OF CASE: Appeal from summary judgment denying award of damages for outrageous conduct.

FACT SUMMARY: After Bodewig's (P) employer put her through a strip search to satisfy a customer, even though it had concluded she had not taken the customer's money, Bodewig (P) sought damages for outrageous conduct against both her employer, K-Mart, Inc. (D), and the customer, Golden (D), only to have the trial court grant summary judgment in their favor.

RULE OF LAW
Where it cannot be said as a matter of law that there is no genuine issue of material fact, summary judgment should not be granted.

FACTS: Bodewig (P), who worked as a part-time checker for K-Mart, Inc. (D), was accused by Golden (D), a customer, to have taken four five-dollar bills on top of merchandise on Bodewig's (P) counter when Golden (D) went to check on a sale price. Bodewig (P) told Golden (D) she had not seen any money, but Golden (D) continued in a loud, abrupt voice to demand her money from Bodewig (P), causing a general commotion. After the store manager searched Bodewig's (P) jacket pockets and found nothing, Golden (D) remained dissatisfied, at which point Bodewig (P) was told to accompany a female assistant manager into the women's public restroom for a strip search. With the assistant manager and Golden (D) watching, Bodewig (P) stripped to her underwear, but no money was found. The next day Bodewig (P) returned to work and believed K-Mart (D) was monitoring her work. She quit and then filed suit for damages for outrageous conduct against K-Mart (D) and Golden (D). K-Mart (D) and Golden (D) successfully moved for summary judgment. Bodewig (P) appealed, arguing that the matter should have gone to trial because there were unresolved issues of fact.

ISSUE: Where it cannot be said as a matter of law that there is no genuine issue of material fact, should summary judgment be granted?

HOLDING AND DECISION: (Buttler, J.) No. Where it cannot be said as a matter of law that there is no genuine issue of material fact, summary judgment should not be granted. The relationship between Bodewig (P) and K-Mart (D) was a special relationship, based on which liability may be imposed if K-Mart's (D) conduct, though not deliberately aimed at causing emotional distress, was such that a jury might find it to be beyond the limits of social toleration and reckless of the conduct's predictable effects on Bodewig (P). A jury could find that the K-Mart (D) manager, a 32-year-old male who, after concluding that Bodewig (P) did not take the customer's money, still put her through the degrading and humiliating experience of submitting to a strip search, exhibited conduct that exceeded the bounds of social toleration and was in reckless disregard of its predictable effects on Bodewig (P). Because there was no special relationship between Bodewig (P) and Golden (D), the evidence must be such that a jury could find Golden's (D) conduct not only socially intolerable, but that it was deliberately aimed at causing Bodewig (P) emotional distress. Golden's (D) insistence that Bodewig (P) still had her money after the register checked out perfectly, her eager participation in the strip search, and her continuing to stare angrily at Bodewig (D) over an extended period, even after all efforts to find her money failed, would permit a jury to find Golden's (D) conduct deliberately calculated to cause Bodewig (P) emotional distress and beyond the bounds of social toleration. Reversed and remanded for trial.

ANALYSIS

The court pointed out that the relatively short history and development of the tort of outrageous conduct, at least in Oregon, was summarized in *Brewer v. Erwin*, 287 Or. 435, 600 P.2d 398 (1979), and that the exact elements of the tort were still in the process of clarification. There were at least two versions of the tort. One involved intentional conduct, the very purpose of which was to inflict psychological and emotional distress on the plaintiff. The other involved a lack of wrongful purpose, but the tortious element could be found in the breach of some obligation that attaches to defendant's relationship to plaintiff. In this case, the former would relate to the customer and the latter to the employer.

Quicknotes

INTENT The existence of a particular state of mind whereby an individual seeks to achieve a specific result by his action.

OUTRAGEOUS CONDUCT Conduct exceeding societal standards of decency.

SPECIAL RELATIONSHIP A relationship between two persons that imposes a fiduciary responsibility to act where one is threatened with injury, such as the relationship between a parent and child.

Continued on next page.

SUMMARY JUDGMENT Judgment rendered by a court in response to a motion by one of the parties, claiming that the lack of a question of material fact in respect to an issue warrants disposition of the issue without consideration by the jury.

TORT A legal wrong resulting in a breach of duty.

Hernandez v. Hillsides, Inc.

Employees (P) v. Employer (D)

Cal. Sup. Ct., 211 P.3d 1063 (2009).

NATURE OF CASE: Appeal from intermediate appellate court ruling that reversed the trial court's granting of the defendant's motion to dismiss.

FACT SUMMARY: After suspecting that someone was using an employee's computer after hours to view pornography, Hillsides, Inc. (D) installed a video camera in the shared office of two employees. The video camera was only viewed at night and was never operated while the employees who used the office were at work.

> ## RULE OF LAW
> To recover for the tort of intrusion, a plaintiff must prove both that the defendant intentionally intruded into an area where the plaintiff had a reasonable expectation of privacy and that the intrusion was highly offensive to a reasonable person.

FACTS: Hillsides, Inc. (D) operates the Hillsides Children Center, Inc. (collectively, "Hillside") (D), a residential home for abused and neglected children. Plaintiffs Hernandez (P) and Lopez (P) shared an enclosed office and performed clerical work for the facility. A Hillside (D) supervisor, Hitchcock, learned that someone was using one of their computers after hours to view pornographic websites. Concerned that children in the facility could be exposed to pornography, Hitchcock set up a hidden video camera in their office. The camera could be controlled remotely and could be viewed live. The camera was not operated during business hours and Hernandez (P) and Lopez (P) were never seen on the video at any time. Hillside (D) did not suspect Hernandez (P) and Lopez (P) of viewing pornography, but some other staffer who would had access to their office. After discovering the camera, Hernandez (P) and Lopez (P) brought this claim for intrusion against Hillside (D). At their depositions, Hernandez (P) and Lopez (P) testified they would often use their office to change into workout gear before the end of the day. The trial court dismissed the complaint but the intermediate court of appeals reversed, finding issues of fact regarding the zone of privacy. Hillside (D) appealed to the California Supreme Court.

ISSUE: To recover for the tort of intrusion must a plaintiff prove both that the defendant intentionally intruded into an area where the plaintiff had a reasonable expectation of privacy and that the intrusion was highly offensive to a reasonable person?

HOLDING AND DECISION: (Baxter, J.) Yes. To recover for the tort of intrusion, a plaintiff must prove both that the defendant intentionally intruded into an area

where the plaintiff had a reasonable expectation of privacy and that the intrusion was highly offensive to a reasonable person. The expectation of privacy must be objectively reasonable. To determine reasonableness, a court should review the identity of the intruder, the extent to which others had access to the area and the means of the intrusion. Regarding the "highly offensive" element, factors in that analysis include the degree and setting of the intrusion, and the motives of the intruder. Each intrusion claim can only be reviewed on a case by case basis. This court agrees that Hernandez (P) and Lopez (P) have met the first element. Hillside (D) installed a hidden camera in an enclosed office without informing the employees who worked in that office. Even though the camera was not viewed during the day, it was operational and could have been viewed by Hitchcock if he chose to do so. However, the intrusion was not highly offensive. The court reaches this conclusion because of the diligent efforts Hillside (D) took to not view the camera during the day. The appellate court's decision is reversed and summary judgment should be granted to Hillside (D) on all counts. Reversed.

⏵ ANALYSIS

Cameras in closed offices are usually not permitted by law. However, with the emphasis on security in workplaces over recent years, the use of cameras has grown significantly. Cameras in common areas and entrances are usually allowed due to the lack of an expectation of privacy in those areas.

━━

Quicknotes

INTRUSION To recover for the tort of intrusion, a plaintiff must prove both that the defendant intentionally intruded into an area where the plaintiff had a reasonable expectation of privacy and that the intrusion was highly offensive to a reasonable person.

━━

City of Ontario v. Quon

Employer (D) v. Employee (P)

130 S. Ct 2619 (2010).

NATURE OF CASE: Appeal from Ninth Circuit Court's reversal of a district court decision.

FACT SUMMARY: After the City of Ontario's (City's) (D) police department became aware that Quon (P) was sending unusually high numbers of text messages on his department issued pager, the City (D) obtained and then reviewed those text messages to determine if the messages were work related.

🏛 RULE OF LAW
A government employer's warrantless search shall be reasonable if it is justified at its inception and is narrowly and reasonably tailored to the objectives of the search.

FACTS: In 2001, the City of Ontario (City) (D) issued pagers to several police officers. The City (D) also created a Computer Usage and Email Policy which informed all officers that the City (D) had a right to review emails sent using the City's (D) computer system. The policy did not mention text messages. The text messages at issue here did not rout through the City's (D) computer system. Rather, an outside vendor, Arch Wireless, handled and stored the text messages sent via the pagers. In 2002, a lieutenant informed all officers at a staff meeting that Quon (P) attended that text messages would be treated in the same manner as emails. The lieutenant's comments were later put into memorandum to the police department. In 2002, Quon (P) exceeded his monthly allowance for text messages and agreed to pay the City (D) for the overage costs. After this happened several more times, the City (D) was interested in determining if the allowable text message amount should be increased and that whether Quon (P) was incurring charges for work related messages. Arch Wireless then provided transcripts of Quon's (P) text messages to the City (D) for the period of two months. For one of the months, Quon (P) sent 456 messages, with only 57 of them work related. An internal investigation ensued regarding Quon's (P) conducting of personal matters while on duty. The City (D) disciplined Quon (P) as a result of the investigation. Quon (P) then brought this action for, among other things, a Fourth Amendment violation for the City's (D) alleged unlawful search of his text messages. After a trial, the district court concluded the City's (D) search was not unreasonable. The Ninth Circuit reversed and the City (D) appealed to the United States Supreme Court.

ISSUE: Shall a government employer's warrantless search be reasonable if it is justified at its inception and is narrowly and reasonably tailored to the objectives of the search?

HOLDING AND DECISION: (Kennedy, J.) Yes. A government employer's warrantless search shall be reasonable if it is justified at its inception and is narrowly and reasonably tailored to the objectives of the search. Warrantless searches are per se unreasonable under the Fourth Amendment, unless an exception applies. One recognized exception exists due to the "special needs" of the workplace. Under this exception, the search must be both justified at the inception and narrowly tailored to the objectives of the search. "Justified at the inception" means the initial reason for the search must be for a noninvestigatory work-related purpose. The City (D) satisfied this element because it sought to determine if Quon (P) and others were being forced to pay out of pocket expenses for work related text messages. The City (D) also satisfied the second element regarding the scope of the search. Reviewing the text messages was a reasonable and expedient way of determining if the messages were work related. The search was also tailored to a review of two months only, even though Quon (P) had gone over the allotted text message amount many other months. Lastly, it was not reasonable for Quon (P) to assume the text messages were private. Quon (P) was well aware that the text messages would be treated as emails pursuant to the City's (D) policy. Reversed.

▶ ANALYSIS

Many states have enacted statutes defining the scope of employer initiated searches of employee emails and text messages. Due to the prevalence of personal cell phones, both public and private employers likely now have more right to search the content of emails and text messages on employer-issued mobile devices. A prudent employer should have a policy making all employees aware that employer-issued mobile devices are for work related use only and subject to audit without notification to the employee.

Quicknotes

FOURTH AMENDMENT Provides that persons be secure as to their person and private belongings against unreasonable searches and seizures.

SEARCH An inspection conducted in order to obtain evidence to be utilized for the prosecution of a crime.

Rankin v. McPherson

Company (D) v. Woman seeking backpay (P)

483 U.S. 378 (1987).

NATURE OF CASE: Appeal from award of reinstatement and backpay for wrongful discharge.

FACT SUMMARY: When she was discharged by Rankin (D) from her clerical position in the office of the constable for saying after an assassination attempt on the life of the President that "if they go for him again, I hope they get him," McPherson (P) filed suit, alleging that her First Amendment rights were violated under color of state law.

🏛 RULE OF LAW
Whether a public employer has properly discharged an employee for engaging in speech requires a balance between the interests of the employee, as a citizen, in commenting upon matters of public concern and the interest of the state, as an employer, in promoting the efficiency of the public services it performs through its employees.

FACTS: McPherson (P) was appointed a deputy in the office of the constable, Rankin (D), of Harris County, Texas, although her duties were purely clerical. Her work station was a desk at which there was no telephone, in a room to which the public did not have ready access. After she and some fellow employees heard on an office radio that there had been an attempt to assassinate the President of the United States, McPherson (P) was overheard saying to a coworker (and boyfriend), "If they go for him again, I hope they get him." When Rankin (D) summoned her, McPherson (P) readily admitted making the statement, but said she didn't mean anything by it. Rankin (D) then fired McPherson (P). She brought suit, alleging that in discharging her, Rankin (D) had violated her First Amendment rights under color of state law. She sought reinstatement, backpay, costs and fees, and other equitable relief. The district court found that McPherson's (P) speech did not address a matter of public concern. The court of appeals rejected this conclusion, finding that the life and death of the President are obviously matters of public concern.

ISSUE: Does a determination as to whether a public employer has properly discharged an employee for engaging in speech require a balance between the interests of the employee, as a citizen, in commenting upon matters of public concern, and the interest of the state, as an employer, in promoting the efficiency of the public services it performs through its employees?

HOLDING AND DECISION: (Marshall, J.) Yes. Whether a public employer has properly discharged an employee for engaging in speech requires a balance between the interests of the employee, as a citizen, in commenting upon matters of public concern and the interest of the state, as an employer, in promoting the efficiency of the public services it performs through its employees. The threshold question in applying this balancing test is whether McPherson's (P) speech addresses a matter of public concern. Considering it in context, the statement plainly dealt with a matter of heightened public attention: an attempt on the life of the President. Because it addressed a matter of public concern, McPherson's (P) interest in making the statement must be balanced against the interest of the state in promoting the efficiency of the public services it performs through its employees. The state bears a burden of justifying the discharge on legitimate grounds. The manner, time, and place of the employee's expression are relevant, as is the context in which the dispute arose. Where, as here, an employee serves no confidential, policy-making, or public contact role, the danger to the agency's successful function from that employee's private speech is minimal. At some point, such concerns are so removed from the effective function of the public employer that they cannot prevail over the free speech rights of the public employee. This is such a case; Rankin (D) failed to demonstrate a state interest that outweighed McPherson's (P) First Amendment rights. Affirmed.

CONCURRENCE: (Powell, J.) McPherson (P) made an ill-considered, but protected, comment during a private conversation, and Rankin (D) made an instinctive, but intemperate, employment decision on the basis of this speech.

DISSENT: (Scalia, J.) Rankin's (D) interest in maintaining both an esprit de corps and a public image consistent with his office's law enforcement duties outweighed any interest his employees may have had in expressing at work a desire that the President be killed. Even assuming that this expression of desire addressed a matter of public concern, it should not be protected under the First Amendment.

▌ ANALYSIS

The Court declared that the balancing was necessary in order to accommodate the dual role of the public employer as a provider of public services and as a government entity operating under the constraints of the First Amendment. On the one hand, public employers are simply like any other employer, concerned with the efficient function of

Continued on next page.

their operations; review of every personnel decision made by a public employer could hamper the performance of public functions. On the other hand, the threat of dismissal from public employment is a potent means of inhibiting speech. Vigilance is necessary to ensure that public employers do not use authority over employees to silence discourse, not because it hampers public functions but simply because superiors disagree with its content.

■══■

Quicknotes

FIRST AMENDMENT Prohibits Congress from enacting any law respecting an establishment of religion, prohibiting the free exercise of religion, abridging freedom of speech or the press, the right of peaceful assembly and the right to petition for a redress of grievances.

■══■

Garcetti v. Ceballos

Public employer (D) v. Employee (P)

547 U.S. 410 (2006).

NATURE OF CASE: Appeal of Ninth Circuit's ruling in favor of employee.

FACT SUMMARY: A deputy district attorney (P) testified that a sheriff lied on an affidavit. After his office (D) retaliated against him, he filed suit on grounds that the retaliation violated his First Amendment right to free speech. The trial court rejected the claims on the basis of sovereign immunity, and the Ninth Circuit reversed.

RULE OF LAW

The First Amendment of the U.S. Constitution does not protect a public employee from discipline based on speech made in the course of the employee's official duties.

FACTS: Deputy District Attorney Richard Ceballos (P) wrote a memo that questioned the truth of a deputy sheriff's affidavit in support of a search warrant. His supervisor instructed him to change the memo to make it less accusatory of the deputy sheriff, and Ceballos (P) complied. Ceballos (P) then met with representatives of the district attorney's office and sheriff's department to voice his concerns, but the DA's office decided to continue with the prosecution while an evidence-suppression motion filed by defense counsel in the case was processed. Ceballos (P) told the defense counsel that he believed the search warrant affidavit included false statements. At the subsequent suppression hearing, he testified under subpoena about his conclusions. After testifying, Ceballos (P) charged that he experienced retaliation, including removal of many of his duties, denial of a promotion, and the threat of transfer to a lower-level position. He filed a lawsuit against the county alleging violations of his First Amendment right to free speech. A trial court rejected the claims, citing sovereign immunity. The U.S. Court of Appeals for the Ninth Circuit reversed.

ISSUE: Does the First Amendment of the U.S. Constitution protect a public employee from discipline based on speech made in the course of the employee's official duties?

HOLDING AND DECISION: (Kennedy, J.) No. The First Amendment of the U.S. Constitution does not protect a public employee from discipline based on speech made in the course of the employee's official duties. When public employees make statements pursuant to their official duties, the employees are not speaking as citizens for First Amendment purposes, and the Constitution does not insulate their communications from employer discipline. Allowing Ceballos (P) to be protected by the First Amendment when he merely is performing his job would require

the courts to become immersed in the employee-supervisor relationship of government employers. Reversed and remanded.

DISSENT: (Stevens, J.) The majority's ruling is "misguided." The proper answer to the question "whether the First Amendment protects a government employee from discipline based on speech made pursuant to the employee's official duties," is "sometimes" not "never." While a supervisor can take corrective action when such speech is "inflammatory or misguided," courts should be aware of situations where "it is just unwelcome speech because it reveals facts that the supervisor would rather not have anyone else discover."

DISSENT: (Souter, J.) Although public employers have an interest in supervising employees and making sure decisions are carried out, when employees act as whistleblowers, there should be protection. Private and public interests in addressing official wrongdoing and threats to health and safety can outweigh the government's stake in the efficient implementation of policy, and when they do, public employees who speak on these matters in the course of their duties should be eligible to claim First Amendment protection.

DISSENT: (Breyer, J.) It is true that government employers need discretion in managing their operation and that the Constitution should not interfere with managerial discretion, but there is a middle ground. The First Amendment sometimes does authorize judicial actions based upon a government employee's speech that both (1) involves a matter of public concern and also (2) takes place in the course of ordinary job-related duties. But it does so only in the presence of a larger need for constitutional protection and diminished risk of undue judicial interference with governmental management of the public's affairs.

▶ ANALYSIS

This five-to-four decision represents a significant win for public employers, but it puts public employees who find it necessary to expose corruption in a bind. The majority failed to specify what exactly was involved in an employee's job responsibilities, and that issue is likely to be litigated extensively as a result of this decision.

∎❑∎

Continued on next page.

Quicknotes

FIRST AMENDMENT Prohibits Congress from enacting any law respecting an establishment of religion, prohibiting the free exercise of religion, abridging freedom of speech or the press, the right of peaceful assembly and the right to petition for a redress of grievances.

■━━■

Curay-Cramer v. Ursuline Academy

Employee (P) v. Employer (D)

450 F.3d 130 (3d Cir. 2006).

NATURE OF CASE: Appeal of judgment for employer.

FACT SUMMARY: A schoolteacher (P) was fired by her Catholic employer (D) when she signed her name to a pro-choice advertisement in the local newspaper.

🏛 RULE OF LAW
A Catholic school teacher who signed her name to a pro-choice newspaper advertisement commemorating *Roe v. Wade* did not engage in protected activity for purposes of Title VII of the 1964 Civil Rights Act.

FACTS: Michele Curay-Cramer (P), who was a teacher at Ursuline Academy (Ursuline) (D), a private Catholic school, was fired when she signed her name to a pro-choice advertisement in the local newspaper. She claimed it was a violation of Title VII of the 1964 Civil Rights Act and the Pregnancy Discrimination Act to fire her for opposing Ursuline's (D) illegal employment practice of firing anyone who has or contemplates an abortion. She also claimed she was discriminated against, because male employees who had committed more serious transgressions were treated less harshly.

ISSUE: Did a Catholic schoolteacher who signed her name to a pro-choice newspaper advertisement commemorating *Roe v. Wade* engage in protected activity for purposes of Title VII of the 1964 Civil Rights Act?

HOLDING AND DECISION: (Roth, J.) No. A Catholic school teacher who signed her name to a pro-choice newspaper advertisement commemorating *Roe v. Wade*, 410 U.S. 113 (1973), did not engage in protected activity for purposes of Title VII of the 1964 Civil Rights Act. Curay-Cramer (P) argued that Title VII's opposition clause protects any employee who has had an abortion, who contemplates having an abortion, or who supports the rights of women who do so. Even if it were assumed that Title VII has within its ambit properly structured opposition and association activity directed toward an employer's practice of discriminating against women who have or contemplate abortions, Curay-Cramer (P) has still failed to state a claim for retaliation under Title VII or the Pregnancy Discrimination Act. The pro-choice newspaper advertisement Curay-Cramer (P) signed did not mention employment, her employer, or pregnancy or gender discrimination, and so by signing it she did not engage in protected activity under federal job-bias law. Therefore, summary dismissal on the retaliation claim in favor of the Ursuline (D) is affirmed. In addition, because she did not

identify a male coworker who publicly attacked the church's position on abortion, assessing her claim of sex discrimination would impermissibly require an analysis of Catholic doctrine, i.e., whether her endorsement of abortion was an affront of Catholic doctrine of at least the same seriousness as that allegedly committed by her proffered comparators.

▶ ANALYSIS

The significance of this decision is the parameters it draws with respect to Title VII. Title VII, it holds, does not protect a Catholic schoolteacher's pro-choice stance, because it was unconnected to employment. The court wrote: "To turn pro-choice advocacy, unconnected to employment practices, into conduct protected by Title VII would inappropriately stretch the concept of protected activity." It is not sufficient that the pro-choice advocacy became connected to her employment; her advocacy had to be connected to employment in order to trigger Title VII protection.

━━━

Quicknotes

COMPARATOR The person against whom a claimant compares him- or herself.

━━━

NLRB v. Washington Alum. Co.

National Labor Relations Board (P) v. Employer (D)

370 U.S. 9 (1962).

NATURE OF CASE: Appeal from denial of enforcement of a National Labor Relations Board order of reinstatement.

FACT SUMMARY: When they were discharged for walking off the job in protest over the bitterly cold conditions in the machine shop where they worked, seven of Washington Alum. Co.'s (Washington) (D) employees filed a complaint with the National Labor Relations Board (NLRB), but the court of appeals refused to enforce the NLRB's (P) order that Washington (D) reinstate the seven employees.

🏛 RULE OF LAW
Employees shall have the right to engage in concerted activities for the purpose of collective bargaining or other mutual aid or protection.

FACTS: Seven machine shop employees working for Washington Alum. Co. (Washington) (D) walked out in protest over the extreme cold in the shop. The machine shop was not insulated and had a number of doors to the outside that had to be opened frequently. An oil furnace located in an adjoining building was the chief source of heat for the shop, although there were two gas-fired space heaters that contributed heat to a lesser extent. Several of the eight machinists who made up the day shift had previously complained about the cold working conditions. The night before the walkout, the large oil furnace had broken down and had not yet been repaired. The outside temperature for the day was 22°F and the inside temperature was so cold that the foreman remarked that if they had any guts at all, they would go home. After seven walked out, Washington's (D) president discharged them. On these facts, the National Labor Relations Board (NLRB) (P) found that the conduct of the workers was a concerted activity to protest Washington's (D) failure to supply adequate heat in its machine shop, that such conduct was protected under the provision of § 7 of the National Labor Relations Act, and that their discharge amounted to an unfair labor practice under § 8(a)(1) of the Act (employers forbidden to interfere with, restrain, or coerce employees in the exercise of the rights guaranteed in § 7). The NLRB (P) then ordered Washington (D) to reinstate the discharged workers to their previous positions and to make them whole for losses resulting from the unlawful termination. The court of appeals denied enforcement of this order, holding that because the workers simply left their place of employment without affording Washington (D) an opportunity to grant a concession to a demand,

their walkout did not amount to a protected concerted activity. The NLRB (P) appealed.

ISSUE: Shall employees have the right to engage in concerted activities for the purpose of collective bargaining or other mutual aid or protection?

HOLDING AND DECISION: (Black, J.) Yes. Employees have the right to engage in concerted activities for the purpose of collective bargaining or other mutual aid or protection. The language of § 7 is broad enough to protect concerted activities whether they take place before, after, or at the same time such a demand is made. To compel the NLRB (P) to apply the interpretation urged by Washington (D) might place burdens upon employees so great that it would effectively nullify the right to engage in concerted activities that the section protects. The findings of the NLRB (P), which are supported by substantial evidence, show a running dispute between the machine shop employees and Washington (D) over the heating of the shop on cold days—a dispute that culminated in the decision of the employees to act concertedly in an effort to force Washington (D) to improve that condition of their employment. The conduct of these workers was far from unjustified under the circumstances. Having no bargaining representative and no established procedure by which they could take advantage of their unanimity of opinion in negotiations with Washington (D), the men took the most direct course to make clear that they wanted a warmer place in which to work. Therefore, the NLRB (P) correctly interpreted and applied the Act to the circumstances of this case. Reversed and remanded [with directions to enforce the order in its entirety].

▶ ANALYSIS

The Court declared that it could not agree that employees necessarily lose their right to engage in concerted activities under § 7 merely because they do not present a specific demand upon their employer to remedy a condition they find objectionable. Indeed, Washington's (D) own foreman expressed the opinion that the shop was so cold that the men should go home. According to the Court, concerted activities by employees for the purpose of protecting themselves from inhuman working conditions are unquestionably activities to correct conditions that modern labor-management legislation treats not to be tolerated in a civilized society.

■━■

Continued on next page.

Quicknotes

NATIONAL LABOR RELATIONS ACT Guarantees employees the right to engage in collective bargaining, and regulates labor unions.

UNFAIR LABOR PRACTICE Conduct by labor unions and employers that is proscribed by the National Labor Relations Act.

■▬■

Rulon-Miller v. IBM Corp.

Employee (P) v. Employer (D)

Ca. Ct. App., 208 Cal. Rptr. 524 (1984).

NATURE OF CASE: Appeal from award of compensatory and punitive damages for wrongful discharge and intentional infliction of emotional distress.

FACT SUMMARY: After she was dismissed by International Business Machines (D) on an alleged conflict of interest due to her relationship with an employee of a rival firm, Rulon-Miller (P) filed suit, claiming wrongful discharge and intentional infliction of emotional distress.

🏛 **RULE OF LAW**
Company policy insures to the employee both the right of privacy and the right to hold a job so long as off-the-job activities do not present a conflict of interest or interfere with the employee's work.

FACTS: Rulon-Miller (P) was a low-level marketing manager at International Business Machines (IBM) (D) in its office products division in San Francisco. Her termination as a marketing manager came about as a result of an accusation made by her immediate supervisor, Callahan (D), of a romantic relationship with Blum, before he became the manager of a rival office-products firm, QYX. Rulon-Miller (P) had dated Blum while he was employed as an account manager by IBM (D). IBM (D) knew about Rulon-Miller's (P) relationship with Blum and was assured by her supervisor that it was not a problem. However, a week after she was given a merit raise and was told that she was doing a good job, Callahan (D) told her to stop dating Blum or lose her job. The next day Callahan (D) told Rulon-Miller (P) he had made up her mind for her, and when she protested, he dismissed her. IBM (D) had a policy governing possible conflict of interest between an employee and the company. Callahan (D) based his action against Rulon-Miller (P) on a conflict of interest. IBM (D) and Callahan (D) claimed, however, that he merely transferred her to another division. Rulon-Miller (P) sued for wrongful discharge and intentional infliction of emotional distress and was awarded compensatory and punitive damages. IBM (D) appealed.

ISSUE: Does company policy insure to the employee both the right of privacy and the right to hold a job so long as off-the-job activities do not present a conflict of interest or interfere with the employee's work?

HOLDING AND DECISION: (Rushing, J.) Yes. Company policy insures to the employee both the right of privacy and the right to hold a job so long as off-the-job activities do not present a conflict of interest or interfere with the employee's work. The record showed that IBM

(D) did not interpret its conflict-of-interest policy to prohibit a romantic relationship. Moreover, Callahan (D) admitted that there was no company rule or policy requiring an employee to terminate friendships with fellow employees who leave and join competitors. Callahan's (D) superior also confirmed that IBM (D) had no policy against employees socializing with competitors. While Rulon-Miller (P) was successful, her primary job did not give her access to sensitive information that could have been useful to competitors. Abundant evidence demonstrated there was no conflict of interest by Rulon-Miller (P). In the initial confrontation between Rulon-Miller (P) and her superior, the assertion of the right to be free of inquiries concerning her personal life was based on substantive direct contract rights she had flowing to her from IBM (D) policies. Furthermore, there was no doubt that the jury could have so found, and on this record it must be assumed that it did so find. Affirmed.

▶ **ANALYSIS**

According to the court, when Rulon-Miller (P) was being considered for her promotion to manager, neither her immediate supervisor nor the regional manager raised any issue of conflict of interest because of her relationship with Blum. In a footnote, the court noted that, interestingly enough, Blum continued to play on an IBM (D) softball team while working for QYX. As to private employers, the first limitations imposed upon their control of off-work activities of employees were the constitutional protections afforded public employees. Recently, however, certain protections have been extended to private sector employees, but these are limited and depend on collective-bargaining agreements, implied contract rights, and other sources.

■▭■

Quicknotes

EMPLOYMENT-AT-WILL The rule, an employment relationship is subject to termination at any time, or for any cause, by an employee or an employer in the absence of a specific agreement otherwise.

INTENTIONAL INFLICTION OF EMOTIONAL DISTRESS Intentional and extreme behavior on the part of the wrongdoer with the intent to cause the victim to suffer from severe emotional distress, or with reckless indifference, resulting in the victim's suffering from severe emotional distress.

Continued on next page.

RIGHT TO PRIVACY   Those personal liberties or relationships that are protected against unwarranted governmental interference.

WRONGFUL DISCHARGE   Unlawful termination of an individual's employment.

Nelson v. McClatchy Newspapers, Inc.

Employee (P) v. Employer (D)

Wash. Sup. Ct., 936 P.2d 1123 (1997).

NATURE OF CASE: Appeal from summary judgment in favor of defendant on plaintiff's claim of federal statutory and constitutional violations.

FACT SUMMARY: Nelson (P), a reporter for [The News Tribune] (TNT) (D), commenced suit against the newspaper on the basis that it violated her statutory and constitutional rights by requiring her to refrain from political activity as a condition of her employment.

🏛 RULE OF LAW
A statute depriving a newspaper of its editorial discretion is unconstitutional in violation of the First Amendment right to freedom of the press.

FACTS: Nelson (P) was hired as a writer for [The News Tribune] (TNT) (D). Three years later, the newspaper was purchased by McClatchy Newspapers, Inc. (D). TNT (D) imposed a code of ethics in order to regulate its operational activities and to minimize the public's perception of bias. Nelson (P) was a lesbian and a political activist. Nelson (P) was observed by a TNT (D) reporter and photographer demonstrating for abortion rights outside a local hospital. TNT (D) informed her that such conduct was not acceptable. Nelson (P) stated that she would nevertheless continue such political activities. Subsequently, Nelson (P) promoted a ballot initiative to enact an antidiscrimination ordinance. TNT (D) transferred Nelson (P) from her position as education reporter to that of copy editor until after the election. That position became permanent after Nelson (P) again refused to comply with the newspaper's (D) ethics code. Nelson (P) sought reinstatement of her position as a reporter. Nelson (P) filed suit against TNT (D) alleging violations of state and federal statutes and of her constitutional rights. Summary judgment was granted to TNT (D) on the federal claims. Nelson (P) appealed.

ISSUE: Is a statute depriving a newspaper of its editorial discretion unconstitutional in violation of the First Amendment right to freedom of the press?

HOLDING AND DECISION: (Sanders, J.) Yes. A statute depriving a newspaper of its editorial discretion is unconstitutional in violation of the First Amendment right to freedom of the press. Absent a demonstration of ambiguity, in construing the meaning of a statute, its plain language controls. Washington law RCW 42.17.680(2) of the Fair Campaign Practices Act prohibits an employer or labor organization from discriminating against an officer or employee regarding the terms or conditions of his or her employment for the failure to contribute or support, or for the opposition of, a candidate, ballot proposition, political party or political committee. The issue in the present case is whether Nelson (P) is covered by the statute based on discrimination for her refusal to abstain from political activity regarding the ballot initiative. The intent behind RCW 42.17.680(2), and the act as a whole, was to prohibit employers from disproportionately influencing the political activities of its employees by requiring them to embrace a particular political position, or to abstain from political activity, as a condition of employment. Nelson (P) clearly falls within the purviews of the statute. However, the statute is unconstitutional in its application to TNT (D). The Supreme Court has held that state statutes attempting to regulate the content of newspapers are prohibited. A fundamental aspect of the right to free press under the First Amendment is the right to editorial discretion. In order to effectuate this purpose, newspapers are permitted to enact policies and procedures tailored to minimize the public's perception of bias. A statute infringing on that discretion is constitutionally impermissible. Trial court affirmed and case remanded.

▶ ANALYSIS

A majority of jurisdictions have enacted statutes safeguarding employees against company policies restricting their rights to engage in political activities outside the workplace. Note that the court declined to resolve the state law issues due to the constitutional violations. However, the court stated that regardless of whether a state or federal statute is implicated, the Constitution requires that freedom of the press be the minimum level of protection afforded to news publications.

▬▭▬

Quicknotes

AMBIGUOUS TERMS Contract terms that are capable of more than one interpretation.

FIRST AMENDMENT Prohibits Congress from enacting any law respecting an establishment of religion, prohibiting the free exercise of religion, abridging freedom of speech or the press, the right of peaceful assembly and the right to petition for a redress of grievances.

FREEDOM OF THE PRESS The right to publish and publicly disseminate one's views.

▬▭▬

Chambers v. Omaha Girls Club, Inc.

Employee (P) v. Employer (D)

834 F.2d 697 (8th Cir. 1987).

NATURE OF CASE: Appeal from denial of injunction and damages for civil rights and Title VII employment discrimination.

FACT SUMMARY: After she became pregnant, Chambers (P), a single, black woman, was fired from her job as an arts and crafts instructor at the Omaha Girls Club, Inc. (D).

🏛 RULE OF LAW

An employer's role-model rule is an employment practice that is consistent with Title VII employment discrimination because it is justifiable as a business necessity or a bona fide occupational qualification.

FACTS: Chambers (P), a single, black woman, was fired from her job as an arts and crafts instructor at the Omaha Girls Club Inc. (Club) (D) after she became pregnant and informed her supervisor of that fact. Among the Club's (D) many activities were programs directed at pregnancy prevention. Staff members were trained and expected to act as role models for the girls, with the intent that the girls would seek to emulate their behavior. Ninety percent of the members at the Club (D) where Chambers (P) was employed were also black. The Club (D) formulated its role-model rule banning single-parent pregnancies among its staff members in pursuit of this role-model approach. Soon after her termination, Chambers (P) filed charges with the Nebraska Equal Opportunity Commission (NEOC), alleging discrimination on the basis of sex and marital status. When the NEOC found no reasonable cause to believe that unlawful employment discrimination had occurred, Chambers (P) brought this action in the district court, seeking injunctions and damages for wrongful discharge. The district court found that Chambers (P) had succeeded in establishing a prima facie case of discrimination but concluded that the role-model rule had a manifest relationship to the Club's (D) fundamental purpose. The court relied in part on expert testimony to the effect that the role-model rule could be helpful in preventing teenage pregnancy. On appeal, Chambers (P) argued that the district court erred in finding business necessity because the role-model rule had not been validated by any studies showing that it prevented pregnancy among the Club's (D) members. Chambers (P) argued further that the district court erred in discounting alternative practices that could have ameliorated the discriminatory effects of the rule.

ISSUE: Is an employer's role-model rule an employment practice that is consistent with Title VII employment discrimination and justifiable as a business necessity or a bona fide occupational qualification?

HOLDING AND DECISION: (Wollman, J.) Yes. An employer's role model rule is an employment practice that is consistent with Title VII employment discrimination because it is justifiable as a business necessity or a bona fide occupational qualification (BFOQ). Business necessity determinations in disparate impact cases are reviewed under the clearly erroneous standard of review applied to factual findings. Thus, the district court's finding of business necessity may be set aside only if this court is left with the definite and firm conviction that a mistake has been committed. Because the district court's account of the evidence is plausible in light of the record viewed in its entirety, it cannot be said that the court's finding of business necessity is clearly erroneous. Moreover, it appeared that Chambers (P) could not be transferred to a noncontact position because no such positions existed at the Club (D). Accordingly, the district court's finding that the role-model rule was justified by business necessity and a violation of Title VII under the disparate impact theory is not clearly erroneous. Moreover, the court's finding of business necessity itself was persuasive as to the existence of a BFOQ. Affirmed.

DISSENT: (McMillian, J.) Even under the deferential clearly erroneous standard, the BFOQ or business necessity exceptions offered by the Club (D) should be rejected because there is no evidence to support a relationship between teenage pregnancies and the employment of an unwed pregnant instructor.

▶ ANALYSIS

The Club (D) served 1,500 members, 90 percent of them black, at the facility where Chambers (P) was employed. The testimony of board members made it clear that the policy was not based upon a morality standard but on a belief that teenage pregnancies severely limit the available opportunities for teenage girls and that the policy was just one prong of a comprehensive attack on the problem of teenage pregnancy. However, two other cases are difficult to distinguish. In *Dolter v. Wahlert High School*, 483 F. Supp. 266 (N.D. Iowa 1980), the court held that the firing by a Roman Catholic high school of an unmarried English teacher who became pregnant violated Title VII. In the other, *Lewis v. Delaware State College*, 455 F. Supp. 239 (D. Del. 1978), the court held that refusal by a state college to renew the contract of the director of residence halls for

Continued on next page.

women because she bore a child out of wedlock violated
the Due Process Clause of the Fourteenth Amendment.

■━■

Quicknotes

BONA FIDE OCCUPATIONAL QUALIFICATION   A statutory exception to the prohibition on discrimination in employment
if the individual's sex, religion or national origin is a necessary qualification for the operation of the business.

DISPARATE IMPACT   Unequal treatment of employees or
of applicants for employment due to practices that appear neutral, but are not.

DISPARATE TREATMENT   Unequal treatment of employees
or of applicants for employment without justification.

TITLE VII OF THE CIVIL RIGHTS ACT OF 1964   States that it shall
be an unlawful employment practice for an employer to fail
or refuse to hire or otherwise discriminate against any
individual with respect to his employment because of such
individual's race, color, religion, sex, or national origin.

■━■

Occupational Safety and Health

Quick Reference Rules of Law

Frank Diehl Farms v. Secretary of Labor

Employer (D) v. Government agency (P)

696 F.2d 1325 (11th Cir. 1983).

NATURE OF CASE: Petition challenging assessment for violation of Occupational Safety and Health Administration (OSHA) standards.

FACT SUMMARY: After an administrative law judge determined that employer-provided housing violated the requirements of the Occupational Safety and Health Act (Osh Act/Act) under the directly-related-to-employment standard, Diehl Farms (D) petitioned for review of the order and the Secretary of Labor's (P) new interpretation of the statutory workplace as it related to housing.

🏛 RULE OF LAW
The Occupational Safety and Health Administration (OSHA) may regulate employer-provided housing if employees are required to live in such housing as a condition of their employment.

FACTS: Diehl Farms (D), an employer of seasonal workers, made housing available to them on a voluntary basis at little or no cost. The workers were not required, either implicitly or explicitly, to live in the housing, and some workers chose not to live in the housing provided. When work was available, the housed workers were required to work on the farm that provided the housing. At other times, however, they could continue to use the housing while working for other employers. To determine whether occupational safety and health regulations applied to employer-provided housing, the Occupational Safety and Health Administration (OSHA) had previously applied the condition-of-employment test, but had recently rejected that test in favor of a directly-related-to-employment standard. The parties in the case agreed that the temporary workers' occupancy of the provided housing, while not a condition of employment, was directly related to employment. Diehl Farms (D) challenged the new test standard, under which it was assessed for violations. The Secretary of Labor (P) argued that it was not material whether laborers were compelled to live in the camp as long as the camp was "directly beneficial, convenient, or advantageous to the employer." The administrative law judge (ALJ) determined that the new test was valid and held that the temporary housing provided by Diehl Farms (D) was a workplace within the meaning of the Occupational Safety and Health Act (Osh Act/Act) and, thus, was subject to its requirements. Diehl Farms (D) petitioned the court to review the agency determination.

ISSUE: May OSHA regulate employer-provided housing if employees are required to live in such housing as a condition of their employment?

HOLDING AND DECISION: (Vance, J.) Yes. OSHA may regulate employer-provided housing if employees are required to live in such housing as a condition of their employment. Nothing in the legislative history of the Act indicates that Congress intended it to apply to places that are not places of work. With the workplace as the central focus of the legislation, the question is whether OSHA has authority to extend its jurisdiction beyond the place where work is performed to encompass a residence. In order for coverage under the Act to be properly extended to a particular area, the conditions to be regulated must fairly be considered working conditions, the safety and health hazards to be remedied occupational, and the injuries to be avoided work related. Only if company policy or practical necessity forces workers to live in employer-provided housing is the degree of coercion such that the hazards of apartment living are sufficiently related to employment to come under the scope of the Act. [The condition-of-employment test previously used by OSHA is the essential bridge that links the residence to the workplace for the purpose of jurisdiction under the Act. The directly-related-to-employment test did not meet these requirements.] Reversed.

DISSENT: (Johnson, J.) The directly-related-to-employment standard should be applied, and the citations should be enforced.

▸ ANALYSIS

OSHA regulations state that living in employer-provided housing is construed as a condition of employment if (1) employers require employees to do so or (2) geographical circumstances require employees to do so (i.e., lack of comparable alternative housing in the area). In 1972, the National Congress of Hispanic American Citizens petitioned OSHA to require portable toilets, hand-washing facilities, and drinking water for migrant farm workers. After ten years of litigation, the case was settled in 1982 when OSHA finally agreed to consider issuing a standard. When a proposed standard was issued in 1984, but withdrawn in 1985, the D.C. Circuit held in *Farmworker Justice Fund v. Brock*, 811 F.2d 613 (D.C. Cir. 1987), that the Secretary had acted contrary to law. It ordered that a standard be issued in 30 days. Even with standards in place, employers have raised various defenses to avoid compliance, making enforcement difficult.

■=■

Continued on next page.

Quicknotes

COERCION The overcoming of a person's free will as a result of threats, promises, or undue influence.

CONDITION OF EMPLOYMENT A requirement necessary in order for an individual to obtain or maintain employment.

OCCUPATIONAL SAFETY AND HEALTH ACT Regulates employee health and safety. Regulations are promulgated and enforced by the Occupational Safety and Health Administration of the Labor Department.

OCCUPATIONAL SAFETY AND HEALTH ADMINISTRATION (OSHA) Oversees safety and health standards in the workplace.

SCOPE OF EMPLOYMENT Those duties performed pursuant to a person's occupation or employment.

STANDARD A measure of comparison.

■■■

Chao v. OSHRC (Erik K. Ho)

Secretary of Labor (P) and Employer (D) v. Government commission (Respondent)

401 F.3d 355 (5th Cir. 2005).

NATURE OF CASE: Challenge by Labor Department (P) and Employer (D) of Occupational Safety and Health Review Commission's (OSHRC's) modification of Employer's (D) penalty for violation of the Occupational Safety and Health Act (Osh Act), as assessed by Labor Department (P).

FACT SUMMARY: Erik K. Ho (D) employed illegal immigrants to move asbestos without training, in violation of the Occupational Safety and Health Act (Osh Act). The Secretary of Labor (P) cited him on a per-employee basis for violations. The Occupational Safety and Health Review Commission (OSHRC) ruled that the Secretary improperly cited Ho (D) on a per-employee basis. The Secretary (P) and Ho (D) appealed the OSHRC's ruling.

RULE OF LAW
(1) The Secretary of Labor (P) does not have discretion under the respirator portion of the asbestos standard to charge employers with per-employee citations.
(2) The Secretary of Labor (P) has discretion under the asbestos training standard to charge employers with per-employee citations.

FACTS: The "egregious penalty" policy adopted by Occupational Safety and Health Administration (OSHA) in 1990 says the Secretary of Labor can propose penalties based on each employee exposed to a single condition that violates Occupational Safety and Health Act (OSH Act), rather than on each standard violated. The policy was created to address situations where the employer's conduct is so egregious that normal enforcement is not sufficient. In late 1997, Ho (D) hired illegal immigrant labor to remove asbestos from an abandoned Houston hospital without proper equipment or training. After a city inspector ordered that the work stop, Ho (D) continued the work at night. Three workers were seriously injured when some of the workers mistakenly opened a gas line, thinking it was a water line, and caused an explosion. After an investigation, OSHA cited Ho (D) and two companies he owned—Ho Ho Ho Express Inc. and Houston Fruitland Inc.—with serious and willful violations of OSH Act. Because 11 workers were involved, Ho's (D) citations included 11 willful violations each of the asbestos standard's respirator and training requirements. The agency proposed a penalty of $1.48 million. Ho (D) contested the citations before an administrative law judge, who upheld 28 willful and 12 serious violations but reduced the penalties to $1.14 million. On review, the Occupational Safety and Health Review Commission ruled that the Secretary (P) improperly cited Ho (D) on a per-employee basis for violating the asbestos respirator and training standards, affirmed one willful violation of each, and reduced the businessman's penalties to $658,000. The Secretary (P) appealed the Occupational Safety and Health Review Commission's (OSHRC's) decision, and Ho (D) filed a cross-appeal.

ISSUE:
(1) Does the Secretary of Labor (P) have discretion under the respirator portion of the asbestos standard to charge employers with per-employee citations?
(2) Does the Secretary of Labor (P) have discretion under the asbestos training standard to charge employers with per-employee citations?

HOLDING AND DECISION: (DeMoss, J.)
(1) No. The Secretary of Labor (P) does not have discretion under the respirator portion of the asbestos standard to charge employers with per-employee citations. The plain language of the respirator portion of the asbestos standard at issue does not give the Secretary of Labor (P) the discretion to charge employers with per-employee citations.
(2) Yes. The Secretary of Labor (P) has discretion under the asbestos training standard to charge employers with per-employee citations. But while the asbestos-training standard allows the Secretary (P) to propose per-employee penalties, the Secretary's (P) decision to cite Ho (D) on a per-employee basis was unreasonable. Review denied and Commission affirmed.

ANALYSIS

The majority's decision was a balancing act that essentially leaves intact OSHA's egregious/willful penalty policy while at the same time affirming the conclusions of the OSHRC.

Quicknotes

OCCUPATIONAL SAFETY AND HEALTH ACT Regulates employee health and safety. Regulations are promulgated and enforced by the Occupational Safety and Health Administration of the Labor Department.

OCCUPATIONAL SAFETY AND HEALTH ADMINISTRATION (OSHA) Oversees safety and health standards in the workplace.

Industrial Union Department v. American Petroleum Institute (The Benzene Case)

OSHA (D) v. Employer (P)

448 U.S. 607 (1980).

NATURE OF CASE: Appeal from decision invalidating an Occupational Safety and Health Administration (OSHA) permanent standard.

FACT SUMMARY: When the Occupational Safety and Health Administration (OSHA/Agency)) (D) promulgated a new standard for concentrations of benzene lower than the standard it had previously set, American Petroleum Institute (P) filed an action that resulted in the standard being invalidated by the Fifth Circuit.

> ## 🏛 RULE OF LAW
> Before issuing any permanent standard under the Occupational Safety and Health Act, the Secretary must determine that the standard is reasonably necessary and appropriate to remedy a significant risk of material health impairment.

FACTS: The Occupational Safety and Health Administration (OSHA/Agency) (D) adopted a threshold limit for benzene of ten parts per million (ppm). After OSHA (D) conducted hearings on a new standard of one ppm, it promulgated the new permanent standard because of evidence that exposure to benzene over a long period caused leukemia. The Fifth Circuit invalidated the standard in response to American Petroleum Institute's (P) suit, holding that the Agency (D) failed to show that the new standard would achieve the desired benefits. On appeal, the Government (D) argued that § 3(8) of the Act imposed a minimal requirement of rationality that would not prevent it from requiring employers to do whatever would be reasonably necessary to eliminate all risks of any harm from their workplaces. With respect to toxic substances and harmful physical agents, the Government (D) took an even stronger position. Relying on § 6(b)(5)'s direction to set a standard that most adequately assures that no employee will suffer material impairment of health or functional capacity, the Government (D) contended that the Secretary of Labor was required to impose standards that either guaranteed workplaces that were free from any risk of material health impairment, however small, or that came as close as possible to doing so without ruining entire industries.

ISSUE: Before issuing any permanent standard under OSHA, must the Secretary determine that it is reasonably necessary and appropriate to remedy a significant risk of material health impairment?

HOLDING AND DECISION: (Stevens, J.) Yes. Before issuing any permanent standard under OSHA, the

Secretary must determine that it is reasonably necessary and appropriate to remedy a significant risk of material health impairment. If the purpose of the statute were to eliminate completely and with absolute certainty any risk of serious harm, it would be proper for the Secretary to interpret §§ 3(8) and 6(b)(5) as he has. But it is clear that the statute was not designed to require employers to provide absolutely risk-free workplaces whenever it is technologically feasible to do so, so long as the cost is not great enough to destroy an entire industry. Rather, both the language and structure of the Act, as well as its legislative history, indicate that it was intended to require the elimination, as far as feasible, of significant risks of harm. Thus, before he can promulgate any permanent health or safety standard, the Secretary is required to make a threshold finding that a place of employment is unsafe, in the sense that significant risks are present and can be eliminated or lessened by a change in practices. The burden was on the Agency (D) to show, on the basis of substantial evidence, that it was at least more likely than not that long-term exposure to 10 ppm of benzene presented a significant risk of material health impairment. In this case, the Agency (D) did not even attempt to carry its burden of proof. Although the Agency (D) has no duty to calculate the exact probability of harm, it does have an obligation to find that a significant risk is present before it can characterize a place of employment as "unsafe." So long as its findings are supported by a body of reputable scientific thought, the Agency (D) is free to use conservative assumptions in interpreting the data with respect to carcinogens, risking error on the side of over-protection rather than under-protection. The record in this case makes it perfectly clear that the Secretary relied squarely on a special policy for carcinogens that imposed the burden on industry of proving the existence of a safe level of exposure, thereby avoiding his threshold responsibility of establishing the need for more stringent standards. In so interpreting his statutory authority, the Secretary exceeded his power. Affirmed.

CONCURRENCE: (Rehnquist, J.) The legislative history demonstrated that the feasibility requirement was a legislative mirage. Thus, the first sentence of § 6(b)(5) of the Act as applied to any toxic substance or harmful physical agent for which a safe level was, according to the Secretary, unknown or otherwise infeasible should have been invalidated.

Continued on next page.

DISSENT: (Marshall, J.) The Secretary's decision was reasonable and in full conformance with the statutory language requiring that he "set the standard which most adequately assures, to the extent feasible, on the basis of the best available evidence, that no employee will suffer material impairment of health or functional capacity, even if such employee has regular exposure to the hazard dealt with by such standard for the period of his working life."

▶ ANALYSIS

The Court noted that in setting a permissible exposure level in reliance on less-than-perfect methods, OSHA would have the benefit of the results gleaned from monitoring and medical testing. Thus, it could keep a constant check on the validity of the assumptions made in developing the permissible exposure limit, giving it a sound evidentiary basis for decreasing the limit if it was initially set too high. Moreover, in this way it could ensure that workers who were unusually susceptible to benzene could be removed from exposure before suffering any permanent damage.

■══■

Quicknotes

BURDEN OF PROOF The duty of a party to introduce evidence to support a fact that is in dispute in an action.

OCCUPATIONAL SAFETY AND HEALTH ACT Regulates employee health and safety. Regulations are promulgated and enforced by the Occupational Safety and Health Administration of the Labor Department.

RATIONALITY The ability to reason; sanity.

■══■

Durez Division of Occidental Chemical Corp. v. OSHA

Employer (P) v. Government agency (D)

906 F.2d 1 (D.C. Cir. 1990).

NATURE OF CASE: Petition for review of agency's interpretation and application of disclosure requirements.

FACT SUMMARY: The Occupational Safety and Health Review Commission (OSHRC) contended that Durez Division of Occidental Chemical Corp. (P) was required to disclose to its employees using the chemical Durez 153 the potential health hazards associated with that substance.

🏛 RULE OF LAW

The Hazard Communications Standard requires that labels of containers containing hazardous chemicals, and their corresponding Material Safety Data Sheets, list all potential health risks associated with their contents, regardless of anticipated exposure levels to those chemicals by their users.

FACTS: Durez Division of Occidental Chemical Corp. (Durez) (P) manufactured Durez 153, a compound containing phenol and formaldehyde, which was used to make heat-resistant products. When the substance was molded, it released small amounts of phenol vapor. The Health Communications Standard (HCS) required manufacturers to investigate the potential hazards of each chemical produced or used in production, to label containers holding those chemicals, and to provide a Material Safety Data Sheet (MSDS) to downstream users disclosing potential hazards. The downstream employer was also required to instruct its employees in the avoidance of the potential hazards of contact with the chemical. Following an inspection by Occupational Safety and Health Administration (OSHA) (D), Durez (P) was issued a citation charging that the MSDS for Durez 153 was in violation of the HCS for failure to disclose potential risks of kidney, liver and heart damage to persons exposed to the chemical. The administrative law judge held that Durez (P) was required to make such disclosures regardless of the amount of Durez 153 to which the employees were actually exposed. The Occupational Safety and Health Review Commission (OSHRC) entered a final order based on the administrative law judge's finding. Durez (P) petitioned for review.

ISSUE: Does the HCS require that labels of containers containing hazardous chemicals, and their corresponding MSDSs, list all potential health risks associated with their contents, regardless of anticipated exposure levels to those chemicals by their users?

HOLDING AND DECISION: (Ginsburg, J.) Yes. The HCS requires that labels of containers containing hazardous chemicals, and their corresponding MSDSs, list all

potential health risks associated with their contents, regardless of anticipated exposure levels to those chemicals by their users. The HCS requires manufacturers to evaluate and communicate all potential hazards presented by a chemical and the downstream employer to supplement this information by instructing its employees in regard to the particular types of exposure they may encounter in the scope of their employment. The rationale supporting this policy is that the downstream employer is better situated to anticipate the particular uses and levels of exposure to which its employees will be exposed. The MSDS is intended to provide more detailed information than the labels of the hazardous chemicals. Since the labels are required to list all potential health risks associated with the hazardous substance, irrespective of anticipated exposure levels, the corresponding MSDS must also contain such information. Petition denied.

▶ ANALYSIS

The court is required to uphold the Secretary's (D) interpretation of regulations as long as it finds that interpretation to be reasonable. Here, the court upheld the Secretary's (D) application of the HCS to chemical mixtures as well as to their constituents. The HCS requires an employer to presume that the same health hazards are present when chemicals are combined in a mixture, and comprise 1 percent or greater of that mixture, as when they are used separately, absent a demonstration to the contrary. Although the court was not required to resolve the issue, it states its opinion that a chemical produced as the result of a reaction from the interaction of chemicals requires the disclosure by an employer of all potential health hazards presented by the hazardous ingredients retaining their chemical identity in the reaction product, regardless of the percentage of that ingredient.

■═■

Quicknotes

DISCLOSURE The communication of certain facts to another.

OCCUPATIONAL SAFETY AND HEALTH ACT Regulates employee health and safety. Regulations are enforced by the Occupational Safety and Health Administration of the Labor Department.

REGULATIONS Rules promulgated by an administrative body pursuant to its legal authority.

■═■

Pepperidge Farm, Inc.

Secretary of Labor (P) v. Employer (D)

17 OSHC 1993, 1997 OSHD ¶31,301 (1997).

NATURE OF CASE: Commission review of administrative law judge's dismissal of a citation item relating to employee grievances in respect to lifting and repetitive-motion hazards.

FACT SUMMARY: Employees of Pepperidge Farm (D) sought penalties for alleged violations of Occupational Safety and Health Act (OSH Act) § 5(a)(1) on the basis that they were required to perform tasks involving repetitive motions and in positions resulting in or likely to result in injury.

🏛 RULE OF LAW
The Secretary of Labor may apply the general duty clause of Occupational Safety and Health Act (OSH Act) § 5(a)(1) to issues involving lifting and repetitive-motion hazards.

FACTS: Employees of Pepperidge Farm (D) alleged 175 separate willful violations of Occupational Safety and Health Act (OSH Act) § 5(a)(1) on the basis that they were required to perform tasks involving repetitive motions and in positions that resulted in or were likely to result in cumulative trauma disorders. The repetitive motions consisted of the lifting of heavy items and the performance of assembly line tasks. The employees sought penalties of $5,000 per violation, for a total of $875,000.

ISSUE: May the Secretary of Labor apply OSH Act § 5(a)(1), the general duty clause, to issues involving lifting and repetitive-motion hazards?

HOLDING AND DECISION: [Commissioner not stated in casebook excerpt.] Yes. The Secretary of Labor may apply the general duty clause of OSH Act § 5(a)(1) to issues involving lifting and repetitive-motion hazards. A violation of § 5(a)(1) exists where a hazardous condition, likely to cause death or serious bodily harm, exists in the workplace of which the employer is aware and there are alternative means available to eliminate or reduce the hazard. First, the plaintiff must demonstrate the existence of a hazard by showing actual or potential physical harm and a sufficient causal connection between the injury and the employee's workplace. Actual physical harm was demonstrated here by the evidence that Pepperidge Farm (D) reported that 28 of its employees underwent 42 surgical procedures, 32 of which were for the treatment of carpal tunnel syndrome. Moreover, the record supported the conclusion that such physical harm was attributable to the workplace. Expert testimony supported the finding that the repetitive motion used in the Downington plant may give rise to some of the injuries suffered. Next, the court

must determine whether the employer was aware of the hazards existing in the workplace. The record clearly supported a finding that Pepperidge Farm (D) was aware of the actual injury to its employees in its Downington plant and of the causal connection of those injuries to the workplace. Those injuries were documented by physicians retained by Pepperidge Farm (D) in order to examine and treat its injured employees. However, § 5(a)(1) only requires the employer to abate hazards causing or likely to cause death or serious bodily harm. The record here showed that the injuries sustained by the employees constituted serious bodily harm. Physical disorders precluding employees from performing their jobs necessarily constitutes serious bodily harm. Approximately half of the 68 employees sustaining injuries were permanently prevented from or severely restricted in the performance of their duties. Other employees were absent from work for several weeks as the result of recovering from surgical operations. Last, it must be shown that alternative means exist to eliminate or reduce the hazards. Based on the demonstration of actual injury and a causal connection, the Secretary (P) may within her discretion require Pepperidge Farm (D) to initiate an abatement plan to ascertain what procedures may reduce the potential risks. Here the Secretary (P) failed to show that Pepperidge Farm (D) did not commence the requisite abatement process or that the actions not taken were materially likely to reduce the possibility of injury. Thus, the administrative law judge properly dismissed the citation. Affirmed.

▌ANALYSIS

Note that Pepperidge Farm (D) did in fact commence actions toward the abatement of hazards in its workplace. The Secretary (P) did not challenge whether Pepperidge Farm (D) took such actions, but rather the extent to which Pepperidge Farm (D) implemented the particular actions, and to which it was required to implement additional measures. Here, Pepperidge Farm (D) attempted to reduce the number of repetitions performed by its employees and to eliminate certain varieties of those repetitions through automated and improved work methods. The Secretary (P) sought the implementation of additional actions to abate the hazards as suggested by its expert witnesses. However, the Secretary (P) failed to sustain her burden of demonstrating that those suggested alternatives would reduce the risk of injury in the workplace.

■━■

Continued on next page.

Quicknotes

ABATEMENT A decrease or lessening of something; in equity, a suspension or dismissal of a cause of action.

DUTY An obligation owed by one individual to another.

HAZARDOUS CONDITIONS Dangerous circumstances with potential risk of injury.

OCCUPATIONAL SAFETY AND HEALTH ACT Federal statute enacted to ensure safe and healthful working conditions via mandatory standards promulgated by the Occupational Safety and Health Administration.

∎≡∎

Brennan v. OSHRC (Republic Creosoting Co.)

Secretary of Labor (P) v. Employer (D)

501 F.2d 1196 (7th Cir. 1974).

NATURE OF CASE: Appeal from reversal of finding of Occupational Safety and Health Administration (OSHA) violations.

FACT SUMMARY: Brennan (P) issued two citations to Republic Creosoting Co. (D) for Occupational Safety and Health Administration (OSHA) violations after one of its employees was killed during the unloading of a truckload of wood ties destined for use as railroad ties.

🏛 RULE OF LAW
Each employer shall furnish to each of his employees employment and a place of employment that is free from recognized hazards causing or likely to cause death or serious physical harm.

FACTS: Republic Creosoting Co. (Republic) (D) operated five railroad-tie yards where it seasoned wood for use as railroad ties. The ties arrived at the yards by truck, with 20 to 25 percent of them bound together into packages of 25 to 45 ties held together by a single narrow steel band. Each tie weighed about 150 to 235 pounds. Generally the truck driver delivering the ties cut the steel band holding each package together but only after Republic's (D) unloader was in place and supporting the package. Davis, a recent hire, sorted and stacked ties after they were unloaded. On Davis's fourth day at work, the unloader operator suggested he come to the unloading to help sort the ties. Republic's (D) field superintendent warned Davis not to get around the trucks because the unloader did all the unloading. Although Davis initially watched from a safe distance, he went up to the truck and while standing next to it, without being ordered to do so or informing anyone of what he intended to do, used an ax to cut the steel band on a package. As a result, five ties fell on and killed Davis. Brennan (P), Secretary of Labor, issued two citations, one serious and one nonserious, to Republic (D) for alleged violations of the Occupational Safety and Health Act (OSH Act). Brennan (P) contended that where an inexperienced, untrained employee was placed at the site of a potentially dangerous operation, the employer should foresee that the employee is likely, because of ignorance, to injure himself and that in such a situation, the employee should be instructed in the safe procedure for the operation being performed in his presence. An administrative law judge (ALJ) affirmed, raising the second citation to a serious violation and imposing a $1,300 penalty. Republic (D) petitioned the Occupational Safety and Health Review Commission (OSHRC) (D) for discretionary review. After

OSHRC (D) reversed and vacated the citations, Brennan (P) appealed.

ISSUE: Shall each employer furnish to each of his employees employment and a place of employment that is free from recognized hazards causing or likely to cause death or serious physical harm?

HOLDING AND DECISION: (Pell, J.) Yes. Each employer shall furnish to each employee employment and a place of employment that is free from recognized hazards causing or likely to cause death or serious physical harm. A "serious violation" is present only where there is "a substantial probability that death or serious physical harm could result from a condition that exists or from one or more practices, means, methods, operations, or processes that have been adopted or are in use, unless the employer did not, and could not with the exercise of reasonable diligence, know of the presence of the violations." The issue on appeal is whether an employer, using reasonable diligence, would have foreseen the danger in question. The Act does not require that a new employee always be trained in proper procedures for a task simply because he is required to be present at the place of an operation in which he is not a participant. OSHRC (D) accurately recognized that training may be unnecessary for an employee who is wholly disassociated with the operation in question and who would not be foreseeably exposed to danger. The instruction given to Davis by Republic's (D) field superintendent was sufficient to satisfy the employer's duty under the OSH Act. Davis was clearly told to stay away from the trucks during unloading. The fact that he did not know the correct procedure for unloading a truck is immaterial. Affirmed.

▶ ANALYSIS

The court noted that whether training was necessary and the amount of any training required would depend on a number of factors, such as the experience of the employee in the particular field of work, the extent of the employee's participation in the operation in question, and the complexity and danger involved in the operation. Where an employee was directly participating in a job, however, the employer may well have a duty under the Act to instruct him on the safe procedure for handling the job. This case demonstrates an employer's use of the unpreventable employee-misconduct defense.

■=■

Continued on next page.

Quicknotes

DEFENSE An argument set forth by a defendant in a law suit seeking to defeat or oppose a plaintiff's claim.

DILIGENCE The exercise of care or attentiveness; the law sets forth three degrees of diligence: ordinary, slight, and extraordinary.

DUTY An obligation owed by one individual to another.

OCCUPATIONAL SAFETY AND HEALTH ACT Federal statute enacted to ensure safe and healthful working conditions via mandatory standards promulgated by the Occupational Safety and Health Administration.

Whirlpool Corp. v. Marshall

Employer (D) v. Secretary of Labor (P)

445 U.S. 1 (1980).

NATURE OF CASE: Appeal from reversal of denial of injunctive relief for compensation for lost pay.

FACT SUMMARY: When Whirlpool Corp. (D) took action against two of its employees after they reported an unsafe condition to the Occupational Safety and Health Administration (OSHA) and refused to follow a subsequent work order on the ground that it was unsafe to do so, Marshall (P), Secretary of Labor, filed this suit against Whirlpool (D).

🏛 RULE OF LAW
Without being subject to discharge or discrimination, an employee has the right to choose not to perform his assigned task because of a reasonable apprehension of death or serious injury coupled with a reasonable belief that no less drastic alternative is available.

FACTS: In Whirlpool Corp.'s (D) manufacturing plant, overhead conveyors transported appliance components to workers throughout the factory. A horizontal wire mesh guard screen about 20 feet above the plant floor protected employees from objects that sometimes fell from the conveyors. To remove objects from the screen and perform occasional maintenance work on the conveyors, employees could usually stand on the angle-iron frames that supported the screen but sometimes found it necessary to step onto the steel mesh screen itself. Whirlpool (D) began to replace the screen with heavier wire after several employees partly fell through the old screen. After a maintenance employee subsequently fell to his death through a section of old screen, two employees met with the plant maintenance superintendent to voice their safety concerns and point out dangerous, unrepaired areas. Unsatisfied with Whirlpool's (D) response, they contacted an official of the regional Occupational Safety and Health Administration (OSHA) office. When directed to perform their usual maintenance duties on a section of old screen, the two employees refused. Ordered to punch out early and unpaid for the remaining six hours of their shift, they subsequently received written reprimands, which were placed in their employment files. Marshall (P), Secretary of Labor, filed suit, alleging Whirlpool's (D) actions constituted discrimination in violation of the Act and requested the reprimands be expunged from the personnel files and that a permanent injunction be issued requiring Whirlpool (D) to compensate the two employees for their lost pay. The district court found the employees acted in good faith but denied relief, holding that the regulation was

inconsistent with the Act and therefore invalid. The court of appeals reversed, and this appeal followed.

ISSUE: Does an employee have the right to choose, without being subject to discharge or discrimination, not to perform his assigned task because of a reasonable apprehension of death or serious injury coupled with a reasonable belief that no less drastic alternative is available?

HOLDING AND DECISION: (Stewart, J.) Yes. An employee has the right to choose, without being subject to discharge or discrimination, not to perform his assigned task because of a reasonable apprehension of death or serious injury coupled with a reasonable belief that no less drastic alternative is available. Nothing in the Act suggests that those few employees who have to face this dilemma must rely exclusively on the remedies expressly set forth in the Act at the risk of their own safety. But nothing in the Act explicitly provides otherwise. The Secretary (P) thus exercised his rulemaking power to promulgate the above standard. The question is whether this interpretative regulation constitutes a permissible gloss on the Act in light of the Act's language, structure, and legislative history. The regulation clearly conforms to the fundamental objective of the Act, i.e., to prevent occupational deaths and serious injuries. The Act does not wait for an employee to die or be injured; it authorizes the promulgation of health and safety standards and the issuance of citations to help prevent deaths or injuries from ever occurring. In addition, Marshall's (P) regulation is an appropriate aid to full effectuation of the Act's general duty clause, which places on employers a mandatory obligation independent of the specific health and safety standards to be promulgated by the Secretary (P). The regulation furthers the overriding purpose of the Act and rationally complements its remedial scheme. Affirmed.

▌ ANALYSIS

The Act creates an express mechanism for protecting workers from employment conditions believed to pose an emergent threat of death or serious injury. As here, however, circumstances may sometimes exist in which the employee justifiably believes that the express statutory arrangement does not sufficiently protect him from death or serious injury. Where an employer does not respond as expected by voluntarily and speedily eliminating the danger, the court, through a temporary restraining order or preliminary injunction, may require the employer to avoid,

Continued on next page.

correct, or remove the danger or to prohibit employees from working in the area.

■■■

Quicknotes

DUTY An obligation owed by one individual to another.

GOOD FAITH An honest intention to abstain from any unconscientious advantage of another.

OCCUPATIONAL SAFETY AND HEALTH ACT Federal statute enacted to ensure safe and healthful working conditions via mandatory standards promulgated by the Occupational Safety and Health Administration.

REGULATIONS Rules promulgated by an administrative body pursuant to its legal authority.

■■■

Marshall v. Barlow's, Inc.

Secretary of Labor (D) v. Employer (P)

436 U.S. 307 (1978).

NATURE OF CASE: Appeal from injunction against warrantless Occupational Safety and Health Administration (OSHA) inspections.

FACT SUMMARY: When Occupational Safety and Health Administration (OSHA), under authority of the Occupational Safety and Health Act (Osh Act/Act), attempted a warrantless search of Barlow's (P) premises, Barlow (P) challenged the statute.

🏛 RULE OF LAW
Except in certain carefully defined classes of cases, a search of property, private or business, without proper consent is unreasonable unless it has been authorized by a valid search warrant.

FACTS: Section 8(a) of the Occupational Safety and Health Act (Osh Act/Act) empowered agents of Marshall (D), Secretary of Labor, to search the work area of any employment facility within the Act's jurisdiction. The purpose of the search was to inspect for safety hazards and violations of Occupational Safety and Health Administration (OSHA) regulations. No search warrant or other process was expressly required under the Act. Barlow's, Inc. (P) challenged the statute. Marshall (D) argued that an exception from the search warrant requirement had been recognized for pervasively regulated businesses and for closely regulated industries long subject to close supervision and inspection. Marshall (D) further argued that warrantless inspections were essential to the proper enforcement of the Act and that requiring a warrant for OSHA inspectors would mean that warrantless search provisions in other regulatory statutes were also constitutionally infirm. The district court enjoined OSHA's warrantless inspections, finding they violated the Fourth Amendment of the U.S. Constitution.

ISSUE: Except in certain carefully defined classes of cases, is a search of property, private or business, without proper consent unreasonable unless it has been authorized by a valid search warrant?

HOLDING AND DECISION: (White, J.) Yes. Except in certain carefully defined classes of cases, a search of property, private or business, without proper consent is unreasonable unless it has been authorized by a valid search warrant. Certain industries have such a history of government oversight that no reasonable expectation of privacy could exist for a proprietor of such an enterprise. A central difference between those cases and this is that businessmen engaged in such federally licensed and regulated enterprises accept the burdens as well as the benefits of their trade, whereas Barlow (P) was not engaged in any regulated or licensed business. Regarding proper enforcement of the Act, the risk is, that during the interval between an inspector's initial request to search a plant and his procuring a warrant following the owner's refusal of permission, violations could be corrected and thus escape the inspector's notice. The arguments that requiring warrants to inspect will impose serious burdens on the inspection system or the courts are not convincing. The great majority of business owners can be expected to consent to inspection without warrant. In those cases where an owner does insist on a warrant, inspection efficiency will not be impeded by the advance notice and delay. Moreover, for purposes of an administrative search such as this, probable cause justifying the issuance of a warrant may be based not only on specific evidence of an existing violation but also on a showing that reasonable legislative or administrative standards for conducting an inspection are satisfied with respect to a particular establishment. Finally, the reasonableness of a warrantless search will depend upon the specific enforcement needs and privacy guarantees of each statute, not on this ruling's real or imagined effect on other, different administrative schemes. Thus, the concerns expressed by Marshall (D) do not justify warrantless inspections under the Act or vitiate the general constitutional requirement that for a search to be reasonable a warrant must be obtained. Barlow (P) was therefore entitled to a declaratory judgment that the Act is unconstitutional insofar as it purports to authorize inspections without a warrant or its equivalent and to an injunction enjoining the Act's enforcement to that extent. Affirmed.

▶ ANALYSIS

The Court noted that the authority to make warrantless searches gives almost unbridled discretion to executive and administrative officers, particularly those in the field, as to when to search and whom to search. A warrant, by contrast, would provide assurances from a neutral officer that the inspection was reasonable under the Constitution, authorized by statute, and pursuant to an administrative plan containing specific neutral criteria. Also, a warrant would then and there advise the owner of the scope and objects of the search, beyond which limits the inspector could not proceed. In prior decisions, the Court had held that the Warrant Clause applies to inspections for compliance with regulatory statutes.

■—■

Continued on next page.

Quicknotes

FOURTH AMENDMENT Provides that persons be secure as to their person and private belongings against unreasonable searches and seizures.

OCCUPATIONAL SAFETY AND HEALTH ACT Federal statute enacted to ensure safe and healthful working conditions via mandatory standards promulgated by the Occupational Safety and Health Administration.

SCOPE OF EMPLOYMENT Those duties performed pursuant to a person's occupation or employment.

■══■

International Union, UAW v. Johnson Controls, Inc.

Union (P) v. Employer (D)

499 U.S. 187 (1991).

NATURE OF CASE: Appeal of grant of defense motion for summary judgment in an employment-discrimination action.

FACT SUMMARY: Johnson Controls, Inc. (D) refused to allow any fertile women to hold jobs involving lead exposure.

🏛 RULE OF LAW
Employers may not exclude fertile females from certain jobs merely because of concern for the health of the fetus the woman might conceive.

FACTS: Johnson Controls, Inc. (D), a battery manufacturer, adopted a policy that excluded any fertile women, whether or not they planned to become pregnant, from jobs where they might be exposed to lead. This resulted in women losing their jobs, being transferred, or facing sterilization in order to keep their jobs. The UAW (P) filed a class action alleging that the policy constituted sexual discrimination under Title VII of the Civil Rights Act of 1964. The trial court held that Johnson Controls's (D) fetal protection policy was valid under a business necessity defense and granted its motion for summary judgment. The appellate court affirmed.

ISSUE: May employers exclude fertile females from certain jobs merely because of concern for the health of the fetus the woman might conceive?

HOLDING AND DECISION: (Blackmun, J.) No. Employers may not exclude fertile females from certain jobs merely because of concern for the health of the fetus the woman might conceive. Johnson Controls's (D) policy was facially sexually discriminatory because it required only female employees to produce proof that they were not capable of reproducing. Such sex discrimination is allowed under Title VII only if there is a bona fide occupational qualification (BFOQ) reasonably necessary to the normal operation of the particular business or enterprise. Sex discrimination because of safety is allowed only when sex or pregnancy interferes with the employee's job performance. In this case, Johnson Controls (D) could not establish a BFOQ, as fertile women can manufacture batteries as efficiently as anyone else. Additionally, if Johnson Controls (D) is complying with Occupation Safety and Health Administration (OSHA) standards, it should not have any increased tort liability due to danger to a fetus or newborn child. Reversed and remanded.

CONCURRENCE: (White, J.) The Court erroneously holds that the BFOQ defense is so narrow that it could never justify a sex-specific fetal-protection policy.

CONCURRENCE: (Scalia, J.) An employer may not discriminate against fertile women at all; it is up to parents to make occupational decisions affecting their families.

⏵ ANALYSIS

The Court dismissed the possibility of employer tort liability if the employer has informed employees of the risk and has not acted negligently. However, it is difficult for an employer to determine in advance what will constitute negligence, and compliance with Title VII does not insulate an employer from state tort liability. Also, while warnings may reduce or preclude employee claims, depending on whether the Court follows a theory of comparative or contributory negligence, such warnings will not preclude claims by injured children. Finally, if the manufacturing process is labeled "abnormally dangerous," employers may be held strictly liable despite taking all proper precautions.

■=■

Quicknotes

ABNORMALLY DANGEROUS ACTIVITY An activity, as set forth in Restatement (Second) of Torts § 520, giving rise to strict liability on the part of the actor for damages caused thereby.

BONA FIDE OCCUPATIONAL QUALIFICATION A statutory exception to the prohibition on discrimination in employment if the individual's sex, religion or national origin is a necessary qualification for the operation of the business.

NEGLIGENCE Conduct falling below the standard of care that a reasonable person would demonstrate under similar conditions.

STRICT LIABILITY Liability for all injuries proximately caused by a party's conducting of certain inherently dangerous activities without regard to negligence or fault.

TITLE VII OF THE CIVIL RIGHTS ACT OF 1964 Enacted to end employment discrimination based on race and gender.

■=■

Disabling Injury and Illness

Quick Reference Rules of Law

Eckis v. Sea World Corp.

Employee (P) v. Employer (D)

Cal. Ct. App., 134 Cal. Rptr. 183 (1976).

NATURE OF CASE: Appeal from award of compensatory damages for personal injuries.

FACT SUMMARY: After Eckis (P), a secretary employed by Sea World Corp. (D), was injured while riding Shamu, a killer whale, at the request of her employer, she filed a workers' compensation claim and a civil action seeking compensatory and punitive damages.

🏛 RULE OF LAW
When an employee's injuries are compensable under the Workers' Compensation Act, the right of the employee to recover the benefits provided by the Act is his exclusive remedy against the employer.

FACTS: Eckis (P) held various jobs as a full-time employee at Sea World Corp. (D) until she became a secretary for Burgess (D), the director of the animal-training department. Because Eckis (P) was an excellent swimmer and had occasionally worked as a model, she was asked, in April, if she would like, while wearing a bikini, to ride Shamu, the killer whale, for some publicity pictures for Sea World (D). She was trained for the ride by Sea World (D) during normal office working hours. Burgess (D) knew that Shamu was conditioned to being ridden only by persons wearing wetsuits and that Shamu had in the past attacked those who wore an ordinary bathing suit when attempting to ride the animal. In addition, he knew that Shamu had been behaving erratically since early March. When Eckis (P) expressed some apprehension, Burgess (D) told her that the ride was "as safe as it could be" but did not tell her about any of the earlier problems involving Shamu. Thus reassured, Eckis (P) took three rides while wearing a bikini paid for by Sea World (D). During the second ride, one of the trainers noticed Shamu's tail was fluttering, a sign the animal was upset. During the third ride, Eckis (P) fell off when Shamu refused to obey a signal. Shamu then bit her on her legs and hips and held her in the tank until she could be rescued. Eckis (P) had 18 to 20 wounds, which required 100 to 200 stitches and left permanent scars. She was hospitalized five days, out of work for several weeks, and also suffered some psychological problems. Sea World (D) paid all her medical expenses and continued to pay her salary as usual during this period. Eckis (P) then filed a workers' compensation claim and this personal-injury action. Eckis (P), framing her complaint on the theories of fraud, negligence, and liability for an animal with vicious or dangerous propensities, seeking both compensatory and punitive damages, maintained that she was not injured in the course and scope of her employment since she was hired to be a secretary, not to ride a whale. Before the case was submitted to the jury, the trial court denied Sea World's (D) motion for a nonsuit on the fraud cause of action. Later, its motions for judgment notwithstanding the verdict and for a new trial were also denied. The jury awarded Eckis (P) $75,000 in compensatory damages. Sea World (D) appealed.

ISSUE: When an employee's injuries are compensable under the Workers' Compensation Act, is the right of the employee to recover the benefits provided by the Act his exclusive remedy against the employer?

HOLDING AND DECISION: (Ault, J.) Yes. When an employee's injuries are compensable under the Workers' Compensation Act, the right of the employee to recover the benefits provided by the Act is his exclusive remedy against the employer. Where a reasonable doubt exists as to whether an act of an employee is contemplated by the employment or as to whether an injury occurred in the course of the employment, § 3202 requires courts to resolve the doubt against the right of the employee to sue for civil damages and in favor of the applicability of the Compensation Act. The undisputed evidence shows that at the time she was injured, Eckis (P) was an employee of Sea World (D). She was injured on Sea World (D) premises during her regular working hours while engaging in an activity that Sea World (D) requested her to perform and for which it provided the training and means. It is immaterial that the activity causing the injury was not related to the employee's normal duties or that the circumstances surrounding the injury were unusual or unique. Far less than a direct request by the employer operates to bring an injury-causing activity within the provisions of the Compensation Act. On these facts, the conditions imposing liability for compensation under the Act are met as a matter of law. Reversed.

▶ ANALYSIS

An employee is entitled to a percentage of lost income plus medical expenses under workers' compensation. As long as that employee's income is low, the benefits under workers' compensation are less desirable than the possible award of compensatory and punitive damages in a civil suit. Because her salary at Sea World (D) was $450 a month, any award Eckis (P) might have received under workers' compensation would have most likely not come close to the amount the jury awarded her.

Continued on next page.

Quicknotes

COMPENSATORY DAMAGES Measure of damages necessary to compensate victim for actual injuries suffered.

LABOR CODE § 3600 Enacted to impose liability on an employer for injuries received by employees.

PREEMPTION Doctrine stating that certain matters are of a national character so that federal laws preempt or take precedence over state or local laws.

PUNITIVE DAMAGES Damages exceeding the actual injury suffered for the purposes of punishment, deterrence and comfort to plaintiff.

WORKERS' COMPENSATION ACT The statutory right of an employee to claim fixed benefits (primarily loss of earnings and medical expenses) from her employer for injury or disease arising out of and in the course of employment.

■▬■

Perry v. State

Employee (P) v. State (D)

Wyo. Sup. Ct., 134 P.3d 1242 (2006).

NATURE OF CASE: Appeal of denial of workers' compensation benefits.

FACT SUMMARY: Because Eleanor Perry (P) was injured at work as a result of violating a safety rule, she was denied workers' compensation benefits.

🏛 RULE OF LAW

An employee acts outside the scope of employment by violating a work restriction if the employer tells the employee not to perform a specific task and the employee knows and understands the specific restriction that is imposed.

FACTS: Eleanor Perry (P) worked at the Mountain Towers Healthcare and Rehabilitation Center. On her first day of work, Perry (P) was told that the nursing home had a written safety policy classifying certain patients as "two-person lifts," and violation of the policy by employees could result in termination. Perry (P) signed a document acknowledging the safety rule. On Oct. 26, 2003, a patient who was classified as a two-person lift asked to be helped to the bathroom. Perry (P) could not get the patient to wait until the other certified nurse assistant was available to help, so she assisted the patient on her own. The patient's wheelchair moved while Perry (P) was trying to lift the patient, and Perry (P) twisted and strained her lower back while trying to prevent the patient from falling. Perry's (P) claim for workers' compensation benefits was contested by the employer and denied by the Wyoming Workers' Safety and Compensation Division. An Office of Administrative Hearings (OAH) hearing examiner found that Perry (P) violated the employer's safety rule and thus was not entitled to workers' compensation benefits based on the state supreme court's decision in *Smith v. Husky Terminal Restaurant, Inc.*, 762 P.2d 1193 (Wyo. 1988). The trial court affirmed OAH's ruling, and Perry (P) appealed.

ISSUE: Does an employee act outside the scope of employment by violating a work restriction if the employer tells the employee not to perform a specific task and the employee knows and understands the specific restriction that is imposed?

HOLDING AND DECISION: (Kite, J.) Yes. An employee acts outside the scope of employment by violating a work restriction if the employer tells the employee not to perform a specific task and the employee knows and understands the specific restriction that is imposed. OAH properly applied the *Smith* rule in denying workers' compensation benefits to Perry (P) because she was injured while violating a safety rule; and its decision was supported

by the evidence. Perry's (P) argument that *Smith* is inconsistent with the state's no-fault-based workers' compensation system also failed. The "no fault" concept applies as long as the employee is injured in the course of employment. The *Smith* ruling simply states a method for determining the parameters of the work that is covered by workers' compensation. It does not inappropriately incorporate fault principles into the workers' compensation analysis. Affirmed.

▶ ANALYSIS

In a dissent that is omitted from the casebook, Judge Hill argued that OAH's decision was not supported by record. It was not clear Perry (P) knew and understood the specific rule she supposedly violated, because the record did not include any specifics about the rule. Hill further argued that *Smith* is not in line with the modern cases on the subject, and the decision has "never since been cited in support of the rule adopted therein—in this jurisdiction or in any other."

Quicknotes

WORKERS' COMPENSATION Fixed awards provided to employees for job-related injuries.

Guess v. Sharp Manufacturing of America

Employee (P) v. Employer (D)

Tenn. Sup. Ct., 114 S.W.3d 480 (2003).

NATURE OF CASE: Appeal of judgment for employee.

FACT SUMMARY: Mary Guess (P) obtained workers' compensation benefits for trauma she experienced after she was exposed to a coworker's blood who she believed was HIV positive, even though she was not infected. Sharp Manufacturing of America (D) appealed.

🏛 RULE OF LAW
A worker who was traumatized after being exposed to the blood of a coworker whom the worker suspected was HIV positive cannot collect workers' compensation benefits for the trauma if she was not actually infected.

FACTS: A coworker of Mary Guess (P) cut his hand on the job, and some of his blood got on Guess's (P) hand. She did not have an injury at that time, but had open cuts on her hand and a recent manicure. Guess (P) became hysterical because she thought the blood was HIV positive. She based this conclusion on her observations that her coworker was sick all of the time, had been isolated while at work, had friends at work who had died of AIDS, appeared frail, received mailings from a gay-rights organization, and "looked and acted gay." Guess (P) began having panic attacks about a week later and took medical leave for six weeks. She was diagnosed with post-traumatic stress disorder caused by the incident. Her psychiatrist prescribed various medications and classified her as moderately impaired. He testified that she was vocationally impaired because she should not engage in assembly line or production work where blood could be shed, work involving the public, or work that would involve a great deal of concentration or focus. Another doctor testified that Guess (P) had been tested five times for HIV and all five tests were negative, and that her chance of becoming infected was infinitely small. The trial court found that Guess (P) had a vocational disability as a result of the psychological consequences of her injury and awarded her partial disability benefits. Sharp Manufacturing of America (Sharp) (D) appealed, arguing that Guess (P) did not suffer a compensable injury. Guess (P) also appealed, arguing that she was entitled to a larger amount of benefits because of her severe limitations.

ISSUE: Can a worker who was traumatized after being exposed to the blood of a coworker whom the worker suspected was HIV positive collect workers' compensation benefits for the trauma, even if she was not actually infected?

HOLDING AND DECISION: (Barker, J.) No. A worker who was traumatized after being exposed to the blood of a coworker whom the worker suspected was HIV positive cannot collect workers' compensation benefits for the trauma if she was not actually infected. Under Tennessee law, injuries are compensable if they arise out of and in the course of employment. An accidental injury arises out of and is in the course of employment if it has a rational connection to the work and occurs while the employee is engaged in the duties of employment. Absent proof of actual exposure to HIV, Guess (P) has not suffered a compensable injury under the Workers' Compensation Law because Guess (P) could not show that her mental injury arose out of her employment with Sharp (D). Guess's (P) subjective evidence that she suspected her coworker had HIV because he was frail and "looked and acted gay" is rejected. If a plaintiff were allowed to recover under the facts of the present case, anybody suffering from a mental injury stemming from any perceived or imagined exposure to harmful substances or situations would be entitled to recovery. Such a result is contrary to the original purpose and continued viability of the Tennessee Workers' Compensation Law. Chancery court reversed.

▶ ANALYSIS

It seems that what lost the case for Guess (P) is not so much that she was not infected, but that her post-traumatic stress "arose out of" her subjective belief, not an injury "arising out of employment." The court stated that a mental injury is compensable if it results from an identifiable stressful, work-related event that produced a sudden mental stimulus like fright, shock, or excessive anxiety, and acknowledged that post-traumatic stress disorder can be a compensable injury. But in this case, Guess's (P) injury in this case did not "arise out of" her employment, but out of her subjective beliefs about her coworker's health and sexual orientation.

Quicknotes

WORKERS' COMPENSATION Fixed awards provided to employees for job-related injuries.

Turner v. American Mutual Insurance Co.

Employee (P) v. Employer's Insurer (D)

La. Sup. Ct., 390 So. 2d 1330 (1980).

NATURE OF CASE: Appeal from termination of workers' compensation benefits.

FACT SUMMARY: Turner (P) appealed when the lower courts upheld termination of the workers' compensation he received after his right foot was crushed in a job-related accident.

> ### 🏛 RULE OF LAW
> An injured employee is entitled to total permanent disability compensation if he can perform no services other than those that are so limited in quality, dependability, or quantity that a reasonably stable market for them does not exist.

FACTS: Turner (P), a 20-year-old, mentally retarded black man, had his right foot crushed while employed as a sawhand for a logging contractor. The injury required two operations, which eventually left Turner (D) with a 30 to 40 percent residual disability in his foot. American Mutual Insurance Co. (American Mutual) (D) terminated Turner's (P) workers' compensation payments when Dr. Lowrey, the orthopedist who performed Turner's (P) surgery, notified the insurer that he felt Turner (P) could resume work on a trial basis. Turner (P) sued, claiming that the payments were improperly discontinued because he was permanently disabled. Dr. Lowrey acknowledged that Turner's (P) foot could be reinjured easily and that he could not do work that required him to put a great deal of weight or pressure on his toes. The doctor confessed that he was not familiar with logging but said he did not think it involved standing or pushing up on one's toes. Another orthopedist, Dr. Joffrion, who was familiar with the physical requirements of logging jobs, testified that Turner (P) could not work as a logger because he could no longer stand or walk for extended periods. Although an industrial psychologist and vocational rehabilitationist gave Turner (P) a battery of tests showing him to be mentally retarded, quite limited in academic skills, with eye-hand motor coordination consistent with his level of intellect, achievement, and experience, the psychologist was allowed to testify that Turner (P) could work on an assembly line, do custodial work, or even drive a pulpwood truck or a skidder used in logging. Based on this testimony, the trial court found that Turner (P) was not totally disabled. The court of appeals affirmed, finding that Turner (P) failed to prove to a legal certainty and by a reasonable preponderance of the evidence that he was unable to pursue any type of gainful employment due to the injury.

ISSUE: Is an injured employee entitled to total permanent disability compensation if he can perform no services other than those that are so limited in quality, dependability, or quantity that a reasonably stable market for them does not exist?

HOLDING AND DECISION: (Dennis, J.) Yes. An injured employee is entitled to total permanent disability compensation if he can perform no services other than those that are so limited in quality, dependability, or quantity that a reasonably stable market for them does not exist. The rule stated embodies the odd-lot doctrine that was not applied by either of the lower courts. Thus, neither of those courts focused on the question of whether Turner (P), considering both his physical and mental limitations, could successfully obtain and hold regular employment in actual jobs available to him within reasonable proximity to his residence. Under the odd-lot doctrine, Turner's (P) evidence makes a prima facie case for his classification in that category. All concerned agree that he is mentally and intellectually unable to do any work outside of manual labor. It was also shown that he cannot do work which requires prolonged standing, walking, stooping, or climbing. It has not been shown, however, that there is an occupation available within a reasonable area in which Turner (P) can work considering his physical disability, education, and mental deficiencies. Since it is possible that an actual job in Turner's (P) vicinity exists that might afford him gainful employment, American Mutual (D) should be allowed an opportunity to make this showing. On remand, Turner (P) will also be allowed to introduce further evidence to support his case under the doctrine. If the employer is successful in rebutting Turner's (P) prima facie showing of total disability, the trial judge should reconsider the appropriateness of compensation for partial disability. Reversed and remanded.

▶ ANALYSIS

The term "odd lot" first appeared in a 1911 English case when the court stated "that if the accident leaves the workman's labour in the position of an 'odd lot' in the labour market, the employer must shew [sic] that a customer can be found who will take it." Judge Cardozo was the first to apply the doctrine in this country in his ruling in *Jordan v. Decorative Co.*, 230 N.Y. 522, 130 N.E. 634 (1921). The burden of proof in most jurisdictions is, as it was here, initially on the employee to demonstrate that the former job is beyond his or her capability, whereupon the burden shifts to the employer, who must demonstrate that other jobs exist for which the employee has the requisite skills.

■=■

Continued on next page.

Quicknotes

BURDEN OF PROOF The duty of a party to introduce evidence to support a fact that is in dispute in an action.

PRIMA FACIE CASE An action where the plaintiff introduces sufficient evidence to submit the issue to the judge or jury for determination.

REBUTTABLE PRESUMPTION A rule of law, inferred from the existence of a particular set of facts, which is conclusive in the absence of contrary evidence.

WORKERS' COMPENSATION ACT The statutory right of an employee to claim fixed benefits (primarily loss of earnings and medical expenses) from her employer for injury or disease arising out of and in the course of employment.

Stone Container Corp. v. Castle

Employer (D) v. Employee (P)

Iowa Sup. Ct., 657 N.W.2d 485 (2003).

NATURE OF CASE: Appeal of appellate court judgment for employer.

FACT SUMMARY: Walker Castle (P) was seriously injured on the job, and requested from his employer (D) a laptop with assistive devices, but the employer denied the request. The Iowa Industrial Commissioner ruled in Castle's (P) favor, the trial court affirmed, and the appellate court reversed.

🏛 RULE OF LAW
An assistive device that is not necessary for medical care may be covered by Iowa's workers' compensation law.

FACTS: While he was on the job at Stone Container Corp. (D), Walker Castle (P) fell through a chute used to collect scrap cardboard and landed in a bailing machine that crushed his legs and lower body. He was 19 years old at the time. Doctors amputated both legs at the hip, and he had numerous surgeries, including skin grafts and colon resections. Castle's (P) skin problems require that he stay in a cool environment, and often prevent him from sitting in a wheelchair, so he instead uses a "prone cart" on which he lies face down. Stone Container's (D) insurer granted Castle's (P) initial request for a laptop computer, which he used to complete ten credit hours of college courses. When the computer broke down, he requested a new one, this time with assistive devices that would facilitate using the laptop while in the wheelchair or the prone cart. When Stone Container (D) and/or the insurer did not respond, Castle (P) turned to the industrial commission, which held a hearing, at which Castle's (P) attorney argued he needed a laptop computer to assist with his education and rehabilitation and to replace function lost because of the injury. A computer teacher and a licensed occupational therapist also testified on Castle's (P) behalf. Stone Container (D) argued that the computer was not needed for medical care, and that it therefore should not have to pay for it. The commission decided the computer and assistive devices were appropriate expenses. The Woodbury County District Court affirmed, but the state appeals court ruled that the computer does not qualify as a covered appliance under the workers' compensation law.

ISSUE: Can an assistive device that is not necessary for medical care be covered by Iowa's workers' compensation law?

HOLDING AND DECISION: (Ternus, J.) Yes. An assistive device that is not necessary for medical care may be covered by Iowa's workers' compensation law. The

Iowa workers' compensation law requires employers to provide their injured employees with "reasonable and necessary . . . appliances." Stone Container's (D) argument that a covered appliance must be necessary for medical care is rejected. A device is covered if it replaces a function lost by the employee as a result of the employee's work-related injury. In this case, a laptop computer provides Castle (P) with access to the outside world that has been denied to him by his devastating injuries, and access that can only be gained through this artificial device. Vacated.

▶ ANALYSIS

The court liberally construed the workers' compensation law in this case to accommodate Castle (P). The court acknowledged this, and stated that liberal construction was required.

Quicknotes

WORKERS' COMPENSATION ACT The statutory right of an employee to claim fixed benefits (primarily loss of earnings and medical expenses) from her employer for injury or disease arising out of and in the course of employment.

Weinstein v. St. Mary's Medical Center

Employee (P) v. Employer (D)

Cal. Ct. App., 68 Cal. Rptr. 2d 461 (1997).

NATURE OF CASE: Appeal from summary judgment dismissing action for compensatory damages sustained as a result of an accident.

FACT SUMMARY: Weinstein (P), an employee of St. Mary's Medical Center (D), sought compensatory damages pursuant to an accident she suffered while receiving treatment in the hospital for a prior injury.

🏛 RULE OF LAW
In order to overcome the "dual-capacity" exception to the exclusive remedy of workers' compensation, the employer must demonstrate that the employee at the time of the injury was performing services arising from, and incidental to, her employment and was acting within the scope of that employment.

FACTS: Weinstein (P), an employee of St. Mary's Medical Center (Hospital) (D), injured her left foot in the course of her employment. She ceased working due to her injury, although she was still employed, and filed a workers' compensation claim. Weinstein (P) began receiving temporary disability and ongoing medical payments from the Hospital's (D) workers' compensation administrator. Weinstein (P) went to the Hospital (D) to receive treatment for her injury. As she was being escorted through the Hospital (D) by a technician, she slipped and fell on a liquid substance in one of the hallways, resulting in a chronic injury to her already-injured foot. Weinstein (P) was subsequently laid off from her position. The Hospital (D) continued to pay the costs of treatment associated with the second injury to Weinstein's (P) foot. Weinstein (P) then filed a personal-injury claim against the Hospital (D), seeking compensatory damages for the second accident. The Hospital (D) filed a motion for summary judgment, and the trial court granted the motion. Weinstein (P) appealed.

ISSUE: In order to overcome the "dual-capacity" exception to the exclusive remedy of workers' compensation, must the employer demonstrate that the employee at the time of the injury was performing services arising from, and incidental to, her employment and was acting within the scope of that employment?

HOLDING AND DECISION: (Walker, J.) Yes. In order to overcome the "dual-capacity" exception to the exclusive remedy of workers' compensation, the employer must demonstrate that the employee at the time of the injury was performing services arising from, and incidental to, her employment and was acting within the scope of that employment. The dual-capacity doctrine allows an employee to recover in tort for negligent aggravation of an already-existing work-related injury against an employer who undertakes to render treatment to the plaintiff's injury. The test turns on whether that undertaking by the employer imposes a new set of obligations on the employer. Thus, the employer must have a duty of care that is unrelated to the employment relationship. Moreover, the employer's duty is dependent on the circumstances present at the time of the accident. Thus, in order to overcome the dual-capacity exception, the Hospital (D) was required to demonstrate that Weinstein's (P) aggravated injury was sustained while she was acting within the scope of her employment. At the time Weinstein's injury was sustained, however, the Hospital (D) was acting in the capacity of a medical-care provider toward Weinstein (D) and not as an employer. Thus, the conditions of compensation did not exist between the Hospital (D) and Weinstein (P) at the time of the aggravating injury. Therefore, Weinstein (P) was not limited to the exclusive remedy of workers' compensation. Reversed.

▶ ANALYSIS

Many state workers' compensation statutes employ language stating that such compensation provides the employee with his or her "exclusive" remedy. However, many exceptions have evolved in response to the rule of exclusivity. The dual-capacity exception originated from the separate duties of the employer to its employees arising from its obligations as an employer and its other common-law duties of care. When an employer imposes a contractual duty on the employee to receive medical care from the employer, then the medical treatment rendered may be considered as arising in the scope of employment. However, where such service is rendered independent of that relationship, the employer acts in the capacity of a property owner to an invitee and has a duty to provide the concomitant duty of care to that invitee.

■━■

Quicknotes

DUTY OF CARE A principle of negligence requiring an individual to act in such a manner as to avoid injury to a person to whom he or she owes an obligatory duty.

WORKERS' COMPENSATION ACT Imposes liability on employer for injuries received by employers on the course of their employment.

■━■

Mandolidis v. Elkins Industries, Inc.

Employee (P) v. Employer (D)

W.Va. Sup. Ct., 246 S.E.2d 907 (1978).

NATURE OF CASE: Appeal from grant of motion to dismiss action for damages for work-related personal injury.

FACT SUMMARY: Mandolidis (P), a machine operator for Elkins Industries, Inc. (D), filed an action for damages after he lost two fingers on his right hand and part of the hand itself while using a ten-inch table saw with an unguarded blade in the course of his employment.

⚖ RULE OF LAW
An employer loses immunity from common-law actions where its conduct constitutes an intentional tort or willful, wanton, and reckless misconduct.

FACTS: Mandolidis (P) lost two of the fingers on his right hand and part of the hand itself while operating, in the course of his employment with Elkins Industries, Inc. (Elkins) (D), a ten-inch table saw not equipped with a safety guard. He then sought damages, alleging that Elkins (D) wholly, willfully, wrongfully, deliberately, maliciously, and with intent to injure or kill Mandolidis (P) refused to provide reasonably safe equipment and a reasonably safe place to work. He further contended that Elkins's (D) conduct warranted a specific finding of a deliberate intent to inflict bodily harm or injury upon its employees in general and Mandolidis (P) in particular. Depositions from seven former employees of Elkins (D) confirmed that (1) numerous violations existed in the plant because guards had been removed from saws due to the claim of a foreman that they slowed down production; (2) that Elkins (D) had violated an Occupational Safety and Health Administration (OSHA) order not to operate a table saw without installing a guard; (3) and that employees had been told they would be sent home or fired for refusing to run a saw without a guard. The foreman's affidavit asserted that he had been helping Mandolidis (P) just before the accident and that when he had to leave for a few minutes, he expressly instructed Mandolidis (P) not to operate the saw alone, but Mandolidis (P) ignored the warning. Elkins (D) moved to dismiss, denying in an affidavit all charges and any deliberate intent to injure Mandolidis (P). The trial court sustained the motion and dismissed the action with prejudice. Mandolidis (P) appealed.

ISSUE: Does an employer lose immunity from common-law actions where its conduct constitutes an intentional tort or willful, wanton, and reckless misconduct?

HOLDING AND DECISION: (McGraw, J.) Yes. An employer loses immunity from common-law actions where its conduct constitutes an intentional tort or willful, wanton, and reckless misconduct. Notwithstanding the wording of the trial court's dismissal order, its consideration of affidavits and depositions converted the motion to dismiss to a motion for summary judgment. Thus, the sole issue became whether the trial court erred in concluding there was no genuine issue of material fact entitling Elkins (D) to judgment as a matter of law. The record discloses that there were material facts at issue. Was Mandolidis (P) told by a company agent that he would be discharged if he refused to run an unguarded saw? Did the foreman tell Mandolidis (P) to wait until his return before continuing to run the saw? Mandolidis (P) is entitled to prove these facts in support of his case because they render the desired inference, when taken together with other facts Mandolidis (P) clearly intends to prove, i.e., that Elkins (D) acted with deliberate intent, more probable than it would be without those facts. The trial court determined that reasonable men could not infer deliberate intent from all the facts given. This court does not believe that reasonable men could not infer the necessary intent from the facts of this case. The trial court's determination of this issue was erroneous. Reversed and remanded.

▶ ANALYSIS

Workers' compensation completely supplanted the common-law tort system only with respect to negligently caused industrial accidents. However, entrepreneurs were not given the right to carry on their enterprises without any regard to the life and limb of the participants in the endeavor and free from all common-law liability. A distinction was recognized between negligence, including gross negligence, and willful, wanton, and reckless misconduct. The court stated that the latter conduct required a subjective realization of the risk of bodily injury created by the activity, and employees retained the right to file a civil cause of action for such conduct. The *Mandolidis* opinion, however, represents the minority rule.

■▬■

Quicknotes

IMMUNITY Exemption from a legal obligation.

INTENT The existence of a particular state of mind whereby an individual seeks to achieve a specific result by his action.

Continued on next page.

MOTION FOR SUMMARY JUDGMENT Motion for judgment rendered by a court brought by one of the parties, claiming that the lack of a question of material fact in respect to an issue warrants disposition of the issue without consideration by the jury.

PREMEDITATION Contemplation of undertaking an activity prior to action; any length of time is sufficient.

TORT A legal wrong resulting in a breach of duty.

WILLFUL, RECKLESS MISCONDUCT Unlawful intentional conduct without regard to the consequences.

WORKERS' COMPENSATION ACT The statutory right of an employee to claim fixed benefits (primarily loss of earnings and medical expenses) from her employer for injury or disease arising out of and in the course of employment.

York v. Union Carbide Corp.

Employee's widow (P) v. Manufacturer (D)

Ind. Ct. App., 586 N.E.2d 861 (1992).

NATURE OF CASE: Appeal from grant of defense motion for summary judgment in a wrongful death action.

FACT SUMMARY: The administrator (P) of York's estate commenced a wrongful death action against Union Carbide Corp. (D), the manufacturer of argon gas, on the basis that it failed to properly warn the employees of U.S. Steel regarding the potential dangers of that product.

🏛 RULE OF LAW
(1) The savings clause of 29 U.S.C.A. § 653 operates to exempt from preemption tort-law claims brought pursuant to state law.
(2) The duty to warn an employee of the hazards associated with the use of a product is satisfied by informing the employee responsible for receiving and setting up the product of the hazards associated with the use of that product.

FACTS: Michael York was employed by U.S. Steel as a millwright. U.S. Steel shut down production of a steel-making furnace called the "Evelyn vessel" in order to reline its interior. As part of the relining, a scaffold was erected to hold an industrial elevator carrying employees from a re-pair platform eight feet above the vessel to the vessel floor. While the vessel was in production, it produced argon gas, which flows through a main pipeline and was injected into molten steel from the bottom of the chamber through 16 nozzles. When the vessel is not in production, that gas is diverted to a small supply line also leading to the 16 nozzles. During the relining, the pipelines carrying the argon gas were disconnected and reconnected, at which time argon gas commenced flowing into the chamber. The gas was not detected because air was being circulated into the vessel by a high-volume air mover. An oxygen deficiency test was conducted; however, the reading was incorrectly taken from the ten to twelve foot level rather than the five to six foot level. The test showed there was no oxygen deficiency. Subsequently, Michael York took the elevator to the bottom of the vessel in order to prepare for the removal of the scaffolding. Ten to fifteen minutes later, he was found motionless on the vessel floor. He died as a result of asphyxiation from the argon gas. The trial court granted summary judgment in favor of Union Carbide (D) in Mrs. York's (P) wrongful death action, and Mrs. York (P) appealed.

ISSUE:
(1) Does the savings clause of 29 U.S.C.A. § 653 operate to exempt from preemption tort-law claims brought pursuant to state law?

(2) Is the duty to warn an employee of the hazards associated with the use of a product satisfied by informing the employee responsible for receiving and setting up the product of the hazards associated with the use of that product?

HOLDING AND DECISION: (Staton, J.)
(1) Yes. The savings clause of 29 U.S.C.A. § 653 operates to exempt from preemption tort-law claims brought pursuant to state law. Federal law may be found to preempt state law where Congress expressly states that intent, the federal regulatory scheme is sufficiently comprehensive to imply such intent, or the state law poses a restriction in the achievement of Congress's legislative purpose. While the Occupational Safety and Health Act (OSH Act) contains language impliedly stating that where a federal standard is in effect in respect to an occupation-al safety or health issue, then the state agency or court may not assert jurisdiction over that issue under state law. However, the savings clause of § 653 provides that the OSH Act should not be construed as superseding or affecting any state workers' compensation law. Courts have interpreted this provision as saving state torts law from preemption.

(2) Yes. The duty to warn an employee of the hazards as-sociated with the use of a product is satisfied by inform-ing the employee responsible for receiving and setting up the product of the hazards associated with the use of that product. Union Carbide (D) had no duty to train the employees of the purchaser of the argon gas in the use of gas-testing equipment, nor could any additional warning literature have been distributed to improve U.S. Steel's knowledge of the dangers of the argon gas. The record demonstrated that the trained and cer-tified technicians employed by U.S. Steel took the oxygen reading at a point above the normal breathing zone. That action had no relation to Union Carbide's (D) duty to warn. Mrs. York (P) failed to sustain her burden that an issue of material fact existed in respect to that issue. Affirmed.

▶ ANALYSIS

This case represents an alternative category of exceptions to the exclusivity of workers' compensation claims in an action against an employer by an employee for injury or second illness. Such claims are generally brought against additional employers of the victim based on the theory that the third party breached a duty of care owed to the

Continued on next page.

employee. Actions may also be maintained against insurers, unions or government agencies on the ground that their negligence in inspecting the employee's worksite proximately resulted in that employee's injury or illness. The most effective recourse for an injured employee is typically a products liability claim against a third-party manufacturer alleging that the use of the defective product caused the illness or injury sustained by the employee in the workplace.

∎═∎

Quicknotes

DUTY TO WARN An obligation owed by an owner or occupier of land to persons who come onto the premises, to inform them of defects or active operations which may cause injury.

OCCUPATIONAL SAFETY AND HEALTH ACT Regulates employee health and safety. Regulations are promulgated and enforced by the Occupational Safety and Health Administration of the Labor Department.

PREEMPTION Doctrine stating that certain matters are of a national character so that federal laws preempt or take precedence over state or local laws.

PRODUCT LIABILITY The legal liability of manufacturers and sellers for damages and injuries suffered by buyers, users, and even bystanders because of defects in goods purchased.

∎═∎

Teal v. E.I. DuPont de Nemours & Co.

Employee (P) v. Employer of independent contractor (D)

728 F.2d 799 (6th Cir. 1984).

NATURE OF CASE: Appeal from denial of damages for personal injuries.

FACT SUMMARY: After he was injured while working in DuPont's (D) plant as an employee of an independent contractor, Teal (P) brought this suit against DuPont (D) for recovery for his injuries sustained as a result of his falling off a fixed ladder.

🏛 RULE OF LAW

Once an employer is deemed responsible for complying with Occupational Safety and Health Administration (OSHA) regulations, it is obligated to protect every employee in its workplace.

FACTS: While working for the Daniel Construction Company, an independent contractor hired by E.I. DuPont de Nemours & Co. (DuPont) (D) to dismantle and remove hydraulic bailers from its plant, Teal (P) fell about 17 feet from a straight and permanently affixed ladder at the DuPont (D) plant. Teal (P) sued DuPont (D), alleging that his fall and injuries were the direct and proximate result of DuPont's (D) negligence. One of Teal's (P) negligence theories concerned DuPont's (D) duty to invitees to "furnish protection against dangers" on its property. The trial court instructed the jury that a landowner's duty to invitees was to give warning of, or use ordinary care to furnish protection against, such dangers to employees of the contractor who were without actual or constructive notice of the dangers. The jury later requested additional instruction, whereupon the court added that an owner or occupant of land who had an independent contractor or who employs employees to perform work owes a duty to warn of hazards but is not under a duty to specify the manner in which those hazards should be avoided. Teal (P) claimed that this instruction was erroneous. In addition, evidence indicated that DuPont's (D) ladder failed to conform to Occupational Safety and Health Administration (OSHA) regulations requiring a clearance of not less than seven inches "from the centerline of the rungs, cleats, or steps to the nearest permanent object in back of the ladder." Because DuPont (D) had breached a regulatory obligation, Teal (P) requested a jury instruction on the issue of negligence per se, but the court refused, informing the jury that the OSHA regulation "may be considered as 'some evidence' of the appropriate standard of care." Teal (P) also claimed the court's refusal to charge on the issue of negligence per se was reversible error. DuPont (D) argued that the stated purposes for OSHA revealed that Congress did not intend to impose a duty upon employers to protect the safety of an independent contractor's employees who

work in the employer's plant. When the jury returned a verdict in favor of DuPont (D), Teal (P) appealed.

ISSUE: Once an employer is deemed responsible for complying with OSHA regulations, is it obligated to protect every employee in its workplace?

HOLDING AND DECISION: (Celebrezze, J.) Yes. Once an employer is deemed responsible for complying with OSHA regulations, it is obligated to protect every employee in its workplace. The primary dispute on appeal is whether an employee of an independent contractor is a member of the class of persons that the OSHA regulation was intended to protect. DuPont's (D) reliance on the plain language of the general duty clause of § 654(a)(1) was misplaced since it was accused of breaching the specific duty imposed on employers by § 654(a)(2), mandating that an employer "comply with Occupational Safety and Health standards promulgated under this chapter." If the special duty provision is logically construed as imposing an obligation on the part of employers to protect all of the employees who work at a particular job site, then the employees of an independent contractor who work on the premises of another employer must be considered members of the class that § 654(a)(2) was intended to protect. This court believes that Congress enacted § 654(a)(2) for the special benefit of all employees, including the employees of an independent contractor who perform work at another employer's workplace. Tennessee case law also establishes that breach of a duty imposed by regulation is negligence per se if the plaintiff is a member of the class of persons that the regulation was intended to protect. Teal (P) was thus entitled to a jury instruction on his negligence per se claim. However, although the court's instruction concerning a landowner's duty to invitees is ambiguous, such ambiguity is harmless here. Affirmed in part, reversed in part, and remanded.

▶ ANALYSIS

Most jurisdictions look at OSHA standards in the same light the trial court did in its instructions to the jury, i.e., as "some evidence" of the appropriate standard of care. Only about one-fourth of the jurisdictions apply the Tennessee rule announced in the instant case. The court explained that the difficulty that courts have experienced in attempting to define a particular employer's responsibilities under OSHA is due primarily to the varying nature of the separate duty provisions. The general duty clause was

Continued on next page.

intended by Congress to cover unanticipated hazards that were not otherwise covered by specific regulations.

■━■

Quicknotes

INDEPENDENT CONTRACTOR A party undertaking a particular assignment for another who retains control over the manner in which it is executed.

INVITEE A person who enters upon another's property by an express or implied invitation and to whom the owner of the property owes a duty of care to guard against injury from those hazards which are discoverable through the exercise of reasonable care.

NEGLIGENCE PER SE Conduct amounting to negligence as a matter of law because it is either so contrary to ordinary prudence or it is in violation of statute.

OCCUPATIONAL SAFETY AND HEALTH ACT Regulates employee health and safety. Regulations are promulgated and enforced by the Occupational Safety and Health Administration of the Labor Department.

■━■

Barnhart v. Thomas

Social Security Administration (D) v. Claimant (P)

540 U.S. 20 (2003).

NATURE OF CASE: Appeal of judgment for Social Security claimant.

FACT SUMMARY: An elevator operator whose job was eliminated throughout much of the country applied for Social Security disability benefits. The federal appeals court ruled in her favor.

🏛 RULE OF LAW
Social Security disability insurance claimants who are sufficiently fit to perform a former job that has been eliminated are ineligible for benefits even if that job has virtually disappeared from the economy.

FACTS: Pauline Thomas (P) was an elevator operator until her job was eliminated. When she applied for disability benefits, the Social Security Administration (D) found she was not disabled, despite having hypertension, cardiac arrhythmia, and cervical and lumbar strain/sprain, because her impairments did not prevent her from performing her past relevant work as an elevator operator. The administration (D) also rejected her argument that she is unable to do her previous work because that work no longer exists in significant numbers in the national economy. The district court affirmed the administration's (D) ruling, holding that whether the claimant's old job exists is irrelevant under the administration's regulations. The U.S. Court of Appeals for the Third Circuit (en banc) reversed, holding that the statute unambiguously makes ability to perform prior work disqualifying only if it is substantial gainful work that exists in the national economy.

ISSUE: Are Social Security disability insurance claimants who are sufficiently fit to perform a former job that has been eliminated ineligible for benefits even if that job has virtually disappeared from the economy?

HOLDING AND DECISION: (Scalia, J.) Yes. Social Security disability insurance claimants who are sufficiently fit to perform a former job that has been eliminated are ineligible for benefits even if that job has virtually disappeared from the economy. To be eligible for disability benefits under 42 U.S.C. § 423(d)(2)(A), the claimant's impairment must be so severe that the claimant "is not only unable to do his previous work but cannot, considering his age, education, and work experience, engage in any other kind of substantial gainful work that exists in the national economy." The statute also defines "work that exists in the national economy" as "work that exists in significant numbers either in the region where such individual lives or in several regions of the country." The commissioner of Social Security (D)

reasonably interpreted the Social Security Act's definition of "disability" to make the existence of a job in significant numbers in the national economy pertinent only to the inquiry of whether the claimant can perform any work other than his or her previous job.

▶ *ANALYSIS*

The ruling resolves a circuit split in favor of the majority view.

Quicknotes

SOCIAL SECURITY ACT Federal law creating the Social Security Administration, which is charged with the administration of a national program where contributions from employers and employees are held until the worker retires or is disabled, at which time they are paid out.

Discharge

Quick Reference Rules of Law

Bard v. Bath Iron Works Corp.

Employee (P) v. Employer (D)

Me. Sup. Jud. Ct., 590 A.2d 152 (1991).

NATURE OF CASE: Appeal of judgment for employer.

FACT SUMMARY: A quality-assurance inspector told his supervisor and the employer's client that he believed processes employed by the employer were in breach of its contract with the client. He was fired and brought a retaliation action under the state's Whistleblower Protection Act.

🏛 RULE OF LAW
To establish a claim of retaliation for whistleblowing, the employee must show that he had reasonable cause to believe that his employer violated any law or rule adopted in Maine or the United States.

FACTS: Leon Bard (P) worked for Bath Iron Works Corp. (D) as an inspector in the quality-assurance department, and as part of his job, he discovered flaws in the process, which, he believed, were contrary to Bath Iron Works' (D) contract with the U.S. Navy. He called the attention of several supervisors and Navy inspectors to the flaws. Evaluations of his job performance were initially good, but became increasingly negative. He was eventually fired for deliberately restricting output and creating a nuisance. Bard (P) filed a complaint charging Bath Iron Works (D) with retaliation in violation of the Whistleblowers' Protection Act, among other things. The trial court found in favor of Bath Iron Works (D).

ISSUE: To establish a claim of retaliation for whistleblowing, must the employee show that he had reasonable cause to believe that his employer violated any law or rule adopted in Maine or the United States?

HOLDING AND DECISION: (Brody, J.) Yes. To establish a claim of retaliation for whistleblowing, the employee must show that he had reasonable cause to believe that his employer violated any law or rule adopted in Maine or the United States. This requirement is in addition to the general prima facie case, which requires that the employee show that (1) he engaged in activity protected by the statute, (2) he was the subject of adverse employment action, and (3) there was a causal link between the protected activity and the adverse employment action. Bard (P) failed to show a belief on his part that Bath Iron Works (D) was acting illegally. He showed only that he believed that a violation of contract provisions with the Navy might have occurred, which is insufficient. Affirmed.

▶ ANALYSIS

This case illustrates that to establish a case of retaliation based on the whistleblower statute in Maine, the employee not only must have a subjective belief that the employer is breaking the law, but that belief must also be reasonable. Courts often use subjective standards to determine the reasonableness of the employee's belief.

━━■

Quicknotes

REASONABLE BELIEF A reasonable basis for believing that a crime is being or has been committed.

RETALIATION The infliction of injury or penalty upon another in return for an injury or harm caused by that party.

SUBJECTIVE STANDARD A standard that is based on the personal belief of an individual.

WHISTLEBLOWER An employee who reports an employer for wrongdoing.

━━■

Goetz v. Windsor Central School District

Employee (P) v. Employer (D)

698 F.2d 606 (2d Cir. 1983).

NATURE OF CASE: Appeal from a grant of the defendant's motion for summary judgment in an action for wrongful discharge.

FACT SUMMARY: When Goetz (P) was arrested and charged with third-degree burglary after a series of thefts occurred at the district offices, Windsor Central School District (D) first suspended Goetz (P) and then terminated his employment.

RULE OF LAW

(1) At-will employees possess no protectable property interest in continued employment.

(2) A liberty interest is implicated and a name-clearing hearing required where an employer creates and disseminates a false and defamatory impression about an employee in connection with the employee's termination.

FACTS: One year after Goetz (P) was hired by the Windsor Center School District (School District) (D) as a "cleaner," he was arrested and charged with third-degree burglary after a series of thefts from the district offices. The School District (D) suspended Goetz (P), terminating his employment when he failed to provide a full written explanation of his involvement in the matter. No information regarding the reasons for Goetz's (P) termination was placed in his personnel file, and no mention of him was contained in a memo directing that the strictest confidentiality be maintained regarding the thefts. Goetz (P) instituted this action, charging that he had been deprived of property and liberty interests without due process of law. The district court granted the School District's (D) motion for summary judgment. Goetz (P) appealed.

ISSUE:

(1) Do at-will employees possess a protectable property interest in continued employment?

(2) Is, a liberty interest implicated and a name-clearing hearing required where an employer creates and disseminates a false and defamatory impression about an employee in connection with the employee's termination?

HOLDING AND DECISION: (Cardamone, J.)

(1) No. At-will employees possess no protectable property interest in continued employment. The sufficiency of a claim of entitlement rests on state law. Goetz (P) concedes that he possesses no protectable property interest under New York State's Civil Service Law because, as an unskilled laborer with less than five years of service, his position was one terminable at will.

(2) Yes. A liberty interest is implicated and a name-clearing hearing required where an employer creates and disseminates a false and defamatory impression about an employee in connection with the employee's termination. The allegation that Goetz (P) is a thief is stigmatizing information arising in connection with his discharge. Whether this information is true or false cannot be resolved on a motion for summary judgment. If school district employees or board members were responsible for public awareness of the defamatory charge made against Goetz (P), notice and an opportunity to be heard are essential to protect his due process rights. Affirmed in part, reversed in part, and remanded.

ANALYSIS

A property interest can be created by local ordinance or by implied contract. In *Board of Regents v. Roth*, 408 U.S. 564 (1972), the Supreme Court noted that a person may possess a protected property interest in public employment if contractual or statutory provisions guarantee continued employment absent "sufficient cause" for discharge. Liberty, as guaranteed by the Fourteenth Amendment, denotes the right of the individual to engage in the common occupations of life and to enjoy the privileges recognized as essential to the orderly pursuit of happiness. The rule applied to this issue was stated in *Codd v. Velger*, 429 U.S. 624 (1977).

Quicknotes

42 U.S.C. § 1983 Defamation by state officials in connection with a discharge implies a violation of a liberty interest protected by the due process requirements of the U.S. Constitution.

EMPLOYMENT-AT-WILL The rule that an employment relationship is subject to termination at any time, or for any cause, by an employee or an employer in the absence of a specific agreement otherwise.

FOURTEENTH AMENDMENT No person shall be deprived of life, liberty, or property, without the due process of law.

Marcy v. Delta Airlines

Employee (P) v. Employer (D)

166 F.3d 1279 (9th Cir. 1999).

NATURE OF CASE: Appeal of the refusal to grant a defense motion for judgment as a matter of law in a wrongful discharge suit.

FACT SUMMARY: When Marcy (P) sued her employer, Delta Airlines (Delta) (D), for wrongful discharge under the Montana Wrongful Discharge from Employment Act, Delta (D) argued that the legislation provided no cause of action to an employee in the absence of a showing of an employer's bad faith.

🏛 RULE OF LAW
The Montana Wrongful Discharge from Employment Act (WDEA) provides a cause of action to an employee discharged for a reason based on mistaken facts even though the employer exercised good faith in reaching its decision.

FACTS: Suzanne Marcy (P) was discharged by her employer, Delta Airlines (Delta) (D), after she submitted payroll records with three incorrect entries that would have allowed her to collect about $250 in unearned wages. She was generally rated as an "outstanding Delta employee." While acknowledging the payroll mistakes, Marcy (P) maintained the mistakes were unintentional and were common in Delta's payroll system. Marcy (P) brought suit against Delta (D) under the Montana Wrongful Discharge from Employment Act (WDEA) in federal district court, which found in her favor. Delta (D) moved for judgment as a matter of law on the grounds that Marcy (P) had presented no evidence of bad faith on the part of Delta (D). The district court denied the motion, and Delta (D) appealed.

ISSUE: Does the Montana Wrongful Discharge from Employment Act (WDEA) provide a cause of action to an employee discharged for a reason based on mistaken facts even though the employer exercised good faith in reaching its decision?

HOLDING AND DECISION: (Boochever, J.) Yes. The Montana Wrongful Discharge from Employment Act (WDEA) provides a cause of action to an employee discharged for a reason based on mistaken facts even though the employer exercised good faith in reaching its decision. In accordance with the viewpoint of the Montana Supreme Court, the stated reason for an employee's discharge is not legitimate under the WDEA if the reason given for the employee's discharge (1) is invalid as a matter of law under the WDEA; (2) rests on a mistaken interpretation of the facts; or (3) is not the honest reason for the discharge, but rather a pretext for some other illegitimate

reason. A discharged employee need only prove that one of these three types is true to demonstrate that the reason for the discharge was not legitimate. Thus, proof that the employer acted in bad faith by using a pretext to discharge its employee is only one possible way of demonstrating that the employer's stated reason was not a legitimate one. Here, Delta's (D) reason for terminating Marcy (P), intentional falsification of payroll records, rested on a mistaken interpretation of the facts. Once Marcy (P) offered sufficient evidence to raise a genuine issue that her recording errors were unintentional, the case properly went to the jury. Lack of Delta's (D) bad faith was irrelevant to whether Delta (D) was mistaken. Affirmed.

DISSENT: (Graber, J.) The WDEA permits an employee to sue an employer for wrongful discharge only if the discharge was not for good cause. Good cause, in this context, means reasonable job-related grounds based on failure to satisfactorily perform job duties. Marcy (P) did not satisfactorily perform her employment duties.

▶ ANALYSIS

As noted in the *Marcy* decision, once the employee claims that the employer's reason for termination (in this case, intentional falsification of records) rests on a mistaken interpretation of the facts, the issue of employer good or bad faith becomes irrelevant.

■■■

Quicknotes

BAD FAITH Conduct that is intentionally misleading or deceptive.

GOOD FAITH An honest intention to abstain from taking advantage of another.

JUDGMENT AS A MATTER OF LAW Judgment given during a jury trial establishing that there is no legal basis for a jury to render a verdict on an issue.

■■■

Gordon v. Matthew Bender & Co.

Employee (P) v. Former employer (D)

562 F. Supp. 1286 (N.D. Ill. 1983).

NATURE OF CASE: Motion to dismiss action for damages for breach of contract.

FACT SUMMARY: Gordon (P) brought this action for breach of contract in response to his discharge by Matthew Bender & Co. (Matthew Bender) (D) for allegedly not meeting the sales objectives set by Matthew Bender (D).

🏛 RULE OF LAW
Satisfactory or acceptable performance language does not transform an at-will contract into a contract that cannot be terminated by either party at any time for any reason.

FACTS: Matthew Bender & Co. (Matthew Bender) (D) employed Gordon (P) for seven years as a law-book sales representative in a territory that included parts of Chicago and the surrounding areas. Their employment agreement stated no definite period during which they remained obligated to each other. Gordon (P) reached or exceeded the sales goals set for him by Matthew Bender (D). His territory was reduced on September 1, 1980, and on October 7, 1980, he was told he would be terminated if he failed to achieve the same sales goals that had been set for his territory before its size was reduced. When Gordon (P) failed to meet those goals, he was fired on January 8, 1981. Gordon (P) then sued Matthew Bender (D), alleging that it was Matthew Bender's (D) policy and practice to condition its sales representatives' continued employment on "acceptable sales performance." Gordon (P) contended that the letter placing him on probationary status and asserting that he would be restored to the same status of acceptable sales performance as other Matthew Bender (D) sales representatives if he met his goals created a contract for continuous employment conditioned upon acceptable sales performance, which Matthew Bender (D) breached by firing him even though he met or exceeded the requirement of acceptable sales performance. Matthew Bender (D) moved to dismiss on grounds that the contract was terminable at will and lacked mutuality; therefore, it was not actionable.

ISSUE: Does satisfactory or acceptable performance language transform an at-will contract into a contract that cannot be terminated by either party at any time for any reason?

HOLDING AND DECISION: (Hart, J.) No. Satisfactory or acceptable performance language does not transform an at-will contract into a contract that cannot be terminated by either party at any time for any reason.

Two Illinois cases, *Kendall v. West*, 196 Ill. 221, 63 N.E. 683 (1902), and *Vogel v. Pekoc*, 157 Ill. 339, 42 N.E. 386 (1895), hold that a satisfactory performance contract is terminable at will. Although Gordon (P) disparaged *Kendall* and *Vogel* as "turn-of-the-century cases," it is clear that at least *Kendall* has continuing vitality, as it formed the basis of a recent decision of the Illinois appellate court. In addition, Illinois courts have shown no disposition to abandon the at-will doctrine except in carefully defined areas. A "condition" of satisfactory performance could be implied in every employment contract. Such an end run around the at-will doctrine would eviscerate it altogether, and the Illinois courts do not seem inclined to do so. Motion to dismiss granted.

▌ ANALYSIS

The court cited two other cases as being precisely on point and as establishing the rule enunciated in the instant case. In *Buian v. J.L. Jacobs and Company*, 428 F.2d 531 (7th Cir. 1970), the court found that a contract terminable at will existed despite language to the effect that the assignment period of 18 months presumed "satisfactory service" by each associate. In *Payne v. AHFI/Netherlands, B.V.*, 522 F. Supp. 18 (N.D. Ill. 1980), the court held that an at-will contract existed even though the duration of the Payne contract was to depend on factors such as "individual performance." For written contracts containing a definite term of employment, the general rule is that an employee may be discharged before the end of that term only for breach of a provision in the contract or for other good cause.

■■■

Quicknotes

EMPLOYMENT-AT-WILL The rule that an employment relationship is subject to termination at any time, or for any cause, by an employee or an employer in the absence of a specific agreement, otherwise.

EMPLOYMENT CONTRACT An agreement entered into by an employee and an employer setting forth the terms of an individual's employment.

GOOD CAUSE Sufficient justification for failure to perform an obligation imposed by law.

■■■

Scribner v. WorldCom, Inc.

Employee (P) v. Employer (D)

249 F.3d 902 (9th Cir. 2001).

NATURE OF CASE: Appeal of a grant of a defense motion for summary judgment in an employee's suit to exercise stock-option rights.

FACT SUMMARY: When WorldCom, Inc. (D) terminated Scribner (P) for business reasons, not deficient job performance, it nevertheless argued that the termination was "with cause" and refused Scribner (P) the right to exercise stock-option rights.

> ## 🏛 RULE OF LAW
> General rules of contract law are applied to employee stock-option plans.

FACTS: Donald Scribner (P), a vice-president of WorldCom, Inc. (D), owned unvested options to purchase shares of WorldCom (D) stock, which were to become immediately exercisable if WorldCom (D) terminated him "without cause." He was an exemplary employee. WorldCom (D) subsequently terminated Scribner (P), not because of shortcomings in his performance, but to facilitate the sale of the division in which he worked. WorldCom (D) argued that although Scribner had not been let go because of poor performance, his termination was nonetheless "with cause" for stock-option purposes. Both parties filed motions for summary judgment. The federal district court granted WorldCom's (D) and denied Scribner's (P). Scribner (P) appealed, arguing that although the stock-option plan did not define the word "cause," the word should carry its ordinary meaning to mean deficient performance.

ISSUE: Are general rules of contract law applied to employee stock-option plans?

HOLDING AND DECISION: (Trott, J.) Yes. General rules of contract law are applied to employee stock-option plans. There is nothing unique about employee stock-option plans. As with any contract, determination of the rights of the parties under a stock-option contract is a fact-specific inquiry. Courts, therefore, look to the facts of the specific case and to general contract-interpretation principles set forth by the courts as to what "cause" means. All of these factors indicate that a termination "with cause" means a termination due to some fault of the employee. In view of the language of Scribner's (P) employment contract, the context in which it was drafted, and the subsequent dealings of Scribner (P) and WorldCom (D), "cause" is a performance-related concept. WorldCom (D) in fact concedes that Scribner's (P) termination was not due to any deficiency on his part. Here, although the WorldCom (D) committee had the discretion to determine whether Scribner (P) had in fact been terminated for deficient performance, the committee did not retain the power to redefine the term "cause" in a manner that would undermine Scribner's (P) justified expectations as to what that word meant. Scribner (P) was therefore terminated "without cause" as a matter of law, hence summary judgment in his favor should have been granted. Reversed.

▌ ANALYSIS

In the *Scribner* decision, the court, although not disputing that the WorldCom (D) committee had a broad grant of discretion to interpret the contract terms of the employee stock-option plan, noted, however, that the committee nonetheless had a duty to exercise its interpretive authority in good faith.

Quicknotes

GOOD CAUSE Sufficient justification for failure to perform an obligation imposed by law.

STOCK OPTIONS The right to purchase or sell a particular stock at a specified price within a certain time period.

Pugh v. See's Candies, Inc.

Employee (P) v. Former employer (D)

Cal. Ct. App., 171 Cal. Rptr. 917 (1981).

NATURE OF CASE: Appeal from dismissal of action for damages for wrongful termination.

FACT SUMMARY: Pugh (P) asserted that he had been fired after 32 years as an employee of See's Candies, Inc. (D) in breach of his employment contract and for reasons that offended public policy.

RULE OF LAW
An implied-in-fact promise for continued employment may exist depending on consideration of the personnel policies or practices of the employer, the employee's longevity of service, employer assurances of continued employment, and practices of the industry.

FACTS: Pugh (P) was fired after 32 years of employment with See's Candies, Inc. (See's) (D), during which he worked his way up the corporate ladder from dishwasher to vice president in charge of production and member of the board of directors. It was the practice of See's (D) not to terminate administrative personnel except for good cause. In fact, when Pugh (P) was first hired, he was told that if he was loyal to See's (D) and did a good job his future was secure. See's (D) never gave Pugh (P) formal or written criticism of his work, notice that there was a problem that needed correction, or any warning that any disciplinary action was being contemplated. Pugh (P) thought his termination might be connected with his objection to a possible "sweetheart" contract See's (D) may have had with the Union (D). Asserting that he had been fired in breach of contract and for reasons that offend public policy, Pugh (P) filed suit against See's (D) and the Union (D), seeking compensatory and punitive damages for wrongful termination. Pugh (P) further alleged, based on his successor's statement, the Union (D) had conspired in or induced the wrongful conduct. At the conclusion of Pugh's (P) case in chief, the trial court granted See's (D) motions for nonsuit, and this appeal followed.

ISSUE: May an implied-in-fact promise for continued employment exist depending on consideration of the personnel policies or practices of the employer, the employee's longevity of service, employer assurances of continued employment, and practices of the industry?

HOLDING AND DECISION: (Grodin, J.) Yes. An implied-in-fact promise for continued employment may exist depending on consideration of the personnel policies or practices of the employer, the employee's longevity of service, employer assurances of continued employment, and practices of the industry. The presumption that an employment contract is intended to be terminable at will is subject, like any presumption, to contrary evidence. This may take the form of an agreement, express or implied, that the relationship will continue for some fixed period of time. Here, there were facts in evidence from which the jury could determine the existence of such an implied promise: the duration of Pugh's (P) employment, the commendations and promotions he received, the apparent lack of any direct criticism of his work, the assurances he was given, and See's (D) acknowledged policies. Pugh (P) demonstrated a prima facie case of wrongful termination in violation of his contract of employment. On remand, the burden of coming forward with the evidence as to the reason for Pugh's (P) termination shifts to See's (D). Pugh (P), however, bears the ultimate burden of proving that he was terminated wrongfully. Evidence as to what Pugh's (P) successor told Union (D) representatives after his termination is sufficient in context, given principles applicable to nonsuits, to justify an inference that Pugh (P) was terminated in response to the Union's (D) insistence. However, the record was inadequate to support such an inference. The judgment of nonsuit was erroneously granted. Reversed.

ANALYSIS

In recent years, statutes have established a variety of specific limitations on the employer's power of dismissal, such as union membership or activities, race, sex, age, or political affiliation. Legislatures in this country have so far refrained from adopting statutes, like those in most other industrialized countries, which would provide more generalized protection to employees against unjust dismissal. Apart from statutory or constitutional protection, two relevant principles have developed to limit the employer's right to terminate employees. The first limitation precludes dismissal when an employer's discharge of an employee violates fundamental principles of public policy and the second when the discharge is contrary to the terms of the agreement, express or implied.

◼▤◼

Quicknotes

BREACH OF CONTRACT Unlawful failure by a party to perform its obligations pursuant to contract.

CASE IN CHIEF The portion of a proceeding where the party with the burden of proof presents evidence to support his case.

Continued on next page.

EMPLOYMENT-AT-WILL The rule that an employment relationship is subject to termination at any time, or for any cause, by an employee or an employer in the absence of a specific agreement otherwise.

IMPLIED PROMISE A promise inferred by law from a document as a whole and the circumstances surrounding its implementation.

NONSUIT Judgment against a party who fails to make out a case.

PUBLIC POLICY Policy administered by the state with respect to the health, safety and morals of its people in accordance with common notions of fairness and decency.

WRONGFUL TERMINATION Unlawful termination of an individual's employment.

Woolley v. Hoffmann-La Roche, Inc.

Employee (P) v. Former employer (D)

N.J. Sup. Ct., 491 A.2d 1257, modified, 499 A.2d 515 (1985).

NATURE OF CASE: Appeal from grant of defense motion for summary judgment in breach of contract action.

FACT SUMMARY: After Hoffmann-La Roche, Inc. (D) fired him, Woolley (P) alleged that Hoffmann-La Roche's (D) employment manual created a contract under which an employee could be fired only for cause, that he was not dismissed for good cause, and, thus, his firing was a breach of contract.

🏛 RULE OF LAW
Absent a clear and prominent disclaimer, an implied promise in an employment manual that an employee will be fired only for cause may be enforceable against an employer even when the employment is for an indefinite term and would otherwise be terminable at will.

FACTS: Woolley (P) worked in Hoffmann-La Roche's (D) central engineering department for a little over eight years, first as an engineering section head and then as a group leader for the civil engineering, the piping design, the plant layout, and the standards and systems sections. Sometime during the month after his employment began, Woolley (P) received and read Hoffmann-La Roche's (D) personnel policy manual. During his eighth year of employment, Woolley (P) was asked to write and submit to his immediate supervisor a report about piping problems in one of Hoffmann-La Roche's (D) buildings. After doing so, Woolley (P) was told that the general manager of the corporate engineering department had lost confidence in him, and Woolley's (P) supervisor requested his resignation. Woolley (P) was fired after refusing this and a second request to resign. He filed a complaint alleging breach of contract, intentional infliction of emotional distress, and defamation but subsequently consented to dismissal of the latter two claims. Woolley (P) contended that the express and implied promises in Hoffmann-La Roche's (D) employment manual created a contract under which he could not be fired at will but rather only for cause and then only after the procedures outlined in the manual were followed. Woolley (P) contended that he was not dismissed for good cause and that his firing was a breach of contract. Hoffmann-La Roche (D) contended that the distribution of the manual was simply an expression of their philosophy and therefore free of any possible contractual consequences. Hoffmann-La Roche's (D) motion for summary judgment was granted by the trial court. The appellate division affirmed, and this appeal followed.

ISSUE: Absent a clear and prominent disclaimer, may an implied promise in an employment manual that an employee will be fired only for cause be enforceable against an employer even when the employment is for an indefinite term and would otherwise be terminable at will?

HOLDING AND DECISION: (Wilentz, C.J.) Yes. Absent a clear and prominent disclaimer, an implied promise in an employment manual that an employee will be fired only for cause may be enforceable against an employer even when the employment is for an indefinite term and would otherwise be terminable at will. Termination clauses of Hoffmann-La Roche's (D) personnel policy manual, including the procedure required before termination occurs, could be found to be contractually enforceable. Unless the language contained in the manual was such that no one could reasonably have thought it was intended to create legally binding obligations, the termination provisions of the policy manual would have to be regarded as an obligation undertaken by the employer. It will not do now for Hoffmann-La Roche (D) to say it did not mean the things it said in its manual to be binding. The manual is an offer that seeks the formation of a unilateral contract in return for the employees' continued work when they have no obligation to continue. Even if good cause existed for Woolley's (P) discharge, he could not be fired unless Hoffmann-La Roche (D) went through the various procedures set forth in the manual, steps designed to rehabilitate that employee in order to avoid termination. On the record, Hoffmann-La Roche (D) failed to follow those procedures. Reversed and remanded for trial.

▶ ANALYSIS

The court several times declared that the provisions of the manual concerning job security shall be considered binding unless the manual elsewhere prominently and unmistakably indicated that those provisions shall not be binding or unless there was some other similar proof of the employer's intent not to be bound. The court maintained that what it was seeking was basic honesty. A number of jurisdictions have followed the same course as that followed by the court in the instant case. Other jurisdictions, however, have been reluctant to bind employers to an "agreement" that was not bargained for under any traditional view of contract law.

Continued on next page.

Quicknotes

BREACH OF CONTRACT Unlawful failure by a party to perform its obligations pursuant to contract.

DISCLAIMER Renunciation of a right or interest.

EMPLOYMENT-AT-WILL The rule that an employment relationship is subject to termination at any time, or for any cause, by an employee or an employer in the absence of a specific agreement otherwise.

IMPLIED PROMISE A promise inferred by law from a document as a whole and the circumstances surrounding its implementation.

UNILATERAL CONTRACT An agreement pursuant to which a party agrees to act, or to forbear from acting, in exchange for performance on the part of the other party.

■■■

Russell v. Board of County Commissioners

Employees (P) v. Employer (D)

Okla. Sup. Ct., 952 P.2d 492 (1997).

NATURE OF CASE: Appeal of judgment for employees.

FACT SUMMARY: Ten deputy sheriffs (P) sued the county for overtime, which they claimed they were entitled to under the employee handbook's stated policies.

🏛 RULE OF LAW
The question of whether an employee manual constitutes an employment contract is not always a matter of law.

FACTS: Ten deputy sheriffs (P) who worked at-will for the county filed a breach-of-employment-contract action against the Board of County Commissioners (D) to recover overtime pay. The deputies (P) claimed the employee manual was an implied contract, and that because the manual states that law enforcement personnel are to be paid overtime compensation, the county owed them overtime compensation. The trial court entered summary judgment for the board (D), and the court of appeals reversed.

ISSUE: Is the question of whether an employee manual constitutes an employment contract always a matter of law?

HOLDING AND DECISION: (Opala, J.) No. The question of whether an employee manual constitutes an employment contract is not always a matter of law. In this case, conflicting inferences may be drawn from various statements made in the handbook. Therefore, whether the handbook creates a binding obligation on the county to pay the deputy sheriffs for overtime can only be resolved through a trial. Court of Civil Appeals vacated, trial court's summary judgment reversed, and remanded.

▶ ANALYSIS

This case simply illustrates that in order for an employee handbook to constitute an employment contract, it must meet all the requirements of any valid contract: competent parties, consent, a legal object, and consideration. Disclaimers made by the company that the manual is not to be considered an employment contract must be clear and direct.

■═■

Quicknotes

IMPLIED CONTRACT An agreement between parties that may be inferred from their general course of conduct.

■═■

Fortune v. National Cash Register Co.

Employee (P) v. Former employer (D)

Mass. Sup. Jud. Ct., 364 N.E.2d 1251 (1977).

NATURE OF CASE: Appeal from reversal of award of damages for breach of contract.

FACT SUMMARY: When Fortune (P) was terminated by National Cash Register Co. (NCR) (D) after receiving only 75 percent of the bonus due him from a $5 million sale, he filed suit for breach of contract to recover the remainder of the commissions.

🏛 RULE OF LAW
When an employer's termination of an at-will contract of employment is motivated by bad faith or malice, such termination constitutes a breach of the employment contract.

FACTS: Fortune (P) was employed as a salesman by National Cash Register Co. (NCR) (D) under a written contract that was terminable at will, without cause, by either party on written notice. Under the contract, Fortune (P) would receive a weekly salary in a fixed amount plus a bonus for sales made within the territory assigned to him for coverage or supervision, whether the sale was made by him or someone else. The amount of the bonus was determined on the basis of bonus credits, which were computed as a percentage of the price of products sold. In addition, NCR (D) reserved the right to sell products in the salesman's territory without paying a bonus. However, this right could be exercised only on written notice. Fortune's (P) territory included First National, an account he had serviced for the preceding six years and from which he had obtained several large orders. After NCR (D) introduced a new model cash register in early 1968, Fortune (P) arranged for a demonstration at First National in October 1968. On November 29, 1968, First National signed a $5 million order for 2,008 of the new machines. Although he did not negotiate the terms of the order, Fortune's (P) name was on the order form in the space marked "salesman credited," thus entitling him to the bonus credit of $92,079.99 shown on the order. On the first working day of 1969, Fortune (P) found a termination notice on his desk at work, addressed to his home and dated December 2, 1968. However, to facilitate a smooth operation of the First National order, Fortune (P) was asked and agreed to stay on as "sales support." After receiving 75 percent of the bonus due on the machines, Fortune (P) was told to forget about the balance. Because he was 61 years old at the time and had a son in college, he did so. About 18 months after receiving the termination notice, Fortune (P), who had worked for NCR (D) for almost 25 years, was asked to retire. After he refused, he was fired. Fortune (P) then brought suit to recover the balance of the commissions allegedly owed to him. By agreement of counsel, the issue of bad faith was submitted to the jury, which, determining that NCR (D) had acted in bad faith when it terminated Fortune's (P) contract, awarded him $45,649.62. The court of appeals reversed, and this appeal followed.

ISSUE: When an employer's termination of an at-will contract of employment is motivated by bad faith or malice, does such termination constitute a breach of the employment contract?

HOLDING AND DECISION: (Abrams, J.) Yes. When an employer's termination of an at-will contract of employment is motivated by bad faith or malice, such termination constitutes a breach of the employment contract. Under the express terms of the contract and a literal reading of that contract, no breach occurred. However, NCR's (D) written contract contains an implied covenant of good faith and fair dealing, and a termination not made in good faith constitutes a breach of the contract. Good faith and fair dealing between parties are pervasive requirements by which parties to contracts or commercial transactions are bound. Moreover, recent decisions in other jurisdictions lend support to the proposition that good faith is implied in contracts terminable at will. The evidence and the reasonable inferences to be drawn therefrom support a jury verdict that Fortune's (P) termination was motivated by a desire to pay him as little of the bonus credit as it could. The fact that Fortune (P) was willing to work under these circumstances did not constitute a waiver or estoppel; it only showed that NCR (D) had him "at their mercy." Affirmed.

▶ ANALYSIS

The court referred to the Restatement of Agency (Second) § 454 in stating that where the principal seeks to deprive the agent of all compensation by terminating the contractual relationship when the agent is on the brink of successfully completing the sale, the principal has acted in bad faith, and the ensuing transaction between the principal and the buyer is to be regarded as having been accomplished by the agent. The same result obtains where the principal attempts, as here, to deprive the agent of any portion of a commission due the agent. Courts have often applied this rule to prevent overreaching by employers and the forfeiture by employees of benefits almost earned by the rendering of substantial services.

Continued on next page.

Quicknotes

AGENT An individual who has the authority to act on behalf of another.

BAD FAITH Conduct that is intentionally misleading or deceptive.

BREACH OF CONTRACT Unlawful failure by a party to perform its obligations pursuant to contract.

EMPLOYMENT-AT-WILL The rule that an employment relationship is subject to termination at any time, or for any cause, by an employee or an employer in the absence of a specific agreement otherwise.

FAIR DEALING An implied warranty that the parties will deal honestly in the satisfaction of their obligations and without intent to defraud.

GOOD FAITH An honest intention to abstain from any unconscientious advantage of another.

IMPLIED COVENANT A promise inferred by law from a document as a whole and the circumstances surrounding its implementation.

PRINCIPAL A person or entity who authorizes another (the agent) to act on its behalf and subject to its authority to the extent that the principal may be held liable for the actions of the agent.

■═■

Cleary v. American Airlines

Employee (P) v. Employer (D)

Cal. Ct. App., 111 Cal. App. 3d 443 (1980).

NATURE OF CASE: Appeal of judgment for employer.

FACT SUMMARY: [Plaintiff not identified in casebook excerpt.] Plaintiff sued American Airlines (D) for breach of an oral employment contract.

🏛 RULE OF LAW
The longevity of the employee's service, together with the expressed policy of the employer to resolve employee disputes in good faith and fair dealing, precludes discharge without good cause.

FACTS: [Plaintiff not identified in casebook excerpt.] Plaintiff sued American Airlines (D) for breach of an oral employment contract, under which he claimed to be a permanent employee of the airline. The terms, plaintiff argued, included American Airlines (D) regulation 135-4, which expressed the Airline's (D) policy and procedure with respect to employee grievances and discharge.

ISSUE: Do the longevity of the employee's service, together with the expressed policy of the employer to resolve employee disputes in good faith and fair dealing, preclude discharge without good cause?

HOLDING AND DECISION: (Jefferson, J.) Yes. The longevity of the employee's service, together with the expressed policy of the employer to resolve employee disputes in good faith and fair dealing, precludes discharge without good cause. There is a continuing trend toward recognition by the courts and the legislature of certain implied contract rights to job security. Termination of employment without legal cause after 18 years of service offends the implied-in-law covenant of good faith and fair dealing contained in all contracts, including employment contracts. In addition, the airline's express policy on the subject compels the conclusion that the employer recognized its responsibility to engage in good faith and fair dealing rather than in arbitrary conduct with respect to all of its employees. Reversed.

▶ ANALYSIS

The court states that plaintiff must establish a cause of action by proving he was terminated unjustly, and American Airlines (D) will have the opportunity to show that it did in fact exercise good faith and fair dealing with plaintiff. Only then will plaintiff have a wrongful discharge action, in tort and contract, which will entitle him to an award of compensatory damages and punitive damages. California was one of the first states to allow tort remedies in good faith and fair dealing claims, but this allowance was short lived.

▬▬■

Quicknotes

FAIR DEALING An implied warranty that the parties will deal honestly in the satisfaction of their obligations and without intent to defraud.

GOOD FAITH An honest intention to abstain from any unconscientious advantage of another.

IMPLIED COVENANT A promise inferred by law from a document as a whole and the circumstances surrounding its implementation.

▬▬■

Foley v. Interactive Data Corp.

Employee (P) v. Former employer (D)

Cal. Sup. Ct., 765 P.2d 373 (1988).

NATURE OF CASE: Appeal from dismissal of action for damages for wrongful discharge.

FACT SUMMARY: When Interactive Data Corp. (Interactive) (D) fired Foley (P) after he reported to an Interactive (D) vice president that his current supervisor was under investigation for embezzlement, Foley (P) sought damages for wrongful discharge.

> ## 🏛 RULE OF LAW
> The covenant of good faith and fair dealing applies to employment contracts and breach of the covenant may give rise to contract damages but not to tort damages.

FACTS: Foley (P), an employee of Interactive Data Corp. (Interactive) (D) for almost seven years, was chosen consultant manager of the year and promoted to branch manager of its Los Angeles office in 1981. Foley (P) reported to his former supervisor that his current supervisor, Kuhne, was under investigation for embezzlement. Foley (P) was told not to discuss "rumors" and to forget what he heard about Kuhne's past, but Kuhne subsequently told Foley (P) that he had the choice of resigning or being fired. Foley (P) was discharged in March 1983, two days after receiving a large merit bonus. He then filed this action, seeking compensatory and punitive damages for wrongful discharge. Foley (P) alleged that Interactive's (D) officers made repeated oral assurances of job security so long as his performance remained adequate, and that during his employment Interactive (D) maintained written "Termination Guidelines" setting forth express grounds for discharge and a mandatory seven-step pretermination procedure. Thus, Foley (P) alleged that he reasonably believed Interactive (D) would not discharge him except for good cause. Foley (P) asserted three distinct theories: a tort cause of action alleging a discharge in violation of public policy, a contract cause of action for breach of an implied-in-fact promise to discharge for good cause only, and a tort cause of action alleging breach of the implied covenant of good faith and fair dealing. The trial court sustained Interactive's (D) demurrer without leave to amend and dismissed Foley's (P) causes of action. The court of appeals affirmed, and Foley (P) appealed.

ISSUE: Does the covenant of good faith and fair dealing apply to employment contracts, and may breach of the covenant give rise to contract damages but not to tort damages?

HOLDING AND DECISION: (Lucas, C.J.) Yes. The covenant of good faith and fair dealing applies to

employment contracts, and breach of the covenant may give rise to contract damages but not to tort damages. The covenant of good faith is read into contracts to protect the express covenants or promises of the contract, not some general public-policy interest not directly tied to the contract's purposes. Thus, the insurance cases that held for a variety of policy reasons that breach of the implied covenant would provide the basis for an action in tort were a major departure from traditional principles of contract law. The reason for this exception lies in the special relationship between an insured and an insurer, since the relationship of insurer and insured is inherently unbalanced, and the adhesive nature of insurance contracts places the insurer in a superior bargaining position. In the insurance relationship, the insurer's and insured's interest are financially at odds. As a general rule, however, it is to the employer's economic benefit to retain good employees, and the interest of employer and employee are most frequently in alignment. Thus, the need to place disincentives on an employer's conduct in addition to those already imposed by law in the employment context is not as great as the need created by the conflicting interests at stake in the insurance context. Thus, Foley's (P) cause of action for breach of an implied-in-fact contract promise to discharge him only for good cause was erroneously dismissed. However, his cause of action for a breach of public policy was properly dismissed. Tort remedies are unavailable generally for contract actions, and specifically for breach of the implied covenant in an employment contract. Affirmed in part; reversed in part.

CONCURRENCE AND DISSENT: (Kaufman, J.) Breach of the duty of good faith and fair dealing may give rise to an action in tort where the contractual relation manifests elements similar to those that characterize the "special relationship" between insurer and insured, i.e., elements of public interest, adhesion, and financial dependency.

▶ ANALYSIS

The court was not convinced that a "special relationship" like that between insurer and insured existed in the usual employment relationship, warranting a tort action for breach of the implied covenant. Foley was the first major employment-law ruling made by the California Supreme Court after three of its liberal justices, including Chief Justice Rose Bird, were replaced by more conservative justices. Other jurisdictions, however, have extended tort

Continued on next page.

liability when an employee's discharge stemmed from an improper motive, demonstrating the employer's bad faith. Interestingly, Kuhne pleaded guilty in federal court to a felony count of embezzlement in September 1983, after Foley's (P) discharge.

■━■

Quicknotes

ADHESION A contract, usually in standardized form, that is prepared by one party and offered to another, whose terms are so disproportionately in favor of the drafting party that courts tend to question the equality of bargaining power in reaching the agreement.

EMPLOYMENT CONTRACT An agreement entered into by an employee and an employer setting forth the terms of an individual's employment.

FAIR DEALING An implied warranty that the parties will deal honestly in the satisfaction of their obligations and without intent to defraud.

GOOD FAITH An honest intention to abstain from any unconscientious advantage of another.

IMPLIED CONTRACT An agreement between parties that may be inferred from their general course of conduct.

WRONGFUL TERMINATION Unlawful termination of an individual's employment.

■━■

Guz v. Bechtel National, Inc.

Employee (P) v. Employer (D)

Cal. Sup. Ct., 8 P.3d 1089 (2000).

NATURE OF CASE: Appeal from upholding a discharged employee's breach of contract suit against his employer.

FACT SUMMARY: When Guz (P) was terminated by his employer Bechtel National, Inc. (D), he sued for breach of contract, arguing that even though he was employed under an at-will employment contract, Bechtel National (D) had breached a duty of good faith and fair dealing which is implied by law into all contracts.

🏛 RULE OF LAW
An at-will employment allows either party to terminate for any, or no, reason.

FACTS: Guz (P), a longtime employee of Bechtel National, Inc. (Bechtel) (D) in California, was released when his work unit was eliminated and its tasks were transferred to another Bechtel (D) office for purposes of budget reduction. Bechtel (D) maintained a written personnel policy that its employees "have no employment agreements guaranteeing continuous service and may resign at their option or be terminated at the option of Bechtel." California legislation permits both employer and employee to terminate the relationship at will at any time without cause in the absence of a contract providing otherwise. Guz (P) brought suit against Bechtel (D), alleging the latter's breach of an implied contract to be terminated only for good cause and breach of an implied covenant of good faith and fair dealing. The trial court granted Bechtel's (D) motion for summary judgment and dismissed the action. The court of appeals reversed, and Bechtel (D) appealed.

ISSUE: Does an at-will employment allow either party to terminate for any, or no, reason?

HOLDING AND DECISION: (Baxter, J.) Yes. An at-will employment allows either party to terminate for any, or no, reason. Although Guz (P), like other Bechtel (D) workers, had implied contractual rights under specific provisions of Bechtel's (D) written personnel policies, neither the policies, nor other evidence, suggest any contractual restriction on Bechtel's (D) right to eliminate a work unit as it saw fit, even where dissatisfaction with unit performance was a factor in the decision. While an implied covenant of employer good faith and fair dealing is implied by law in every contract, such an implied covenant cannot substantively alter contractual terms. If an employment, as here, is at will, and thus allows either party to terminate for any or no reason, the implied covenant cannot decree otherwise. Moreover, although any breach of the actual terms of an employment contract also violates the implied covenant, the measure of damages for such a breach remains solely contractual. Hence, where breach of an actual term is alleged, a separate implied covenant claim, based on the same breach, is superfluous. On the other hand, where an implied covenant alleges a breach of obligations beyond the agreement's actual terms, it is invalid. Reversed and remanded.

▶ ANALYSIS

In California, the Labor Code provides that an employment, having no specified term, may be terminated at the will of either party on notice to the other. An at-will employment, therefore, may be ended by either party at any time without cause, and subject to no procedure except the statutory requirement of notice. The statute does not, however, prevent the parties from agreeing to any limitation, otherwise lawful, on the employer's termination rights. As the *Guz* decision notes, an employee's mere passage of time in the employer's service cannot alone form an implied-in-fact contract that the employee is no longer at will.

Quicknotes

BREACH OF CONTRACT Unlawful failure by a party to perform its obligations pursuant to contract.

EMPLOYMENT-AT-WILL The rule that an employment relationship is subject to termination at any time, or for any cause, by an employee or an employer in the absence of a specific agreement otherwise.

EMPLOYMENT CONTRACT An agreement entered into by an employee and an employer setting forth the terms of an individual's employment.

IMPLIED COVENANT A promise inferred by law from a document as a whole and the circumstances surrounding its implementation.

IMPLIED-IN-FACT CONTRACT Refers to conditions which arise by physical or moral inference: (a) prerequisites or circumstances which a reasonable person would assume necessary to render or receive performance; and (b) the good-faith cooperation of the promisee in receiving the performance of the promisor.

Gantt v. Sentry Insurance

Employee (P) v. Former employer (D)

Cal. Sup. Ct., 824 P.2d 680 (1992).

NATURE OF CASE: Appeal of award of damages for unlawful termination.

FACT SUMMARY: Gantt (P) was forced to quit his job after refusing to give false information or withhold information from the public agency investigating another employee's sexual harassment claim.

🏛 RULE OF LAW
An employee who is terminated in retaliation for supporting a coworker's sexual harassment claim has a valid cause of action for tortious discharge against public policy.

FACTS: When a coworker, Joyce Bruno, reported being sexually harassed by the manager of another Sentry Insurance (Sentry) (D) office, Gantt (P), sales manager of Sentry's (D) Sacramento office, reported the matter to his supervisors. Bruno was fired by Sentry (D), and she filed a claim with the Department of Fair Employment and Housing (DFEH). During the DFEH investigation, Gantt (P) was pressured by Sentry (D) to retract his report. When Gantt (P) refused, he was demoted and forced to quit his job. Gantt (P) filed suit, claiming that as a result of the pressure applied by Sentry (D), he was forced to resign. The trial court, finding Gantt (P) to have been constructively discharged by Sentry (D) in contravention of public policy, awarded him damages. The appellate court affirmed, and Sentry (D) appealed.

ISSUE: Does an employee who is terminated in retaliation for supporting a coworker's sexual harassment claim have a valid cause of action for tortious discharge against public policy?

HOLDING AND DECISION: (Arabian, J.) Yes. An employee who is terminated in retaliation for supporting a coworker's sexual harassment claim has a valid cause of action for tortious discharge against public policy. While an at-will employee may be terminated for no reason or for an arbitrary or irrational reason, there is no right to terminate an employee for an unlawful reason or a purpose that contravenes fundamental public policy. "Public policy" is that principle of law that holds that no citizen can lawfully do that which has a tendency to be injurious to the public or is against the public good. Any attempt to coerce an employee to lie to an investigator contravenes California public policy. Thus, Sentry (D) violated a fundamental public policy when it constructively discharged Gantt (P) in retaliation for his refusal to testify falsely or withhold information in the course of the DFEH investigation. Affirmed.

▶ ANALYSIS

The majority of states have recognized that an at-will employee possesses a tort action when he or she is discharged for performing an action that public policy would encourage or for refusing to do something that public policy would condemn. The difficulty for a court lies in determining whether the claim involves a bona fide public-policy matter or merely an ordinary dispute between an employer and an employee. Generally, courts consider public-policy matters to be those matters that affect society at large, rather than matters that are of purely personal or proprietary interest to the employer and employee.

■≡■

Quicknotes

CONSTRUCTIVE DISCHARGE Involuntary resignation by an employee as a result of intolerable working conditions.

PUBLIC POLICY Policy administered by the state with respect to the health, safety and morals of its people in accordance with common notions of fairness and decency.

RETALIATORY DISCHARGE The firing of an employee in retribution for an act committed against the employer's interests.

SEXUAL HARASSMENT An employment practice subjecting persons to oppressive conduct on account of their gender.

TORT A legal wrong resulting in a breach of duty.

■≡■

Arres v. IMI Cornelius Remcor, Inc.

Employee (P) v. Employer (D)

333 F.3d 812 (7th Cir. 2003).

NATURE OF CASE: Appeal of judgment for employer.

FACT SUMMARY: A human resources administrator disagreed with her employer's approach to a problem involving immigration law, and refused to follow orders. She was fired, and she filed a claim for retaliation.

🏛 RULE OF LAW
An employee is not illegally discharged if it resulted from her opposition to her employer's alleged failure to follow immigration law.

FACTS: Janice Arres (P) was a human-resources administrator for IMI Cornelius Remcor, Inc. (Rencor) (D), a manufacturer of soft-drink dispensing machines. In March 1999, the Social Security Administration told the company (D) that some of the W-2 forms filed by its employees showed discrepancies with federal records. Arres (P) determined that the errors were made by the employees rather than the company (D), and then made the judgment that aliens who lacked work authorization must have filed them. Arres (P) recommended their immediate discharge. But, after consulting with one of Remcor's (D) attorneys and the Social Security Administration, Arres's (P) supervisor instead decided to send letters to the employees asking them to correct any errors. Arres (P) refused to process the documents, because she thought the approach was illegal. After she was fired, she sued for retaliatory discharge in violation of public policy under Illinois law. The company (D) responded that her discharge was for poor performance and a district court judge granted the employer's (D) summary judgment motion. Arres (P) appealed to the Court of Appeals for the Seventh Circuit.

ISSUE: Is an employee illegally discharged if it resulted from her opposition to her employer's alleged failure to follow immigration law?

HOLDING AND DECISION: (Easterbrook, J.) No. An employee is not illegally discharged if it resulted from her opposition to her employer's alleged failure to follow immigration law. Arres (P) had no claim of retaliatory discharge under Illinois law, based on her opposition to the employer's (D) willingness to give workers who submitted the wrong Social Security numbers a second chance, rather than firing them immediately, as Arres (D) had suggested. Arres (P) is wrong to suppose that either state or federal law gives her any right to follow an idiosyncratic view of the law's demands. The company (D) did exactly what the Social Security Administration and its legal counsel suggested by examining the documents for inadvertent errors before firing anyone. That approach followed the requirements of federal immigration law. A human resources manager is not free to impose a different approach unilaterally; that's nothing but insubordination. That Arres (P) did not agree with counsel's view of Remcor's (D) legal obligations is not a justification for insubordination. Affirmed.

▶ ANALYSIS

Note that the court departed from Illinois law prohibiting the discharge of an individual attempting to implement federal law. The court carved out an exception, when the law involves labor and immigration. In that case, the court held, the law must be implemented only as the national government sees fit.

■==■

Quicknotes

PUBLIC POLICY Policy administered by the state with respect to the health, safety and morals of its people in accordance with common notions of fairness and decency.

WRONGFUL TERMINATION Unlawful termination of an individual's employment.

■==■

Hansen v. America Online, Inc.

Employees (P) v. Employer (D)

Utah Sup. Ct., 96 P.3d 950 (2004).

NATURE OF CASE: Appeal of judgment for employer.

FACT SUMMARY: Three America Online, Inc. (AOL) employees (P) who were off duty brought firearms to the AOL parking lot, thus violating AOL's (D) stated prohibition. AOL (D) fired all three, and they brought wrongful discharge claims.

🏛 RULE OF LAW
An employer has a right to restrict weapons in the workplace by contract, despite state public policy protecting the right to keep and bear arms.

FACTS: Hansen (P), Carlson (P), and Melling (P) were employed at America Online, Inc.'s (AOL's) (D) call center in Ogden, Utah. While off duty, they met in the company parking lot so they could go target shooting together. A security camera recorded Melling (P) and Carlson (P) transferring their guns to Hansen's (P) car. Four days later, AOL (D) fired the workers for violating the company's workplace-violence-prevention policy. The state's Uniform Firearms Laws provide that except where provided by law, a local or state entity cannot infringe on an individual's right to keep and bear arms. But the statute also states: "Nothing in this section restricts or expands private property rights." Hansen (P), Melling (P), and Carlson (P) sued AOL (D) for wrongful termination. Although the workers (P) acknowledged they were aware of the anti-violence policy, they argued that AOL (D) was liable for wrongful termination because their possession of firearms was protected by a clear and substantial public policy. A trial court granted summary judgment in the employer's favor, and the workers appealed.

ISSUE: Does an employer have a right to restrict weapons in the workplace by contract, despite state public policy protecting the right to keep and bear arms?

HOLDING AND DECISION: (Nehring, J.) Yes. An employer has a right to restrict weapons in the workplace by contract, despite state public policy protecting the right to keep and bear arms. Based on legislative debates over the statute, the state legislature purposefully declined to give the right to keep and bear arms absolute preeminence over the right to regulate one's own private property. Accordingly, AOL (D) had the right to restrict firearms in its parking lot and to fire workers for violating the policy. Trial court affirmed.

▶ ANALYSIS

In a footnote omitted from the casebook excerpt, the court rejected the workers' argument that by barring guns in its parking lot, AOL had in effect "disarmed" its employees by making it impractical for them to store guns in their cars. The court stated that it declined to create "multiple categories of an employer's property" with different liabilities. "Those who are unnerved by the prospect of engaging unarmed in the human interactions that occur while in transit to and from the workplace are, of course, at liberty to seek employment in a workplace that has adopted the philosophy that a safe and productive work environment is best achieved with armed employees."

Quicknotes

PROPERTY RIGHTS A legal right in specified personal or real property.

PUBLIC POLICY Policy administered by the state with respect to the health, safety and morals of its people in accordance with common notions of fairness and decency.

Gardner v. Loomis Armored, Inc.

Employee (P) v. Employer (D)

Wash. Sup. Ct., 913 P.2d 377 (1996).

NATURE OF CASE: Action for wrongful discharge.

FACT SUMMARY: An armored truck driver left the truck in order to help save a woman's life. A company policy prohibits a driver from leaving the truck for any reasons, and the employer therefore fired the driver. He filed suit for wrongful discharge, arguing his termination violated public policy.

🏛 RULE OF LAW
A public-policy exception to the terminable-at-will doctrine applies where a company work rule that was designed to protect the human lives is broken in order to save a human life.

FACTS: Kevin Gardner (P) worked for Loomis Armored, Inc. (Loomis) (D) as a guard and driver of an armored car. Loomis (D) had a company policy prohibiting the driver from getting out of the armored car for any reason, in order to protect the life of the driver and his partner, because of the dangerous nature of the work. On a scheduled stop at a bank, Gardner's (P) partner got out of the truck and went into the bank. A moment later, the manager of the bank, whom Gardner (P) knew, came running out of the bank screaming, followed by a man with a knife. Gardner (P) got out of the armored car to help. The bad guy then grabbed another woman from the street and dragged her into the bank, with the knife at her throat. Gardner (P) entered the bank, where his suspect had his gun drawn on the bad guy. They were able to subdue the suspect. No one was hurt. Loomis (D) fired Gardner (P) for violating company policy by getting out of the car. Gardner (P) filed suit for wrongful discharge, arguing his termination violated public policy.

ISSUE: Does a public-policy exception to the terminable-at-will doctrine apply where a company work rule that was designed to protect the human lives is broken in order to save a human life?

HOLDING AND DECISION: (Dolliver, J.) Yes. A public-policy exception to the terminable-at-will doctrine applies where a company work rule that was designed to protect the human lives is broken in order to save a human life. The public policy at issue here is to encourage such heroic conduct. The holding does not diminish the importance of Loomis's (D) work rule regarding drivers leaving the truck. But Loomis (D) may not fire Gardner (P) for breaking the rule because he saw a woman who faced imminent life-threatening harm and reasonably believed his intervention was necessary to save her life.

CONCURRENCE: (Guy, J.) The work rule is not in violation of public policy in a general sense. But in this case, Gardner (P) was faced with a choice between watching a person die in order to comply with a company safety rule, and breaking the rule, facts which provide an exception to a normally good rule.

DISSENT: (Madsen, J.) The company work rule is designed to protect the lives of drivers in a highly dangerous occupation, which itself furthers the public policy of saving lives. In addition, the driver can summon help by suing the truck's two-way radio, public-address system, and sirens. Encouraging citizens to jump into the middle of a criminal situation does not further public policy. Looking past the emotionally charged facts of this case, Loomis's (D) maligned work rule actually serves the interests of society and is consistent with public policy and therefore cannot be the basis of a claim for wrongful termination in violation of public policy. And the courts should not be in the business of analyzing company work rules.

▶ ANALYSIS

The company's right to discharge for breaking a company work rule is limited in this case, and despite the majority's disclaimer about not ruling on the utility of the work rule, the holding certainly does place the Loomis (D) work rule, in a general sense, in jeopardy. The concurrence seems to recognize this, and limits the holding to the particular facts of the case.

Quicknotes

EMPLOYMENT AT-WILL The rule that an employment relationship is subject to termination at any time, or for any cause, by an employee or an employer in the absence of a specific agreement otherwise.

PUBLIC POLICY Policy administered by the state with respect to the health, safety and morals of its people in accordance with common notions of fairness and decency.

WRONGFUL TERMINATION Unlawful termination of an individual's employment.

Lingle v. Norge Division of Magic Chef, Inc.

Employee (P) v. Employer (D)

486 U.S. 399 (1988).

NATURE OF CASE: Appeal from denial of application of state-law tort remedy for retaliatory discharge.

FACT SUMMARY: When Lingle (P) was discharged for allegedly filing a "false" workers' compensation claim after being injured in the course of her employment for Norge Division of Magic Chef, Inc. (D), the union filed a grievance under the collective-bargaining agreement, while Lingle (P) began an action in state court under a state statute for retaliatory discharge before final arbitration of the union grievance.

🏛 RULE OF LAW
A state-law claim for retaliatory discharge is preempted by applicable federal law only if such a claim requires the interpretation of a collective-bargaining agreement.

FACTS: Lingle (P), who was employed in the Norge Division of Magic Chef, Inc. (Norge) (D) manufacturing plant in Herrin, Illinois, notified Norge (D) on December 5, 1984, that she had been injured in the course of her employment and requested compensation for her medical expenses under the Illinois Workers' Compensation Act. On December 11, 1984, Norge (D) discharged Lingle (P) for filing a "false" workers' compensation claim. The union representing Lingle (P) promptly filed a grievance under its collective-bargaining agreement (CBA), covering all production and maintenance employees in the plant. The CBA protected those employees from discharge except for proper or just cause and established a procedure for the arbitration of grievances. Ultimately, an arbitrator ruled in Lingle's (P) favor and ordered Norge (D) to reinstate her with full backpay. Meanwhile, Lingle (P) began this action against Norge (D) in the state court, alleging that she had been discharged for exercising her rights under the workers' compensation laws. Norge (D) removed the case to the federal district court, moving that the court either dismiss the case on preemption grounds or stay further proceedings pending the completion of the arbitration. The district court concluded that the claim for retaliatory discharge was "inextricably intertwined" with the collective-bargaining provision prohibiting wrongful discharge or discharge without just cause and that allowing the state-law action to proceed would undermine the arbitration procedures set forth in the parties' contract. The court of appeals agreed that the state-law claim was preempted by § 301 of the National Labor Relations Act (NLRA), rejecting Lingle's (P) argument that the tort action was not "inextricably intertwined" with the CBA because disposition of a retaliatory discharge claim in Illinois did not depend upon an interpretation of the CBA. This appeal followed.

ISSUE: Is a state-law claim for retaliatory discharge preempted by applicable federal law only if such a claim requires the interpretation of a collective-bargaining agreement?

HOLDING AND DECISION: (Stevens, J.) Yes. A state-law claim for retaliatory discharge is preempted by applicable federal law only if such a claim requires the interpretation of a collective-bargaining agreement. To show retaliatory discharge, Lingle (P) must set forth sufficient facts from which it can be inferred that she was discharged or threatened with discharge and that Norge's (D) motive in discharging or threatening to discharge her was to deter her from exercising her rights under the Act or to interfere with her exercise of those rights. Each of these purely factual questions pertains to the conduct of the employee and the conduct and motivation of the employer. Neither of the elements requires a court to interpret any term of a CBA. An employer must show that it had a nonretaliatory reason for the discharge. This purely factual inquiry likewise does not turn on the meaning of any provision of a CBA. Thus, the state-law remedy in this case is independent of the CBA for § 301 preemption purposes since resolution of the state-law claim does not require construing the CBA. This decision should make clear that interpretation of CBA's remains firmly in the arbitral realm, and judges can determine questions of state law involving labor-management relations only if such questions do not require construing CBA's. Reversed.

▶ ANALYSIS

The Court referred to its opinion in *Fort Halifax Packing Co. v. Coyne*, 482 U.S. 1 (1987), which emphasized that preemption should not be lightly inferred in this area since the establishment of labor standards falls within the traditional police power of the state. Specifically, the Maine law in question in that case was not preempted by the NLRA since its establishment of a minimum labor standard did not impermissibly intrude upon the collective-bargaining process. Both federal and state statutes attempt to provide protection for employees against unfair employer practices. To the extent that the trend toward increased recognition of individual rights continues, there will most likely be an increase in the cases where statutory and

Continued on next page.

common-law rights and remedies overlap and sometimes conflict.

■═■

Quicknotes

ARBITRATION An agreement to have a dispute heard and decided by a neutral third party, rather than through legal proceedings.

COLLECTIVE BARGAINING Negotiations between an employer and employee that are mediated by a specified third party.

EMPLOYMENT CONTRACT An agreement entered into by an employee and an employer setting forth the terms of an individual's employment.

LABOR MANAGEMENT RELATIONS ACT OF 1947 Preempts state labor laws in claims for retaliatory discharge. 29 U.S.C. § 185.

RETALIATORY DISCHARGE The firing of an employee in retaliation for an act committed against the employer's interests.

■═■

Wilson v. Monarch Paper Co.

Employee (P) v. Employer (D)

939 F.2d 1138 (5th Cir. 1991).

NATURE OF CASE: Appeal of denial of judgment n.o.v. upon award of damages for intentional infliction of emotional distress.

FACT SUMMARY: Because of his age, Wilson (P), a vice president of Monarch Paper Co. (D), was demoted to an entry-level job in order to force him to quit.

🏛 RULE OF LAW
An employee may sue an employer for intentional infliction of emotional distress if the employer's actions are so outrageous that they are utterly intolerable in a civilized society.

FACTS: Wilson (P), who was hired by Monarch Paper Co. (Monarch) (D) at age 48, was a good employee and eventually became vice president and assistant to the president. Monarch (D) implemented a policy of promoting younger executives, and after its president died, Wilson (P) was ostracized by management and given the choice of quitting or taking a warehouse job. Wilson (P) accepted the warehouse job, an entry-level position consisting of mostly janitorial work. Additionally, the warehouse manager harassed Wilson (P) by putting up signs saying things like "Wilson is old." Wilson (P) fell into a severe clinical depression and required hospitalization. After his release, Wilson (P) brought suit against Monarch (D) for intentional infliction of emotional distress and age discrimination. The trial court found for Wilson (P) and awarded damages. Monarch (D) appealed, challenging the sufficiency of the evidence.

ISSUE: May an employee sue an employer for intentional infliction of emotional distress if the employer's actions are so outrageous that they are utterly intolerable in a civilized society?

HOLDING AND DECISION: (Jolly, J.) Yes. An employee may sue an employer for intentional infliction of emotional distress if the employer's actions are so outrageous that they are utterly intolerable in a civilized society. This test has a high threshold and does not extend to mere insults, indignities, threats, annoyances, or other trivialities. Additionally, the facts of any claim of outrageous conduct must be analyzed in the context of the situation at issue. Here, most of Monarch's (D) conduct, such as management's snubbing Wilson (P) and offering him a less desirable job, failed to reach the required level of outrageousness. What takes this case out of the realm of an ordinary employment dispute is the degrading and humiliating way that Wilson (P) was stripped of his duties and demoted from an executive manager with 30 years of experience to an entry-level warehouse janitorial position with menial and demeaning duties. The evidence supported the judgment. Affirmed.

▶ ANALYSIS

Under the facts of this case, Wilson (P) was an at-will employee. As such, Monarch (D) had the absolute right to terminate his employment for good cause or for no cause. It is conceivable that Monarch (D) tried to coerce Wilson (P) to quit to avoid an age discrimination lawsuit. However, by going beyond mere coercion, Monarch's (D) actions subjected it to liability.

⬛▬◼

Quicknotes

AGE DISCRIMINATION IN EMPLOYMENT ACT 29 U.S.C. § 621 Prohibits age discrimination and retaliation in employment.

EMPLOYMENT-AT-WILL The rule that an employment relationship is subject to termination at any time, or for any cause, by an employee or an employer in the absence of a specific agreement otherwise.

INTENTIONAL INFLICTION OF EMOTIONAL DISTRESS Intentional and extreme behavior on the part of the wrongdoer with the intent to cause the victim to suffer from severe emotional distress, or with reckless indifference, resulting in the victim's suffering from severe emotional distress.

JUDGMENT NOTWITHSTANDING THE VERDICT A judgment entered by the trial judge reversing a jury verdict if the jury's determination has no basis in law or fact.

⬛▬◼

Employees' Duties to the Employer

Quick Reference Rules of Law

Handicapped Children's Education Board v. Lukaszewski

Employer (P) v. Employee (D)

Wis. Sup. Ct., 332 N.W.2d 774 (1983).

NATURE OF CASE: Appeal from denial of award of damages for employee's breach of contract.

FACT SUMMARY: The Handicapped Children's Education Board (P) sued Lukaszewski (D) for breach of her employment contract when she quit her job for one closer to her home due to high blood pressure caused by hypertension.

🏛 **RULE OF LAW**
A health danger will not excuse nonperformance of a contractual obligation when the danger is caused by the nonperforming party.

FACTS: Lukaszewski (D), initially hired by the Handicapped Children's Education Board (Board) (P) for the spring term in 1978 as a speech and language therapist in Sheboygan Falls, commuted 45 miles daily from her home to work rather than move. During the spring term, the Board (P) offered, and Lukaszewski (D) accepted, a contract to continue her position for the 1978–1979 school year at an annual salary of $10,760. Before the 1978 fall term, Lukaszewski (D) was offered a position by the Wee Care Day Care Center, located not far from her home, at an annual salary of $13,000. She submitted a letter of resignation to the Board (P), but it refused to release her from her contract. The Board's (P) attorney directed her to return to work and informed the Wee Care Day Care Center that the Board (P) would take legal action if the Center interfered. Lukaszewski (D) returned to work, although she was emotionally upset having to do so. The circumstances caused her hypertension and high blood pressure to worsen, and her doctor believed that it would be dangerous for her to drive long distances in her agitated state. Lukaszewski (D) resubmitted her resignation with a letter from her doctor and then applied for and obtained employment at the Center. The Board (P) replaced Lukaszewski (D) with the one qualified applicant for the position, although at an additional cost of $1,026.64 per year. The Board (P) then sued Lukaszewski (D) for breach of contract. The trial court, expressly finding that the danger to Lukaszewski's (D) health was self-induced, awarded the Board (P) damages of $1,249.14. The court of appeals affirmed the breach of contract ruling but reversed the damages award, holding that the Board (P) was not damaged. The Board (P) appealed.

ISSUE: Will a health danger excuse nonperformance of a contractual obligation when the danger is caused by the nonperforming party?

HOLDING AND DECISION: (Callow, J.) No. A health danger will not excuse nonperformance of a contractual obligation when the danger is caused by the nonperforming party. It must be determined on review if Lukaszewski (D) breached her employment contract with the Board (P) and whether the Board (P) suffered recoverable damages if she did. It was undisputed that Lukaszewski (D) resigned before her contract with the Board (P) expired. The only question became whether her resignation was somehow justified. However, it would be fundamentally unfair to allow a breaching party to escape liability because of a health danger that by her own fault precluded performance. Lukaszewski (D) could have removed the hazard of commuting simply by moving to Sheboygan Falls. Thus, any health danger associated with performance of the employment contract was her fault, not the Board's (P). Further, because Lukaszewski (D) had a history of hypertension dating back at least five years and was able to commute between her home and Sheboygan Falls during the spring term, the evidence supported the trial court's finding that she resigned for reasons other than her health. Damages for breach of contract are measured by the expectations of the parties. The Board (P) expected to receive the services of a speech therapist with Lukaszewski's (D) education and experience at the salary agreed upon, not a more experienced therapist at a higher salary. Thus, the Board (P) lost the benefit of its bargain and suffered damages for that loss in the amount of the additional compensation it was required to pay Lukaszewski's (D) replacement. Affirmed in part; reversed in part.

DISSENT: (Day, J.) Whether objective symptoms are caused by another party or self-induced, termination of a contract is justified where physical symptoms are medically certifiable as they admittedly are here.

▶ **ANALYSIS**

The court explained that an employer who is injured by an employee's breach of contract must take all reasonable steps to mitigate damages. Since the Board (P) hired the one qualified applicant who applied for the position, it had properly mitigated its damages by hiring the least expensive qualified replacement available. Courts traditionally have not taken kindly to an employer's effort to keep an employee from changing jobs. In particular, the remedy of specific performance for employment or personal service contracts is not available since it could be considered

Continued on next page.

involuntary servitude, in violation of the Thirteenth Amendment.

■━━■

Quicknotes

BREACH OF CONTRACT Unlawful failure by a party to perform its obligations pursuant to contract.

EXPECTATION DAMAGES Damages awarded in actions for nonperformance of a contract, which are calculated by subtracting the injured party's actual dollar position as a result of the breach from that party's expected dollar position had the breach not occurred.

MITIGATION Reduction in penalty.

■━━■

Lamorte Burns & Co. v. Walters

Employer (P) v. Former Employees (D)

N.J. Sup. Ct., 770 A.2d 1158 (2001).

NATURE OF CASE: Appeal from intermediate appellate court's reversal of trial court's decision in favor of the plaintiff.

FACT SUMMARY: While still employed at Lamorte Burns & Co. (Lamorte) (P), Walters (D) and Nixon (D) took steps to establish a new competing business utilizing Lamorte's (P) proprietary and confidential list of clients.

🏛 RULE OF LAW

Although an employee has the right to start his own business, the duty of loyalty requires that the employee shall not solicit the employer's customers while still an employee of the company.

FACTS: Lamorte Burns & Co. (Lamorte) (P) provides claim adjustment services for marine and nonmarine liability insurance companies. Walters (D) joined the company in 1990 while Nixon (D) had been with the company for several years. Walters (D) signed an employment agreement promising to not divulge confidential and proprietary information, including client names. Lamorte (P) never executed the agreement. In 1996, Walters (D) began entertaining the idea of starting a competing business. Nixon (D) joined the endeavor and the two began compiling a list of clients to solicit, using the Lamorte (D) client base. Walters (D) stored that client information with all of their active liability claims on his home computer. On Friday, December 19, 1997, Walters (D) called in sick. He was actually setting up the offices of his new company, the Walters Nixon Group. Phone records from Walters's (D) office revealed he made many phones calls to Lamorte (P) clients that day. On Saturday, December 20, Walters (D) and Nixon (D) faxed their resignation letters to Lamorte (P). On the following morning, they faxed solicitation letters and transfer authorization forms to all but one of Lamorte's (P) clients. Within a few weeks, all but one of the Lamorte (P) clients had requested a transfer of their cases to the Walters Nixon Group. Lamorte (P) filed suit and brought tort claims of breach of the duty of loyalty, tortious interference and misappropriation of confidential material. There was also a separate breach of contract claim against Walters (D). A trial court granted summary judgment to Lamorte (P) and awarded damages, but an appellate division judge reversed the ruling on the tort claims. Lamorte (P) appealed to the New Jersey Supreme Court. [The casebook's portion of the opinion deals only with the breach of the duty of loyalty.]

ISSUE: Although an employee has the right to start his own business, does the duty of loyalty require that the employee shall not solicit the employer's customers while still an employee of the company?

HOLDING AND DECISION: (LaVecchia, J.) Yes. Although an employee has the right to start his own business, the duty of loyalty requires that the employee shall not solicit the employer's customers while still an employee of the company. Customer lists have been defined as trade secrets, but they need not reach that status to be protected. Here, Lamorte's (P) customer list was confidential and proprietary information deserving of legal protection. The information was not available to the general public and Walters (D) would not have been aware of the information but for his employment. Because the client information is protected, Walters' (D) and Nixon's (D) handling of that information constitutes a breach of their duty of loyalty to Lamorte (P). That duty requires that while still employed, an employee, as agent of the employer, must not take actions contrary to the employer's interest. The Restatement (Agency) notes that employees may not solicit customers of the employer while still employed with the company. Here, Walters (D) and Nixon (D) obtained Lamorte's (P) client list while still employed to assist with the development of their new venture. These actions were contrary to Lamorte's (P) interest and therefore a violation of the duty of loyalty. The trial court's decision regarding Lamorte's (P) tort claims is reinstated in full. Reversed.

▶ ANALYSIS

Here, Lamorte (P) had Walters (D) execute an employment agreement, but unfortunately, Lamorte (P) never executed the agreement. Conveniently, the court was able to fall back on the tort claims to provide Lamorte (P) with a recovery. If the contract had been fully executed, it is likely the breach of contract claim would have been Lamorte's (P) primary vehicle to obtain damages.

■■■

Quicknotes

DUTY OF LOYALTY An employee's duty to refrain from taking a position that is adverse to the employer's best interests.

■■■

Mercer Management Consulting, Inc. v. Wilde

Management company (P) v. Former employees (D)

920 F. Supp. 219 (D.D.C. 1996).

NATURE OF CASE: Appeal from denial of motion for summary judgment in tort action.

FACT SUMMARY: Mercer (P), a management-consulting and strategic-planning company, initiated suit against three of its former employees, Wilde (D), Silverman (D), and Dewhurst (D), alleging breach of fiduciary duty, breach of contract, and tortious interference with its contractual relationships.

▣ RULE OF LAW
An employee may make arrangements to compete with his employer prior to terminating his employment, provided that no unfair acts are committed against or any injury sustained by the employer.

FACTS: Mercer Management Consulting, Inc. (Mercer) (P), a management-consulting and strategic-planning company, acquired Strategic Planning Associates (SPA) by merging it with Temple Barker Sloane, which it acquired through one of its subsidiaries. SPA employed Wilde (D), Silverman (D), and Dewhurst (D) as management consultants. The three entered into employment contracts with SPA providing that each would refrain from rendering competitive services to any client or prospective client of the company for a period of one year following their termination of employment. As a condition of the merger, Mercer (P) required that five of SPA's senior employee-stockholders enter into subsequent employment contracts. Wilde (D) and Silverman (D) each executed one of these contracts. The agreements provided for continued employment for a period of three years from the date of the merger at a guaranteed amount. The agreements further provided that Wilde (D) and Silverman (D) would faithfully and satisfactorily perform their obligations. Wilde (D) and Silverman (D) were prohibited from providing competing services within a 50-mile radius, soliciting or accepting business from clients or prospective clients, or soliciting any employees to terminate their employment with the company. The contract also contained an integration clause providing that it constituted the entire agreement between the parties. Wilde (D), Silverman (D) and Dewhurst (D) established a competing business. Mercer (P) filed a complaint charging breach of fiduciary duty, breach of contract and tortious interference with its contractual relationships. Wilde (D) and Silverman (D) counterclaimed for breach of contract based on Mercer's (P) alleged failure to make certain payments to them. The trial court denied Wilde (D) and Silverman's (D) motions for summary judgment, and the case went to trial.

ISSUE: May an employee make arrangements to compete with his employer prior to terminating his employment provided that no unfair acts are committed against or any injury sustained by the employer?

HOLDING AND DECISION: (Green, J.) Yes. An employee may make arrangements to compete with his or her employer prior to terminating his employment provided that no unfair acts are committed against or any injury sustained by the employer. Corporate officers and directors owe a duty of loyalty to the corporation precluding those officers and directors from taking actions in their self-interest. The officer or director also has a duty not to compete with the company in respect to the subject matter of his or her employment. While the right to make arrangements to commence a competing enterprise does not alone constitute a breach of the duty of loyalty, there are nonetheless certain restrictions on the actions an officer may take in attaining that objective. The failure to disclose that objective does not, without more, constitute a breach of loyalty. Rather, that determination is made on a case-by-case basis. Here, Wilde (D) and Silverman (D) commenced actions toward establishing a competing business while still employed by Mercer (P). They did not disclose that objective and continued to service clients and attend board meetings of the company. Mercer (P) contended that the continued serving of its clients constituted a breach of fiduciary duty since such services were rendered with the intent to later solicit those clients for the competing company. However, the maintenance of such client contact prior to the termination of employment does not alone give rise to a breach of fiduciary duty. Since the record is devoid of any solicitation or other improper action taken on the part of Wilde (D), Silverman (D) and Dewhurst (D) prior to leaving Mercer's (P) employment, the continued serving of client contracts did not constitute a breach of their fiduciary duties of loyalty. The breach-of-contract claims are another matter. The anti-competition clause contained in Wilde's (D) and Silverman's (D) contracts was deemed to expire three years following the date of the merger. Because three years had transpired since the merger occurred, Wilde (D) and Silverman (D) were not in violation of those provisions. However, the terms of their original agreements with SPA were still enforceable. Their actions in rendering competing services and hiring of Mercer's (P) employees constituted breaches of those agreements for which they are liable in damages for service

Continued on next page.

rendered in the year following their termination of employment with Mercer (P) in the amount of the profits Mercer (P) would have earned had the services been rendered on its behalf. Judgment for the defendants.

▶ *ANALYSIS*

A finding of a breach of fiduciary duty requires some type of malfeasance on the part of the officer or director. An employee who is preparing to compete with his company is prohibited from committing acts constituting fraud, including the misappropriation of confidential information and the solicitation of clients or employees. A claim alleging a tortious interference with business relationships requires a plaintiff to demonstrate that the defendants knew of the existence of a business relationship and committed an intentional and improper interference with that relationship, resulting in damages. In the above case, the court concluded that while Wilde (D) and Silverman's (D) actions constituted an interference with Mercer's (P) business relationships, that interference did not rise to the level of wrongful intent required by law.

■■■

Quicknotes

BREACH OF CONTRACT Unlawful failure by a party to perform its obligations pursuant to contract.

COVENANT NOT TO COMPETE A provision, typically contained in an employment contract or a contract for the sale of a business, pursuant to which the promisor agrees not to compete with the promisee for a specified time period and/or within a particular geographic area.

FIDUCIARY DUTY A legal obligation to act for the benefit of another, including subordinating one's personal interests to that of the other person.

INTERFERENCE WITH BUSINESS RELATIONSHIPS An intentional tort whereby a defendant intentionally elicits the breach of a valid contract resulting in damages.

■■■

Estee Lauder Cos., Inc. v. Batra

Employer (D) v. Employee (P)

430 F. Supp. 2d 158 (S.D.N.Y. 2006).

NATURE OF CASE: Action to nullify noncompete agreement.

FACT SUMMARY: Batra (D), a senior executive at Estee Lauder, jumped ship despite a noncompetition clause in his contract, and filed suit to nullify it. Estee Lauder Cos., Inc. (D) sought to enforce it.

RULE OF LAW

A noncompetition agreement between an employer and a high-ranking employee that contains a global geographic limitation is reasonable and enforceable if it is limited to a reasonable amount of time.

FACTS: Shashi Batra (P) was a senior executive for two of Estee Lauder Cos., Inc.'s (D) brands, Rodan and Fields and Darphin. His responsibilities included overseeing all aspects of product business, including research and development, marketing and distribution, pricing, and overall accounts management strategies. He had worldwide responsibility for R&F and North American responsibility for Darphin. Batra (P) signed an employment agreement that contained a noncompetition provision. In return for signing the agreement, Batra (P) received a $100,000 signing bonus, a salary of $300,000 per year, and a benefits package. The noncompetition clause provided in part that Batra (P) would not work for any business in competition with Estee Lauder (D) for 12 months after termination or disclose trade secrets in the geographic areas in which he had worked. Batra (P) notified Estee Lauder (D) that he was resigning to join Perricone. Estee Lauder (D) reminded him of his obligations under the noncompetition agreement, and Batra (P) responded that he did not believe that Estee Lauder (D) would be able to enforce the noncompetition agreement under California law. Batra (P) and Perricone then filed a lawsuit in California state court to nullify the noncompetition agreement, and Batra (P) began employment as the president of Perricone.

ISSUE: Is a noncompetition agreement between an employer and a high-ranking employee that contains a global geographic limitation reasonable and enforceable if it is limited to a reasonable amount of time?

HOLDING AND DECISION: (Sweet, J.) Yes. A noncompetition agreement between an employer and a high-ranking employee that contains a global geographic limitation is reasonable and enforceable if it is limited to a reasonable amount of time. A noncompetition agreement that prevented an employee from working with a competitor anywhere in the world for a period of 12 months after termination is enforceable only to the extent that it protected the employer's trade secrets. In this case, the geographic limitation was reasonable, but the 12-month duration was unreasonable, as five months would be a sufficient duration to protect the company. The fact that Estee Lauder (D) contracted to pay Batra (P) his salary of $375,000 per year for the duration of the 12 months helped in finding that the clause was not overbroad. Although, under the contract, Batra (P) essentially was prohibited from working for a competitor of Estee Lauder (D) product lines R&F or Darphin anywhere in the world, the concern that the breadth of such a prohibition would make it impossible for him to earn a living is assuaged by the fact that he will continue to earn his salary from Estee Lauder (D). Partial enforcement granted.

ANALYSIS

The court denied Batra's (P) request that the court abstain from hearing the case until California state litigation involving the same issues was resolved. Batra (P), who was a resident of California, filed that action against Estee Lauder (D). The court acknowledged California's well-known public policy against enforcement of noncompetition agreements, but also stated New York's strong interest in protecting its "undisputed status as the preeminent commercial and financial nerve center of the Nation and the world."

■═■

Quicknotes

NONCOMPETE CLAUSE A provision, typically contained in an employment contract or a contract for the sale of a business, pursuant to which the promisor agrees not to compete with the promisee for a specified time period and/or within a particular geographic area.

TRADE SECRET Consists of any formula, pattern, plan, process, or device known only to its owner and business which gives an advantage over competitors; a secret formula used in the manufacture of a particular product that is not known to the general public.

■═■

Springfield Rare Coin Galleries v. Mileham

Employer (P) v. Employee (D)

Ill. App. Ct., 620 N.E.2d 479 (1993).

NATURE OF CASE: Appeal of judgment for employee.

FACT SUMMARY: A rare-coin dealer tried to enforce a restrictive covenant against a former employee that prohibited the employee from competing with employer within a certain radius of the employer's business, for a period of two years following termination.

🏛 RULE OF LAW
(1) Where an employer did not incur great expense to secure customer lists, and did not keep those lists under tight security, the customer list does not constitute confidential information for the purpose of enforcing a restrictive covenant against a former employee.
(2) Where an employer is not in the business of providing a professional service, the employer cannot have a near-permanent relationship with its customers for the purpose of enforcing a restrictive covenant against a former employee.

FACTS: Steve Mileham (D) worked as a middleman in the rare-coin business for Springfield Rare Coin Galleries (Springfield) (P). Springfield (P) required him to sign a restrictive covenant as a condition of employment, under which Mileham (D) agreed not to compete with Springfield (P) in the county for two years after termination. When he left, Mileham (D) continued to work as a middleman in the business, and Springfield (P) sought and obtained a preliminary injunction against Mileham (D). At trial, Springfield (P) argued that its customer list constitutes confidential information, and that information about the financial reliability of those customers was confidential information, and that Mileham (D) used that information to his benefit, in violation of the covenant. Springfield (P) also argued that it had a near-permanent relationship with its customers, and that Mileham (D) would not have had contact with those customers but for the association with Springfield (P). The trial court found that the restrictive covenant was not enforceable.

ISSUE:
(1) Where an employer did not incur great expense to secure customer lists, and did not keep those lists under tight security, does the customer list constitute confidential information for the purpose of enforcing a restrictive covenant against a former employee?
(2) Where an employer is not in the business of providing a professional service, can the employer have a near-permanent relationship with its customers for the purpose of enforcing a restrictive covenant against a former employee?

HOLDING AND DECISION: (Knecht, J.)
(1) No. Where an employer did not incur great expense to secure customer lists and did not keep those lists under tight security, the customer list does not constitute confidential information for the purpose of enforcing a restrictive covenant against a former employee. Reasonable restrictive covenants are enforceable where the former employee acquired confidential information through his employment and subsequently tried to use it for his own benefit. Springfield (P) failed to show that it incurred great expense for the development of customer lists or the financial reliability of the customers, or that it kept that information under tight security, and the information is therefore not confidential. Even if such information were considered confidential, Mileham (D) did not use the information for his benefit. Where the employee merely learns the trade during his term of employment, the employee has not learned confidential information.
(2) No. Where an employer is not in the business of providing a professional service, the employer cannot have a near-permanent relationship with its customers for the purpose of enforcing a restrictive covenant against a former employee. Reasonable restrictive covenants are also enforceable where, by the nature of the business, the customer relationship is near permanent and, but for his association with the former employer, the employee would not have had contact with the customers in question. Springfield (P) is not engaged in the provision of professional services, and therefore the near-permanency test is not satisfied. Trial court affirmed.

▎*ANALYSIS*

The type of damage an employer must show, and the amount of damage, before invoking trade-secret protection is not clear, especially in light of the state-by-state consideration of the issue. Aside from obvious cases—as where a high ranking executive of Coca Cola steals the formula for the soft drink and sells it to Pepsi—the line is blurred by courts trying to balance the protection of trade secrets with the commercial interest in free trade.

▬▬■

Continued on next page.

Quicknotes

NONCOMPETE CLAUSE A provision, typically contained in an employment contract or a contract for the sale of a business, pursuant to which the promisor agrees not to compete with the promisee for a specified time period and/or within a particular geographic area.

TRADE SECRET Consists of any formula, pattern, plan, process, or device known only to its owner and business which gives an advantage over competitors; a secret formula used in the manufacture of a particular product that is not known to the general public.

Unemployment

Quick Reference Rules of Law

Howard Delivery Services, Inc. v. Zurich American Insurance Co.

Insured employer (D) v. Insurer (P)

547 U.S. 651 (2006).

NATURE OF CASE: Appeal from federal appeals court judgment in favor of the insurer.

FACT SUMMARY: An employer filed for Chapter 11 protection, and one of its insurers sought to have unpaid workers' compensation premiums listed as a priority under the Bankruptcy Code. The U.S. Court of Appeals for the Fourth Circuit ruled in favor of the insurer.

🏛 RULE OF LAW
The unpaid workers' compensation premiums a debtor employer owes his insurance carrier are not employee benefits entitled to priority status under the Bankruptcy Code.

FACTS: When Howard Delivery Services, Inc. (D), a freight company, filed for Chapter 11 protection, the Zurich American Insurance Company (P) sought to have $400,000 in unpaid workers' compensation premiums listed as a priority under Section 507(a)(5) of the Bankruptcy Code, which grants priority status to "unsecured claims for contributions to an employee benefit plan . . . for services rendered" by employees. The U.S. Court of Appeals for the Fourth Circuit ruled in favor of Zurich (P), and the Supreme Court granted certiorari to settle a circuit split on the issue.

ISSUE: Are the unpaid workers' compensation premiums a debtor employer owes his insurance carrier employee benefits entitled to priority status under the Bankruptcy Code?

HOLDING AND DECISION: (Ginsburg, J.) No. The unpaid workers' compensation premiums a debtor employer owes his insurance carrier are not employee benefits entitled to priority status under the Bankruptcy Code. Section 507(a)(4) grants priority status to "wages, salaries, or commissions," and is linked to subsection (a)(5) by a combined cap on the two priorities of $10,000 per employee. Subsection (a)(5) allows the provider of an employee benefit plan to recover unpaid premiums "only after the employees' claims for 'wages, salaries, or commissions' have been paid" under subsection (a)(4). The main purpose of subsection (a)(5) is to capture portions of employee compensation for services rendered not covered by subsection (a)(4). The juxtaposition of the wages and employee benefit plan priorities indicates congressional comprehension that fringe benefits generally complement, or are a substitute for, hourly pay. Unlike pension provisions or group life, health and disability plans, which are negotiated or granted as pay supplements or substitutes, workers' compensation prescriptions have a dominant employer-oriented thrust: They modify, or substitute for, the common-law tort liability to which employers were exposed for work-related accidents. Further, workers' compensation benefits provide a quid pro quo—workers receive limited benefits regardless of fault, and employers lose the risk of large judgments and heavy tort costs generated by tort litigation. No such tradeoff is involved in fringe benefit plans that supplement each covered worker's hourly pay. In addition, employer-sponsored pension plans, and group-health or life-insurance plans, insure the employee only. In contrast, workers' compensation insurance, in common with other liability insurance, shields the insured enterprise. Workers' compensation policies both protect the employer-policyholder from liability in tort, and cover the obligation to pay workers' compensation benefits. Reversed and remanded.

▶ ANALYSIS

Justice Kennedy, joined by Justices Souter and Alito, dissented, arguing that "'employee benefit plan,' whether viewed as a term of art or in accordance with its plain meaning, includes workers' compensation." The dissent was omitted from the casebook excerpt.

■=■

Quicknotes

CHAPTER 11 BANKRUPTCY A legal proceeding whereby a debtor, who is unable to pay his debts as they become due, is relieved of his obligation to pay his creditors through reorganization and payment from future income.

WORKERS' COMPENSATION Fixed awards provided to employees for job-related injuries.

■=■

Law v. Law Trucking Co.

Company president (P) v. Trucking company (D)

R.I. Sup. Ct., 488 A.2d 1225 (1985).

NATURE OF CASE: Appeal from denial of claim for credit or priority.

FACT SUMMARY: When their employer, Law Trucking Co. (D), went into bankruptcy after five of its drivers agreed to a wage-cut proposal to help Law Trucking (D) remain open, the five drivers asked that these moneys be given priority status for payment to the extent permitted by the Bankruptcy Code.

🏛 RULE OF LAW
Priority status for a bankruptcy employee-creditor applies only where moneys withheld by an employer can be considered wages.

FACTS: When Law Trucking Co. (D) fell on hard times, five of its 12 drivers agreed to accept a wage-cut proposal. Under their union contract, the drivers were paid $12.71 an hour for straight time and $19.06 for overtime, based on a 40-hour week. They agreed in writing to accept $10 for straight time and $15 for overtime. In return, company president Robert Law (P) promised to plow the wage concessions back into Law Trucking (D) and to keep it going for a year, reimbursing the drivers for their "loan" if Law Trucking (D) made a profit at the end of that time. After Law Trucking (D) went into receivership, the permanent receiver petitioned for instructions whether or not to pay the wage claims of the five drivers. Besides seeking priority status, the five drivers contended that the alleged agreement should fail because it contained no mutuality of obligation. The trial justice found there was mutual obligation and that the moneys withheld were loans, not wages. This appeal followed.

ISSUE: Does priority status for a bankruptcy employee-creditor apply only where moneys withheld by an employer can be considered wages?

HOLDING AND DECISION: (Bevilacqua, C.J.) Yes. Priority status for a bankruptcy employee-creditor applies only where moneys withheld by an employer can be considered wages. Mutuality consisted of Law's (P) promise to keep Law Trucking (D) open for a year in exchange for the loans. Further, there was ample evidence in the record to support the finding that the moneys in question were loans, not wages. The language in the agreement refers to a loan to Law Trucking (D). Moreover, no taxes, Social Security, and/or disability deductions were withheld from sums earned above the wage-rate ceiling set forth in the new agreement. Affirmed.

▶ ANALYSIS

The text of the agreement signed by the five drivers stated: "I will 'loan' to Law Trucking Company without interest, my earnings over . . . , and the five personal holidays due in 1981." Because the drivers were aware of the financial difficulty facing Law Trucking (D), it could easily be inferred that they understood the risk involved in their agreement. Priorities for payment are set forth in the United States Bankruptcy Code, 11 U.S.C. § 507, which allows unsecured claims for wages, salaries, or commissions, including vacation, severance, and sick leave pay.

Quicknotes

BANKRUPTCY CODE 11 U.S.C.A. § 507 (1979) Gives workers preference over general creditors as to wages earned but uncollected before bankruptcy.

MUTUALITY OF OBLIGATION Requires that both parties to a contract are bound or else neither is bound.

RECEIVERSHIP Proceeding or condition whereby a receiver is appointed in order to maintain the holdings of a corporation, individual or other entity that is insolvent.

In re American Housing Foundation, Debtor

Former Employee (P) v. Employer (D)

2010 WL 2371072 (Bkrtcy. N.D. Tex. 2010).

NATURE OF CASE: Consideration of former employee's claim for vacation time within bankruptcy proceeding.

FACT SUMMARY: American Housing Foundation (D) entered bankruptcy proceedings and subsequently terminated Jack Traeger (P). Traeger (P) submitted a claim for accrued but unused vacation time.

🏛 **RULE OF LAW**
An employer must pay an employee for unused vacation time only if the employee has the right to such benefit via an expressed employment contract.

FACTS: American Housing Foundation (AHF) (D) was a nonprofit corporation created to develop affordable housing. Traeger (P) served as the Portfolio Manager with a salary of $160,000. In 2009, AHF (D) went into bankruptcy proceedings and subsequently terminated Traeger (P). Traeger (P) filed a claim in bankruptcy for payment of $5,641.03 for accrued but unused vacation time. Traeger, like all AHF (D) employees, was actually employed by a staffing agency, Administaff. Administaff had its own vacation policy but it said nothing about payment for unused vacation time in the event of termination.

ISSUE: Must an employer pay an employee for unused vacation time only if the employee has the right to such benefit via an expressed employment contract?

HOLDING AND DECISION: (Jones, J.) Yes. An employer must pay an employee for unused vacation time only if the employee has the right to such benefit via an expressed employment contract. This is usually a direct contract between the company and the individual employee. Employee handbooks or manuals do not constitute contracts between the employer and its employees, unless the handbook contains express language that the employer intends to be bound by the terms of the handbook. Here, even if the Administaff handbook qualified as an employment contract, it contained no provision that would allow Traeger (P) to recover for his unused vacation time after his termination. Traeger's claim for unused vacation time is denied. The court will allow his claim for $1,898.35 for travel expenses as a legitimate administrative claim under Section 507 of the bankruptcy code.

▶ *ANALYSIS*

The decision reflects the generally accepted rule that employees are not entitled to post-termination benefits unless a written contract exists providing them with those benefits. It also correctly states the majority rule that employee handbooks, policies, and manuals do not constitute employment contracts unless express language exists obligating the employer to their terms.

Quicknotes

EMPLOYMENT-AT-WILL The rule that an employment relationship is subject to termination at any time, or for any cause, by an employee or an employer in the absence of a specific agreement otherwise.

EMPLOYMENT CONTRACT A contract or agreement between employer and employee in which the terms and conditions of employment are provided.

In re A.C.E. Elevator Co., Inc.

Benefit Plan (P) v. Corporation (D)

347 B.R. 473 (Bkrtcy. S.D.N.Y. 2006).

NATURE OF CASE: In bankruptcy, consideration of claim by benefit plan against debtor/company for unpaid contributions to the plan.

FACT SUMMARY: After A.C.E. Elevator Co., Inc. (ACE) (D) filed for bankruptcy, the National Elevator Industry Benefit Plan (Plan) (P) filed for an administrative claim for ACE's unpaid contributions to the Plan (P).

🏛 RULE OF LAW
Under the Bankruptcy Code, unpaid contributions to an employee benefit plan may qualify as retiree benefits and thus have a preference within a bankruptcy proceeding as a qualified administrative expense.

FACTS: A.C.E. Elevator Co., Inc. (ACE) (D) installed and serviced the elevators at the World Trade Center in New York. The service contract provided ACE (D) with 90 percent of its revenue. After the events of September 11, 2001, ACE (D) could not remain in business and eventually filed for bankruptcy on December 21, 2004. ACE (D) concedes that it did not pay all of its contributions into the National Elevator Industry Benefit Plan (Plan) for a certain time period prior to the bankruptcy filing date. However, because the unpaid contributions arose before the filing of bankruptcy, ACE (D) argues the Plan's claim cannot qualify as an administrative expense, which would give the Plan's (P) claim a higher preference than other secured creditors. The Plan (P) argues that it did not process ACE's (D) contribution until after the filing of bankruptcy.

ISSUE: Under the Bankruptcy Code, may unpaid contributions to an employee benefit plan qualify as retiree benefits and thus have a preference within a bankruptcy proceeding as a qualified administrative expense?

HOLDING AND DECISION: (Drain, J.) Yes. Under the Bankruptcy Code, unpaid contributions to an employee benefit plan may qualify as retiree benefits and thus have a preference within a bankruptcy proceeding as a qualified administrative expense. An administrative expense deserves priority because it seeks to preserve the bankrupt entity. First, under § 503(b)(1)(A), the delinquent contribution payments do not qualify as administrative expenses. The contributions arise from hours worked by employees "prepetition," before the date of the bankruptcy filing. Accordingly, under that section of the code, the contributions are not accorded priority status. However, the Plan (P) also argues that the contribution payments to the Plan qualify as "retiree" benefits under § 1114(e) of the code. This section states that any payment for retiree benefits required to be

paid prior to the confirmation of a bankruptcy plan shall be accorded priority status. That may be the case here. The contributions must satisfy three factors. First, the contributions must qualify as retirement payments. Second, the payments must not be to a multiemployer plan. Lastly, the payments at issue should only relate to retirees and their spouses, not current employees. Because neither party has briefed the issue, the court will decline to decide the matter until both parties provide further submissions on the applicability of § 1114(e).

▶ ANALYSIS

Note that under the Code, contributions for retirees of the company take precedence over retirement contributions for current employees. Also, under § 1114(e), if the contributions qualify as retiree benefits, it does not matter if they arose from hours worked by employees prepetition or postpetition.

■═■

Quicknotes

ADMINISTRATIVE EXPENSES In determining priority of claims in Chapter 7 liquidation, refers to expenses of preserving the estate, including payment for services rendered after filing of the bankruptcy petition.

BANKRUPTCY A legal proceeding whereby a debtor, who is unable to pay his debts as they become due, is relieved of his obligation to pay his creditors either by liquidation and distribution of his remaining assets or through reorganization and payment from future income.

■═■

Local 1330, United Steel Workers of America v. United States Steel Corp.

Union (P) v. Steel company (D)

631 F.2d 1264 (6th Cir. 1980).

NATURE OF CASE: Appeal from denial of motions for injunctive relief.

FACT SUMMARY: After U.S. Steel Corp. (D) announced the closing of its two steel plants in the Youngstown area the Union (P) sought an order to keep the plants in operation or, alternatively, an injunction to require U.S. Steel (D) to sell the two plants to the Union (P).

🏛 RULE OF LAW
Under the law, an employer has the right to close its plant due to a lack of profitability.

FACTS: The United States Steel Corp. (D) operated two steel mills in Youngstown, Ohio, one since 1901 and the other since 1918. For all the years U.S. Steel (D) operated in Youngstown it was a dominant factor in the lives of its thousands of employees and their families and in the life of the city itself. At the time notice of the closing was given, U.S. Steel (D) employed 3,500 workers at the two plants. The employees were represented by the United Steel Workers of America (P), which had a collective-bargaining agreement with U.S. Steel (D) for many years. Plant closings were attributed to the fact that the plants were obsolete. The Union (P) and others asked the federal courts to order U.S. Steel (D) to keep the two plants in operation or, alternatively, an injunction to require it to sell the plants to the Union (P) under a tentative plan of purchase and operation by a community corporation and to restrain the piecemeal sale or dismantling of the plants until such a proposal could be brought to fruition. The Union (P) argued that a contract, based on an oral promise not to close the plants if the workers increased their productivity and thereby rendered the two plants "profitable," existed under the doctrine of promissory estoppel and also that a property right had arisen from the long-established relation between the community and U.S. Steel (D). U.S. Steel (D) asserted an absolute right to make a business decision to discharge its former employees and abandon Youngstown. The district judge, after originally restraining U.S. Steel (D) from ceasing operations, denied the Union's (P) motions, holding that the plants had become unprofitable. This appeal followed.

ISSUE: Under the law, does an employer have the right to close its plant due to a lack of profitability?

HOLDING AND DECISION: (Edwards, C.J.) Yes. Under the law, an employer has the right to close its plant due to a lack of profitability. In this case, there was no indication that there was ever any formal negotiation or amendment of the collective-bargaining contract in relation to the issues. The doctrine of promissory estoppel recognizes the possibility of the formation of a contract by action or forbearance on the part of a second party, based upon a promise made by the first party under circumstances where the actions or forbearance of the second party should reasonably have been expected to produce the detrimental results to the second party that they did produce. The local management of U.S. Steel's (D) Youngstown plants engaged in a major campaign to enlist employee participation in an all-out effort to make these two plants profitable in order to prevent their being closed, and the employees responded wholeheartedly. However, the condition precedent of the alleged contract and promise, profitability of the Youngstown facilities, was never fulfilled, and an action in contract and for detrimental reliance cannot be found for the Union (P). Furthermore, even though a lengthy, long-established relationship existed between U.S. Steel (D) and the Youngstown area, no constitutional authority, either state or federal, recognizes such a relationship as creating a property right to the extent of compelling U.S. Steel (D) to remain in the Youngstown area or to be restrained from leaving the area in a state of waste. Whatever the future may bring, neither by statute nor by court decision has the Union's (P) claimed property right been recognized to date in this country. Affirmed.

▶ ANALYSIS

The court recognized that the closure of the steel plants would be not only a devastating blow to the workers, their families, and the business community but an economic tragedy of major proportion to the area. Thus far, federal law sought to protect the human values discussed here through means of legislation such as unemployment compensation. The court declared that formulation of public policy on the great issues involved in plant closings and removals was the responsibility of the legislatures of the states or of the U.S. Congress. In 1988, Congress enacted the first federal statute restricting employer authority to shut factories, unless the union, if there was one, or each worker, if there was no union, along with state and local government officials, received 60 days' notice.

■=■

Continued on next page.

Quicknotes

COLLECTIVE BARGAINING Negotiations between an employer and employee that are mediated by a specified third party.

CONDITION PRECEDENT The happening of an uncertain occurrence, which is necessary before a particular right or interest may be obtained or an action performed.

PROMISSORY ESTOPPEL A promise that is enforceable if the promisor should reasonably expect that it will induce action or forbearance on the part of the promisee, and does in fact cause such action or forbearance, and it is the only means of avoiding injustice.

■■■■

Gross v. Hale-Halsell Co.

Employees (P) v. Employer (D)

554 F.3d 870 (10th Cir. 2009).

NATURE OF CASE: Appeal from granting of summary judgment to the defendant.

FACT SUMMARY: After losing its biggest client, Hale-Halsell Co. (HHC) (D) laid off all its employees one week later.

🏛 RULE OF LAW
While employers must give 60 days' notice to employees of mass layoffs, the time frame may be shortened if the layoffs are the result of business circumstances that were not reasonably foreseeable.

FACTS: Hale-Halsell Co. (HHC) (D) was a wholesale grocery warehouse. The company owned 50 percent of United Supermarkets (United), which provided HHC (D) with 40 percent of HHC's (D) total business. By the end of 2003, HHC (D) was struggling and was unable to fill 53 percent of the items requested by United. The two companies had been doing business together for 31 years. At the same time, HHC (D) was negotiating a loan from LaSalle Bank. On January 8, 2004, United informed HHC (D) that it wanted to continue doing business with HHC (D) but was considering ordering from other wholesale grocery suppliers. On January 15, United informed HHC (D) that HHC (D) would no longer be United's primary supplier. On January 20, HHC (D) representatives met with its bank and other creditors and decided the company could not survive. On January 21, HHC (D) representatives informed office staff and warehouse personnel of the decision to cease operations and that all employees would be laid off immediately. On January 22, 2004, HHC (D) formally terminated all staff. The plaintiff employees (P) brought suit alleging that HHC (D) violated the Worker Adjustment and Retraining Notification Act (WARN Act). The WARN Act demands that employers provide employees with 60 days' notice of mass layoffs, unless business circumstances dictate otherwise. The federal district court granted summary judgment to HHC (D) and the plaintiff employees (P) appealed.

ISSUE: While employers must give 60 days' notice to employees of mass layoffs, may the time frame be shortened if the layoffs are the result of business circumstances that were not reasonably foreseeable?

HOLDING AND DECISION: (Kelly, J.) Yes. While employers must give 60 days' notice to employees of mass layoffs, the time frame may be shortened if the layoffs are the result of business circumstances that were not reasonably foreseeable. Under the WARN Act, an employer bears the burden of proof that the circumstances were unforeseeable and that those circumstances caused the layoffs. The foreseeability analysis is an objective one and is not based on the employees' subjective beliefs. A court should review the history of the business and the industry. The evidence does not suggest that United's decision to use another supplier was reasonably foreseeable. The relationship between the companies lasted for 31 years and had survived downturns in the past. One week prior to United's final decision, United expressed its desire to continue working with HHC (D). In addition, HHC (D) informed its employees of the layoffs as soon as was practicable. After receiving the January 15 letter from United, HHC (D) met with its bank and attorneys to determine a course of action. After deciding on January 20 to cease operations, HHC (D) notified the staff orally the next day and then terminated all employees the following day. This notice was sufficient under the WARN Act. Affirmed.

▶ ANALYSIS

As the text notes, the business circumstances exception to the 60 days' notice requirement provides a very large escape hatch for employers caught unawares. While the statute technically places the burden on the employers to show that the circumstances were unforeseeable, the burden is not difficult to satisfy. Because of this exception, the WARN Act operates only to protect employees in the most egregious of cases.

■═■

Quicknotes

BURDEN OF PROOF The duty of a party to introduce evidence to support a fact that is in dispute in an action.

■═■

Administaff v. New York Joint Board

Off-site vendor (D) v. Union (P)

337 F.3d 454 (5th Cir. 2003).

NATURE OF CASE: Appeal of summary judgment for off-site vendor.

FACT SUMMARY: A union sought to hold an off-site human resources vendor liable under the Worker Adjustment and Retraining Notification Act when the factory that employed the off-site vendor closed down without 60 days' notice to the workers.

> **🏛 RULE OF LAW**
> An outside payroll administrator for a factory is not liable for violations of the Worker Adjustment and Retraining Notification Act when the factory closed down its operations without 60 days' notification.

FACTS: TheCustomShop.com, the former owner of a men's clothing production plant in New Jersey, contracted for the services of Administaff (D), which operated an off-site human resources department, providing payroll, personnel, and other services to the factory. In late 2000, the company encountered financial difficulties. When its attempts to raise capital and to sell the business failed, it closed the New Jersey facility, without providing the 60 days' notice required under the Worker Adjustment and Retraining Notification Act (WARN Act). Administaff (D) did not participate in the decision and was not aware of the closing until after it occurred. The union representing employees of the facility demanded that Administaff (D), as an employer under the WARN Act, compensate each member of the bargaining unit for 60 days of pay plus benefits. Administaff (D) moved for summary judgment, arguing that it was not liable under the Act, and a district court granted the motion.

ISSUE: Is an outside payroll administrator for a factory liable for violations of the Worker Adjustment and Retraining Notification Act when the factory closed down its operations without 60 days' notification?

HOLDING AND DECISION: (Jones, J.) No. An outside payroll administrator for a factory is not liable for violations of the Worker Adjustment and Retraining Notification Act when the factory closed down its operations without 60 days' notification. The Act provides that any employer who orders a plant closing or mass layoff in violation of Section 3 of this Act, which is the 60-day notice provision, shall be liable to each aggrieved employee who suffers an employment loss as a result of such closing or layoff for backpay and benefits. The language of the statute clearly imposes liability only on an employer who orders the closing of a plant. Administaff (D) did not participate

in the company's decision to close the plant and therefore was not liable under the Act. Affirmed.

▶ ANALYSIS

The Fifth Circuit distinguished a 1992 ruling by the U.S. Court of Appeals for the Second Circuit, *Local 217 Hotel & Rest. Employees Union v. MHM Inc.*, 976 F.2d 805 (2d Cir. 1992), where a hotel management firm was held liable under the WARN Act, even though the hotel owner had sole control over the timing and decision to close the hotel. In that case, the management company "ran every aspect of the hotel on a day-to-day basis," carried out the closing of the hotel, and was a party to the collective-bargaining agreement. None of those conditions applied in the case of Administaff (D), which did not have the right to manage or make decisions regarding the plant and had nothing to do with the closing.

■■■

Quicknotes

NOTICE Communication of information to a person by an authorized person or an otherwise proper source.

WORKER ADJUSTMENT AND RETAINING NOTIFICATION ACT 29 U.S.C. §§ 2101 et seq. (Sup. 1993) requires employers to provide 60 days' notice to employees who will be laid off or whose hours will be substantially reduced.

■■■

Zambrano v. Reinert

Employee (P) v. State employment agency (D)

291 F.3d 964 (7th Cir. 2002).

NATURE OF CASE: Appeal of denial of unemployment compensation.

FACT SUMMARY: Zambrano (P), who worked for a temporary-staffing firm for a few weeks and worked for a vegetable processor in the state for four months in 1999, sued after the Wisconsin Department of Workforce Development (D) decided he was ineligible for unemployment compensation.

🏛 **RULE OF LAW**
Wisconsin's "cannery rule" governing unemployment compensation eligibility for seasonal fruit- or vegetable-processing workers does not violate the Social Security Act, the Federal Unemployment Tax Act, or the constitutional guarantee of equal protection.

FACTS: Under the cannery rule, work that involves the processing of fresh fruits or vegetables during the active-processing season does not count toward eligibility for unemployment benefits unless the worker had been employed by the processor outside the active-processing season, earned at least four times the weekly benefit rate in relevant quarters, or earned more than $200 in another job in Wisconsin. Rene Zambrano (P) earned $1,250 working for a Wisconsin temporary-staffing firm in May and June 1999 and earned $10,291 working for Seneca Foods Inc., a vegetable processor in Wisconsin from June 11 to October 7, 1999. He did not work for Seneca outside the active-processing season, his earnings during relevant quarters were $40 short of the level needed to be four times the weekly benefit rate, and because his wages from the staffing firm were earned during the same quarter as the start of his work for Seneca and not during the preceding quarter, he did not qualify under the provision requiring at least $200 from another job in Wisconsin. Zambrano (P) sued Jennifer Reinert (D) in her official capacity as secretary of Department for Workforce Development (D), alleging that the cannery rule violated the Social Security Act (SSA), the Federal Unemployment Tax Act (FUTA), and the Equal Protection Clause of the U.S. Constitution. The U.S. District Court for the Western District of Wisconsin granted summary judgment to Reinert (D), upholding the cannery rule.

ISSUE: Does Wisconsin's "cannery rule" governing unemployment compensation eligibility for seasonal fruit or vegetable-processing workers violate the Social Security Act, the Federal Unemployment Tax Act, or the constitutional guarantee of equal protection?

HOLDING AND DECISION: (Kanne, J.) No. Wisconsin's "cannery rule" governing unemployment compensation eligibility for seasonal fruit- or vegetable-processing workers does not violate the Social Security Act, the Federal Unemployment Tax Act, or the constitutional guarantee of equal protection. States that enact qualifying unemployment-insurance laws receive federal funding under the SSA, and the state programs are subject to certification by the Secretary of Labor, which requires that methods of administration are reasonably calculated to insure full payment of unemployment compensation when due. Zambrano (P) argued the cannery rule violates the "when-due" requirement of the SSA, because the cannery rule excludes the wages he earned from the staffing firm, thus making him ineligible under the "other employment" provision. But the focus of the when-due clause is timeliness. Administrative provisions, which govern when eligibility is determined or when benefits are paid, are subject to the when-due clause, but eligibility requirements, which govern who is eligible to receive benefits, do not fall under the when-due clause. In addition, the cannery rule merely sets forth requirements for being eligible to receive unemployment compensation and therefore does not cancel or reduce wage credits or benefit rights in violation of FUTA. Finally, the cannery rule does not violate the Equal Protection Clause because there is a rational basis for treating seasonal fruit and vegetable workers differently from other workers more committed to the Wisconsin labor market. Affirmed.

▶ **ANALYSIS**

The Department of Workforce Development (D) argued that the purpose of the cannery rule is to ensure that workers receiving unemployment compensation benefits are firmly committed to the Wisconsin labor market. The court found that even though fruit and vegetable processing occurs during only three to four months a year, and employment availability and duration in this line of work is therefore necessarily limited, the "other employment" provision nevertheless allows seasonal fruit- and vegetable-processing workers to show a commitment to the Wisconsin labor market and gain eligibility for unemployment compensation.

■=■

Continued on next page.

Quicknotes

EQUAL PROTECTION CLAUSE A constitutional provision that each person be guaranteed the same protection of the laws enjoyed by other persons in like circumstances.

■═■

Jaime v. Director, Department of Employment Security

Employee (P) v. State employment agency (D)

Ill. App. Ct., 704 N.E.2d 721 (1998).

NATURE OF CASE: Appeal of denial of unemployment compensation.

FACT SUMMARY: A worker was denied unemployment compensation, which she applied for after her company moved to the suburbs, and she had no way to get to work. She was denied unemployment compensation because she voluntarily resigned.

🏛 RULE OF LAW
A worker who voluntarily resigns from employment is entitled to unemployment benefits if workplace relocation caused the resignation.

FACTS: Maria Jaime (P) worked for Miniat for 10 years while Miniat was located in Chicago. When the company moved to the suburbs, Jaime (P) had to travel 16 miles to get to work. She rode with a coworker until the coworker quit. Jaime (P) then had no way to get to work, and resigned. She applied for unemployment compensation, but was denied by the Department of Employment Security (D).

ISSUE: Is a worker who voluntarily resigns from employment entitled to unemployment benefits if workplace relocation caused the resignation?

HOLDING AND DECISION: (McNamara, J.) Yes. A worker who voluntarily resigns from employment is entitled to unemployment benefits if workplace relocation caused the resignation. A reasonable person would view Jaime's (P) reason for leaving her employment as a valid one, and not indicative of unwillingness to work on her part. While transportation to and from work is generally not the responsibility of the employer, Jaime's (P) inability to maintain her employment is the direct result of Miniat's moving, which significantly changed the circumstances of her employment. This decision comports with the state legislature's policy that a person who becomes unemployed through no fault of his own should be entitled to unemployment compensation. Affirmed.

▶ ANALYSIS

Jaime's (P) resignation might be considered involuntary, given the circumstances. And, if that is the case and her resignation was directly the cause of the company's relocation, the result is easily squared with the policy underlying unemployment benefits.

■━■

Quik 'N Tasty Foods, Inc. v. Division of Employment Security

Employer (D) v. Employee (P)

Mo. Ct. App., 17 S.W.3d 620 (2000).

NATURE OF CASE: Appeal of grant of unemployment benefits to employee.

FACT SUMMARY: An employee who voluntarily resigned after management suggested to the employee that resignation might be preferable to discharge was granted unemployment compensation. The company appealed.

🏛 RULE OF LAW
A claimant is not entitled to unemployment benefits if she voluntarily quits her job absent good cause attributable to her work or to her employer.

FACTS: Quik 'N Tasty Foods, Inc. (Quik 'N Tasty) (D) reprimanded Wendy Foley (P) for chronic absenteeism. Following a meeting on the subject, Foley (P) resigned. Quik 'N Tasty's management suggested that resignation might be better for Foley (P) than a discharge. Foley (P) then applied for unemployment benefits with the Division of Employment Security (D), which denied her application. The Labor and Industrial Commission reversed, granting Foley (P) benefits, finding that her actions were reasonable, her resignation was in good faith, and that she was therefore not disqualified from benefits. Quik 'N Tasty (D) then appealed.

ISSUE: Is a claimant entitled to unemployment benefits if she voluntarily quits her job absent good cause attributable to her work or to her employer?

HOLDING AND DECISION: (Holliger, J.) No. A claimant is not entitled to unemployment benefits if she voluntarily quits her job absent good cause attributable to her work or to her employer. "Good cause" is judged by the facts of each case, and conditions that motivate the employee to voluntarily leave must be real, substantial, reasonable, and in good faith. Here, the Labor and Industrial Commission argued that Foley (P) acted reasonably and in good faith. But the good cause necessary to support an award of unemployment benefits must be cause attributable to her work or her employment, which means that it must be the work or the employer that creates the condition making it unreasonable to expect this employee to continue work. Here, no condition created by the employer, other than the suggestion to resign rather than be discharged, may constitute good cause sufficient for the exception from benefit disqualification. Reversed and remanded.

▶ ANALYSIS

In this case, it was not the company's suggestion that resignation might be preferable to discharge for the employee that constituted the cause for resignation, but the fact was that other obligations kept the employee from keeping a good attendance record. Her other obligations were not the "good cause" of her resignation. But note also that this case highlights the problems faced by female employees who try to balance the demands of work with the demands of motherhood.

■■■

Quicknotes

GOOD CAUSE Sufficient justification for failure to perform an obligation imposed by law.

■■■

Tri-County Youth Programs, Inc. v. Acting Deputy Director of Division of Employment & Training

Employer (D) v. Employee (P)

Mass. App. Ct., 765 N.E.2d 810 (2002).

NATURE OF CASE: Appeal of grant of unemployment benefits to employee.

FACT SUMMARY: A client sexually assaulted a caseworker at a residence for emotionally troubled adolescents. She resigned when the employer failed to take reasonable steps to keep the caseworker and her assailant separated. She filed for unemployment compensation, which was ultimately granted. The employer appealed.

🏛 RULE OF LAW
An employee need not show that he or she took reasonable steps to preserve his or her employment, in addition to showing that he or she left work involuntarily with good cause attributable to the employer, in cases where the cause for resignation was sexual harassment and the employer's manner of dealing with the harassment.

FACTS: Lawrie (P) was a shift manager in a residence for emotionally troubled adolescents operated by Tri-County Youth Programs, Inc. (Tri-County) (D) in Northampton, Mass. While driving the company van, Lawrie (P) was sexually assaulted by one of the clients, a 14-year-old male. She reported the assault to her superiors and reported the assault to police and pressed charges. The boy was arrested and placed in custody. Tri-County (D) told Lawrie (P) that her assailant would probably be returned to Lawrie's (P) work site, with a "stay-away" order in place. The court eventually found the assailant guilty and ordered him to stay away from Lawrie (P), but he was returned to Tri-County (D). Lawrie (P) then resigned, giving as the reason her dissatisfaction with Tri-County's (D) handling of the sexual assault incident. Lawrie (P) was granted unemployment benefits, and Tri-County (D) appealed.

ISSUE: Must an employee show that he or she took reasonable steps to preserve his or her employment, in addition to showing that he or she left work involuntarily with good cause attributable to the employer, in cases where the cause for resignation was sexual harassment and the employer's manner of dealing with the harassment?

HOLDING AND DECISION: (Gelinas, J.) No. An employee need not show that he or she took reasonable steps to preserve his or her employment, in addition to showing that he or she left work involuntarily with good cause attributable to the employer, in cases where the cause for resignation was sexual harassment and the employer's manner of dealing with the harassment. Generally, it is the employee's burden to show that the employee left work involuntarily with good cause attributable to the employer, and that he or she took reasonable steps to preserve his or her employment, unless the circumstances indicate that such efforts would be futile or result in retaliation. In cases involving allegations of sexual harassment, however, the claimant need not show that she took all or even reasonable steps to preserve her employment. The Division of Employment and Training review board, which granted Lawrie's (P) benefits, could reasonably conclude, based on the facts of the case, that Lawrie (P) left her employment because she was dissatisfied with the way her employer handled the sexual assault, and that her resignation was involuntary, with good cause attributable to Tri-County (D). But even under the more stringent requirement, Lawrie (P) would have sustained her burden, since Tri-County (D) was aware of the existence of the harassment, and it should have taken affirmative steps to transfer Lawrie (P) permanently to another job site. But the employer (D) made no such effort. District court affirmed.

▶ ANALYSIS

Note that the court uses "involuntary" in this case to mean that a reasonable person in the employee's situation would have seen no choice but to resign. It does not mean that she was involuntarily discharged by her employer, even though her resignation was accelerated by the employer. Note also that in many states, racial harassment, like sexual harassment, may constitute good cause for voluntary termination.

■═■

Quicknotes

BURDEN OF PROOF The duty of a party to introduce evidence to support a fact that is in dispute in an action.

GOOD CAUSE Sufficient justification for failure to perform an obligation imposed by law.

■═■

Pesce v. Board of Review

Employee (P) v. State employment office (D)

Ill. App. Ct., 515 N.E.2d 849 (1987).

NATURE OF CASE: Appeal from reversal of denial of unemployment benefits.

FACT SUMMARY: After Pesce (P) was discharged for backing his employer's vehicle into stationary objects four different times, his former employer objected to the district court's reversal of an administrative denial of Pesce's (P) request for unemployment insurance benefits.

🏛 RULE OF LAW
A justifiable discharge does not necessarily disqualify the discharged employee from receiving unemployment benefits.

FACTS: Pesce (P) worked as a driver of a medicar, transporting patients to and from hospitals and nursing homes, for about three and one-half months. During that time, he backed the vehicle into a stationary object four different times. There were no patients in the medicar at the time of these accidents, and none of the accidents caused severe damage. Pesce (P) was suspended from work for three days after the first accident and paid his employer for the damage after the second accident. He was again suspended after the third accident and was discharged after the fourth accident because his involvement in the accidents violated a company rule. Pesce's (P) union had a rule that provided for discharge after two accidents. Pesce's (P) application for unemployment insurance benefits was denied on the ground that his actions constituted misconduct within the meaning of the Unemployment Insurance Act (Act). After the Board of Review (Board) (D) affirmed that denial under § 602A of the Act, Pesce (P) appealed to the circuit court, which reversed, finding the Board's (D) decision incorrect as a matter of law. The Board (D) appealed.

ISSUE: Does a justifiable discharge necessarily disqualify the discharged employee from receiving unemployment benefits?

HOLDING AND DECISION: (Scariano, J.) No. A justifiable discharge does not necessarily disqualify the discharged employee from receiving unemployment benefits. Under the Act, misconduct must evince a willful or wanton disregard of the employer's interests, carelessness or negligence of such a degree or recurrence as to manifest equal culpability, wrongful intent or evil design, or an intentional and substantial disregard of an employer's interests or of a plaintiff's duties and obligations to his employer. Here, there was no showing of an unreasonable and improper course of conduct from which a lack of proper regard for the employer's interests could be imputed. The Board (D) mistakenly equated Pesce's (P) inability to back up the vehicle with gross indifference to the interests of his employer. Affirmed.

▶ ANALYSIS

Pesce (P) was discharged after four accidents rather than after two because it was company policy to allow leeway for accidents that were not the employee's fault. The court explained that a company rule governing the conduct or performance of any employee must be reasonable, and a breach of the rule must be shown to be deliberate or its equivalent. A Massachusetts case, *Cantres v. Director*, 396 Mass. 226, 484 N.E.2d 1336 (1985), shifted to employers the burden of persuading the fact finder that a dismissed employee's conduct evidenced "deliberate misconduct in willful disregard of the employing unit's interest."

Quicknotes

BURDEN OF PROOF The duty of a party to introduce evidence to support a fact that is in dispute in an action.

NEGLIGENCE Conduct falling below the standard of care that a reasonable person would demonstrate under similar conditions.

UNEMPLOYMENT Condition in which an individual is not employed.

WILLFUL AND WANTON MISCONDUCT Unlawful intentional or reckless conduct without regard to the consequences.

Amador v. Unemployment Insurance Appeals Board

Employee (P) v. State employment office (D)

Cal. Sup. Ct., 677 P.2d 224 (1984).

NATURE OF CASE: Appeal from denial of petition for writ of mandate to vacate ruling of ineligibility for unemployment benefits.

FACT SUMMARY: After Amador (P) was discharged from her employment as a histotechnician for refusing to perform a hospital-requested procedure, due to a good-faith belief that it would jeopardize the health of others, she applied for unemployment benefits, which were initially awarded and then denied on subsequent appeals.

🏛 RULE OF LAW
A worker who has been discharged for willfully refusing to perform work that she reasonably and in good faith believed would jeopardize the health of others has not committed misconduct disqualifying her from collecting unemployment insurance benefits.

FACTS: Amador (P), who was licensed as a histotechnician by the American Society of Clinical Pathologists, had worked in such capacity at hospitals operated by Stanford and Oxford Universities before being hired by San Mateo County Community Hospital (Chope) to prepare tissue samples for microscopic analysis by pathologists. On several occasions, two doctors at Chope asked Amador (P) to perform a procedure known as "grosscutting," which consists of the selection and removal of small tissue samples of approximately one centimeter in breadth from organs or other large (gross) specimens removed from a patient by a doctor. Amador (P) refused to perform grosscutting on tissue removed from live patients, believing that it exceeded her capabilities as a histotechnician and that such life-and-death matters should be handled by physicians or by specially trained technicians. Histotechnicians at Stanford and Oxford had not been permitted to perform grosscutting. Amador (P) was willing to perform grosscutting on organs taken from cadavers or to process small-size specimens selected and removed from live patients by doctors. Suspended for her refusal to perform the requested procedure, Amador (P) was eventually discharged for incompetence and insubordination. Unemployment benefits were initially awarded to her by a claims interviewer. Subsequent appeals, including one to the Unemployment Insurance Appeals Board (D), found that Amador's (P) deliberate violation of a reasonable order constituted misconduct within the meaning of § 1256 of the Unemployment Insurance Code. Amador's (P) petition to the superior court for a writ of mandate was denied. This appeal followed.

ISSUE: Has a worker who has been discharged for willfully refusing to perform work that she reasonably and in good faith believed would jeopardize the health of others

committed misconduct disqualifying her from collecting unemployment insurance benefits?

HOLDING AND DECISION: (Bird, C.J.) No. A worker who has been discharged for willfully refusing to perform work that she reasonably and in good faith believed would jeopardize the health of others has not committed misconduct disqualifying her from collecting unemployment insurance benefits. Mere inefficiency, unsatisfactory conduct, failure in good performance as the result of inability or incapacity, inadvertencies or ordinary negligence in isolated instances, or good-faith errors in judgment or discretion are not to be deemed misconduct within the meaning of the statute. Fault is the basic element to be considered in interpreting and applying the code sections on unemployment compensation. The determination of fault is not concluded by a finding that the discharge was justified. Benefits may not be denied solely on the basis of a good-faith error in judgment; a claimant's conduct must evince culpability or bad faith. Applying the substantial-evidence test, the record lacks sufficient evidence to support the denial of benefits. The duty to construe the code liberally to benefit the unemployed precludes the adoption of a draconian rule requiring an employee who reasonably and in good faith feared harm to herself or others to sacrifice her right to unemployment benefits because she acted on that concern. Reversed.

DISSENT: (Mosk, J.) The law does not permit a recalcitrant employee to dictate employment conditions in conflict with the job description pursuant to which she was hired.

▶ ANALYSIS

Section 1256 of the Code states: "An individual is disqualified for unemployment compensation benefits if the director finds that he or she left his or her most recent work voluntarily without good cause or that he or she has been discharged for misconduct connected with his or her most recent work." The term "misconduct," as used in the Code, is limited to conduct that is willful or wanton or rises to the level of an intentional or negligent disregard for the employer's interests. Moreover, in view of the statutory objective of reducing the hardship of unemployment, the concept of good cause cannot be arbitrarily limited. Account must be taken of real circumstances, substantial reasons, objective conditions, palpable forces that operate to produce correlative results, adequate excuses that will

Continued on next page.

bear the test of reason, just grounds for action, and, as always, the element of good faith.

■═■

Quicknotes

GOOD FAITH An honest intention to abstain from any unconscientious advantage of another.

UNEMPLOYMENT Condition in which an individual is not employed.

WILLFUL AND WANTON MISCONDUCT Unlawful intentional or reckless conduct without regard to the consequences.

■═■

Sauerland v. Florida Unemployment Appeals Commission

Unemployment claimant (P) v. Unemployment agency (D)

Fla. Dist. Ct. App., 923 So. 2d 1240 (2006).

NATURE OF CASE: Appeal of denial of unemployment compensation.

FACT SUMMARY: An employee who was discharged for falsifying work records was denied unemployment benefits for the misconduct. He appealed.

🏛 RULE OF LAW
Deliberate falsification of a state logbook, with knowledge that doing so violates employer policies, which provide justification for discharge, also warrants disqualification from unemployment compensation.

FACTS: Jason Sauerland (P) worked as a juvenile-detention officer for the state of Florida. He was required to perform ten-minute visual checks of each room he was assigned to monitor and to record those checks in a logbook. His duties were spelled out in the employee handbook, and he understood that failure to make the checks could result in discharge. Videotapes of Sauerland's (P) shifts showed that he was not making the checks that he was recording in the logbook, and he was fired. He applied for unemployment benefits and was denied, because he was fired for misconduct. He appealed.

ISSUE: Does deliberate falsification of a state logbook with knowledge that doing so violates employer policies, which provide justification for discharge, also warrant disqualification from unemployment compensation?

HOLDING AND DECISION: (Lewis, J.) Yes. Deliberate falsification of a state logbook, with knowledge that doing so violates employer policies, which provide justification for discharge, also warrants disqualification from unemployment compensation. The Florida Unemployment Appeals Commission (Commission) (D) found that Sauerland (P) was observed making his rounds at intervals in excess of ten minutes, that his log entries revealed at least two rounds that did not occur, and that his conduct falls squarely within the state's definition of "misconduct," which includes "conduct demonstrating willful or wanton disregard of an employer's interests and found to be a deliberate violation or disregard of the standards of behavior that the employer has a right to expect of his or her employees." Sauerland (P) also was aware of the employer's policy concerning the necessity to conduct rounds every ten minutes. Because the evidence supports the Commission's (D) findings, and the Commission properly interpreted the law in ruling that Sauerland (P) engaged in misconduct connected with work, the order is affirmed.

DISSENT: (Ervin, J.) Sauerland's (P) conduct that resulted in his discharge was an instance of poor judgment rather than misconduct warranting denial of benefits. He had no prior record of poor performance, and was not the subject of any warnings or disciplinary actions. Misconduct that justifies denial of unemployment benefits usually involves repeated violations of explicit policies after several warnings, and that is not present in this case, even though the employer may have had sufficient grounds to discharge Sauerland (P).

▶ ANALYSIS

The falsification of state records is a serious offense, and probably formed the basis of the court's decision in this case. Had he not falsified state records, the outcome might have been different and along the same lines as the dissent's.

■=■

Quicknotes

MISCONDUCT Conduct that is unlawful or otherwise improper.

■=■

Petty v. University of Delaware

Unemployment claimant (P) v. Employer (D)

Del. Sup. Ct., 450 A.2d 392 (1982).

NATURE OF CASE: Appeal of denial of unemployment benefits.

FACT SUMMARY: A female custodian whose job responsibility had to be severely restricted to accommodate a problematic pregnancy was placed on maternity leave, without pay, and then denied unemployment benefits. She appealed.

RULE OF LAW
A claimant in her second month of pregnancy and under doctor's orders not to lift, climb, or stand for prolonged periods is not "able to work" and is not "available for work" under the state unemployment-compensation law, and is therefore ineligible for unemployment compensation.

FACTS: Mercedes Petty (P) was a custodian for the University of Delaware (D), and while in her second month of pregnancy began to experience some health issues that prompted her doctor to recommend that she not lift, climb, or stand for prolonged periods. Her job classification required her to perform heavy cleaning tasks. The University (D) placed Petty (P) on maternity leave of absence for the duration of her doctor's medical restrictions, without pay, and on termination of her medical restrictions, she could return to work. She then applied for state unemployment compensation benefits, which were denied, because Delaware law requires that any claimant for unemployment benefits be "able to work" and "available for work." The trial court affirmed the unemployment commission's findings.

ISSUE: Is a claimant in her second month of pregnancy and under doctor's orders not to lift, climb, or stand for prolonged periods not "able to work" and not "available for work" under the state unemployment-compensation law, and therefore ineligible for unemployment compensation?

HOLDING AND DECISION: (Horsey, J.) No. A claimant in her second month of pregnancy and under doctor's orders not to lift, climb, or stand for prolonged periods is not "able to work" and is not "available for work" under the state unemployment-compensation law and is therefore ineligible for unemployment compensation. The board correctly found that due to her medical condition, Petty (P) was not able to perform any job for which she was qualified. An individual seeking benefits is "available for work" only to the extent that she is willing, able, and ready to accept employment that she has no good cause to refuse. Due to her physical condition, she was unable to perform her normal job functions. She also lacked training to do other work that did not require standing for a prolonged period. Affirmed.

ANALYSIS

Despite the valid reasoning in this case, the rule puts a woman experiencing a troublesome pregnancy with limited skills relevant to the job market at a severe disadvantage, since under the circumstances, she has no way to generate income.

Quicknotes

GOOD CAUSE Sufficient justification for failure to perform an obligation imposed by law.

Lester v. Department of Employment Security

Unemployment claimant (P) v. State employment agency (D)

Ill. App. Ct., 819 N.E.2d 1143 (2004).

NATURE OF CASE: Appeal of denial of unemployment compensation.

FACT SUMMARY: Following a layoff, a supermarket employee was denied unemployment compensation because she refused to accept a job that was similar to her previous position, and which paid the same as her previous position.

RULE OF LAW
An individual is ineligible for benefits if she fails, without good cause, to accept suitable work when offered.

FACTS: Susan Lester (P), who worked in a supermarket 1.3 miles from her home, was laid off when her job was phased out. She received severance pay for four months. While receiving severance, she was offered a position at another office, which was located 30 miles from her home, which paid the same amount she received prior to her layoff. She refused the position. She applied for unemployment compensation, and was denied. She argued on appeal that the circuit court erred in affirming the Illinois Department of Employment Security's (D) decision because it was based on erroneous factual findings and errors of law.

ISSUE: Is an individual ineligible for benefits if she fails, without good cause, to accept suitable work when offered?

HOLDING AND DECISION: (South, J.) Yes. An individual is ineligible for benefits if she fails, without good cause, to accept suitable work when offered. A claimant who refuses a job offer with suitable wages and conditions is not deemed involuntarily unemployed, but unemployed by his own choosing, thereby making her ineligible for unemployment compensation. A refusal to work must be supported by real, substantial, and reasonable circumstances and cannot be predicated on mere inconvenience. In this case, Lester (P) was offered the same salary as her previous position, more than other employees in a similar job, and the additional travel time, working 40 instead of 35 hours per week, and added managerial responsibility do not make the offered position unsuitable. Affirmed.

▶ ANALYSIS

This case clearly illustrates that some additional responsibility and travel time are not enough to warrant the refusal of a job, and still preserve eligibility for unemployment benefits. The facts would change the outcome, if, for example, Lester (P) was not able to get to the new location by driving or public transportation.

■▬■

Quicknotes

GOOD CAUSE Sufficient justification for failure to perform an obligation imposed by law.

■▬■

Quick Reference Rules of Law

Solon v. Gary Community School Corp.

Class of teachers approaching retirement (P) v. School system (D)

180 F.3d 844 (7th Cir. 1999).

NATURE OF CASE: Appeal of finding of age discrimination.

FACT SUMMARY: Gary Community School Corp. (D) appealed a federal district court's finding that its incentive plan on its face violated the Age Discrimination in Employment Act, arguing that older workers were free to take or leave the retirement incentives offered.

🏛 RULE OF LAW
Early retirement incentives that give greater monetary rewards to teachers who elect to retire at age 58 than those who retire at age 61 violate the Age Discrimination in Employment Act.

FACTS: Following a one-third drop in student enrollment between 1970 and 1984, the school system in Gary, Ind., (D) began laying-off teachers and administrators. In 1982, the local teachers' union proposed that the schools adopt an early retirement incentive plan. The plan's goal was to encourage teachers at the top of the pay scale to retire sooner than they otherwise would have, enabling the schools to retain more teachers who were paid less and had less seniority. Under the plan, teachers who retired on their 58th birthday would receive 48 incentive payments, and those retiring at later ages would receive fewer incentives, up to age 62. A teacher who chose to retire at 62 would get no incentives. The 34 plaintiffs were teachers and administrators who had not yet reached age 58 when the incentive plan was put in place. Because the incentive payments ended when employees reached age 62, the plaintiffs claimed the incentive plan violated the Age Discrimination in Employment Act (ADEA) because it treated persons differently and detrimentally because of their age. The trial court found for the plaintiffs. Gary Schools appealed the court's finding that the Early Retirement Incentive Plain (ERIP) was discriminatory.

ISSUE: Do early retirement incentives that give greater financial rewards to teachers who elect to retire at age 58 than those who retire at age 61 violate the ADEA?

HOLDING AND DECISION: (Rovner, J.) Yes. Early retirement incentives that give greater financial rewards to teachers who elect to retire at age 58 than those who retire at age 61 violate the ADEA. The terms of the incentive plan explicitly establish an employee's eligibility for the early retirement incentives based on his age. The plans are therefore discriminatory on their face. "Bridge" payments, which help span the gap between an employee's age at early retirement and the age at which the employee becomes eligible for reduced or unreduced Social Security benefits, are allowed under ADEA. But in this case, there is no connection between the incentive plan payments and Social Security benefits that early retirees could expect to receive at age 62, when the incentive payments stop.

▶ ANALYSIS

The discrimination inherent in the incentive plan is best illustrated in the court's example of the harm. The plan, the court said, "would permit a 58-year-old teacher with plans to retire at age 62 to retire immediately and receive four years of incentive payments. Yet a 66-year-old teacher with plans to retire at age seventy, but otherwise identically situated with her younger colleague ... would receive nothing if she chose to retire at once, notwithstanding that her retirement would be just as premature as that of her 58-year-old colleague." Individuals like the more senior teacher in the example, the court said, "suffer a concrete injury by virtue of the express terms of the [incentive plan], just as surely as they would if their age disqualified them from receiving performance bonuses, wage increases, or promotions."

■═■

Quicknotes

DISCRIMINATION Unequal treatment of a class of persons.

■═■

LaRue v. DeWolff, Boberg & Associates, Inc.

Individual (P) v. Corporation (D)

552 U.S. 248 (2008).

NATURE OF CASE: Appeal from granting of judgment on the pleadings to the defendant.

FACT SUMMARY: An individual participant in a defined contribution pension plan brought suit under the Employee Retirement Income Security Act of 1974 (ERISA) for breach of a fiduciary duty by a plan administrator.

RULE OF LAW

Under ERISA, an individual may bring a claim for breach of a fiduciary duty that allegedly impaired the plan value of that individual participant's account within a defined contribution pension plan.

FACTS: LaRue (P) is a former employee of DeWolff, Boberg & Associates, Inc. (DeWolff) (D) and had a 401(K) through DeWolff in the form of a defined contribution plan. The Plan allowed LaRue (P) to direct the investments of his contributions. In 2001 and 2002, LaRue (P) alleged he requested investment changes to his plan that were never made. He contends this failure constituted a breach of a fiduciary duty and cost him $150,000 in lost interest. LaRue (P) brought suit under § 502(a)(2) of ERISA against DeWolf (D) and the plan administrator for a violation of § 409 of ERISA. Section 409 imposes fiduciary duties upon plan administrators related to the proper management, administration and investment of fund assets. The federal district court granted DeWolff's (D) judgment on the pleadings and the Fourth Circuit affirmed. LaRue (P) appealed to the United States Supreme Court.

ISSUE: Under ERISA, may an individual bring a claim for breach of a fiduciary duty that allegedly impaired the plan value of that individual participant's account within a defined contribution pension plan?

HOLDING AND DECISION: (Stevens, J.) Yes. Under ERISA, an individual may bring a claim for breach of a fiduciary duty that allegedly impaired the plan value of that individual participant's account within a defined contribution pension plan. In *Massachusetts Mut. Life Ins. Co. v. Russell*, 473 U.S. 134 (1985), this Court held that ERISA did not allow an individual participant in a defined benefit plan to bring her own action to recover for consequential damages arising out of the delay in processing the plaintiff's claim. *Russell* is easily distinguished. When *Russell* was decided, most employees were in defined benefit plans, where the participants did not have individual accounts. In *Russell*, the employee's disability plan would simply pay a fixed benefit amount based upon the employee's salary. Accordingly, disallowing an individual claim made sense because the plan administrators owed a fiduciary duty to the plan as a whole. Moreover, in *Russell*, the plaintiff received her disability benefits, but was seeking consequential damages beyond the scope of recovery allowed by ERISA. A defined contribution plan is different. In defined contribution plans, employees have individual accounts and have discretion as to the size of their contributions and how they are invested. Accordingly, a fiduciary's duty is to the plan and to each participant. Because a fiduciary may act in a way that could harm the plan assets of an individual, such conduct falls under § 409. Accordingly, an individual in a defined contribution plan may bring an action for violation of § 409 to recover for breaches that impair the plan assets within the individual's account. Reversed and remanded.

ANALYSIS

In his concurrence not available in the text, Justice Roberts noted that ERISA does have a separate provision, § 502(a)(1)(B), that allows plan participants to bring direct claims for benefits due to them under the plan, rather than for a breach of fiduciary duty pursuant to § 502(a)(2). The significance is that under § 502(a)(1)(B), participants must exhaust their administration remedies prior to filing suit.

Quicknotes

BREACH OF FIDUCIARY DUTY The failure of a fiduciary to observe the standard of care exercised by professionals of similar education and experience.

EMPLOYEE RETIREMENT INCOME SECURITY ACT OF 1974 (ERISA) Federal law of employee benefits which establishes minimum standards to protect employees from breach of benefit promises made by employers.

Varity Corp. v. Howe

Employer (D) v. Employees (P)

516 U.S. 489 (1996).

NATURE OF CASE: Appeal of judgment for employees.

FACT SUMMARY: An employer deceived employees about the financial health of a benefit plan that the employer encouraged the employees to adopt. The employees sued the employer under Employee Retirement Income Security Act (ERISA).

RULE OF LAW
An employer that administers its own ERISA-backed employee benefit plan violates the fiduciary obligations that ERISA imposes upon plan administrators by deliberately misleading the beneficiaries.

FACTS: Charles Howe (P) and others used to work for Massey-Ferguson, Inc., a farm equipment manufacturer, and a wholly owned subsidiary of the Varity Corporation (D). These employees all participated in Massey-Ferguson's self-funded employee welfare benefit plan, an ERISA-protected plan that Massey-Ferguson administered itself. When certain divisions in Massey-Ferguson stared losing money, Varity (D) decided to transfer them to a separately incorporated subsidiary, Massey Combines. Varity (D) persuaded the employees (P) of the failing divisions to change employers and benefit plans, conveying the message that employees' (P) benefits would remain secure when they transferred. Ultimately, the employees (P) lost their non-pension benefits. The employees filed an action under ERISA, claiming that Varity (D) deceived them into withdrawing from their old plan and forfeiting their benefits. The district court found that Varity (D) and Massey-Ferguson, acting as ERISA fiduciaries, had harmed plan beneficiaries through deliberate deception.

ISSUE: Does an employer that administers its own ERISA-backed employee benefit plan violate the fiduciary obligations that ERISA imposes upon plan administrators by deliberately misleading the beneficiaries?

HOLDING AND DECISION: (Breyer, J.) Yes. An employer that administers its own ERISA-backed employee benefit plan violates the fiduciary obligations that ERISA imposes upon plan administrators by deliberately misleading the beneficiaries. Under the specific factual circumstances, Varity (D) and Massey-Ferguson acted in their capacity as an ERISA fiduciary and violated the fiduciary obligations imposed on them by ERISA by knowingly and significantly deceiving the employees as to the financial viability of the new entity and the future of the new entity's benefits plan, in order to save the employer money at the expense of the beneficiaries; they could thus be sued for

equitable relief by the individual beneficiaries. District court affirmed.

► ANALYSIS

Note that employers usually are not fiduciaries with respect to the plans that they create, but become fiduciaries when they become administrators of the plan. Plans that have no named administrator have the employer as administrator by default.

Quicknotes

BREACH OF FIDUCIARY DUTY The failure of a fiduciary to observe the standard of care exercised by professionals of similar education and experience.

Pension Benefit Guaranty Corp. v. LTV Corp.

Federal government corporation (D) v. Employer (P)

496 U.S. 633 (1990).

NATURE OF CASE: Appeal from decision disallowing restoration of employee pension plan after termination under the Employee Retirement Income Security Act (ERISA).

FACT SUMMARY: Upon determining that the financial factors on which it had relied in terminating LTV Corporation's (P) employment pension plans had changed significantly, the Pension Benefit Guaranty Corporation (D) used its power under ERISA to restore those terminated plans.

RULE OF LAW

The Pension Benefit Guaranty Corporation is authorized to take such action as may be necessary to restore a pension plan terminated under ERISA to its pretermination status, reinstating full benefits and transferring responsibility for the plan's unfunded liabilities back to the employer.

FACTS: Title IV of ERISA includes a mandatory government insurance program that protects the pension benefits of over 30 million private-sector American workers who participate in plans covered by the Title. The Pension Benefit Guaranty Corporation (D) (PBGC) has the power, under § 4042 of ERISA, to terminate a plan "involuntarily" under specified circumstances, notwithstanding the existence of a collective-bargaining agreement. Termination can also be undone by the PBGC (D) under § 4047 of ERISA. LTV Corp. (P) and many of its subsidiaries filed petitions for reorganization under Chapter 11 of the Bankruptcy Code. One of LTV's (P) principal goals in filing the bankruptcy petitions was the restructuring of its three pension obligations, a goal that could be accomplished if the plans were terminated and responsibility for the unfunded liabilities was placed on the PBGC (D). By late 1986, the plans had unfunded liabilities for promised benefits of almost $2.3 billion. Approximately $2.1 billion of this amount was covered by PBGC (D) insurance. However, LTV (P) could not voluntarily terminate the plans because two of them had been negotiated in collective bargaining. Determining that the plans should be terminated in order to protect the insurance program from the unreasonable risk of large losses, PBGC (D) commenced termination proceedings in the district court. With LTV's (P) consent, the plans were terminated effective January 13, 1987. PBGC (D) later objected to new pension agreements between LTV (P) and the unions as follow-on plans, which placed retired participants in substantially the same positions they would have been in had the old plans never been terminated. The PBGC's (D) policy against follow-on plans stemmed from its belief that such plans were "abusive" of the insurance program and resulted in the PBGC's (D) subsidizing an employer's ongoing pension program in a way not contemplated by Title IV. Believing that the steel industry was experiencing a dramatic turnaround and concluding that LTV (P) no longer faced the imminent risk of large unfunded liabilities stemming from plant shutdowns, the PBGC (D) issued a notice of restoration of the terminated plans under § 4047 of ERISA. The court of appeals held that the restoration decision was arbitrary and capricious under the Administrative Procedure Act (APA) because the PBGC (D) did not take account of all the areas of law the court deemed relevant to the restoration decision, namely, bankruptcy and labor law. The PBGC (D) contended that the court of appeals misapplied the general rule that an agency must take into consideration all relevant factors by requiring the agency explicitly to consider and discuss labor and bankruptcy law. This appeal followed.

ISSUE: Is the PBGC authorized to take such action as may be necessary to restore a pension plan terminated under ERISA to its pretermination status, reinstating full benefits and transferring responsibility for the plan's unfunded liabilities back to the employer?

HOLDING AND DECISION: (Blackmun, J.) Yes. The PBGC (D) is authorized to take such action as may be necessary to restore a pension plan terminated under ERISA to its pretermination status, reinstating full benefits and transferring responsibility for the plan's unfunded liabilities back to the employer. The requirement imposed by the court of appeals upon the PBGC (D) cannot be reconciled with the plain language of § 4047, under which the PBGC (D) was operating here. The statute does not direct the PBGC (D) to make restoration decisions that further the "public interest" generally but rather empowers the agency to restore when restoration would further the interests that Title IV of ERISA is designed to protect. Moreover, because the PBGC (D) can claim no expertise in the labor and bankruptcy areas, it may be ill-equipped to undertake the difficult task of discerning and applying the "policies and goals" of those fields. In addition, the PBGC's (D) construction based upon its conclusion that the existence of follow-on plans will lead to more plan terminations and increased PBGC (D) liabilities is "assuredly a permissible one." The PBGC's (D) failure to consider all potentially relevant areas of law did not render its restoration decision arbitrary and capricious.

Continued on next page.

Furthermore, its anti-follow-on policy, an asserted basis for the restoration decision, is not contrary to clear congressional intent and is based on a permissible construction of § 4047. Finally, the procedures employed by the PBGC (D) are consistent with the APA. Reversed and remanded.

DISSENT: (Stevens, J.) Unless there was a sufficient improvement in LTV's (P) financial condition to justify the restoration order, it should be set aside. Furthermore, the follow-on plans are wholly consistent with the purposes of ERISA.

▶ *ANALYSIS*

The Court noted that in enacting Title IV, Congress sought to ensure that employees and their beneficiaries would not be completely "deprived of anticipated retirement benefits by the termination of pension plans before sufficient funds have been accumulated in the plans." Title IV covers virtually all "defined benefit" pension plans sponsored by private employers. A defined benefit plan is one that promises to pay employees, upon retirement, a fixed benefit under a formula that takes into account factors such as final salary and years of service with the employer. It is distinguished from a "defined contribution" plan, which ERISA insurance does not cover because employees are not promised any particular level of benefits, only that they will receive the balances in their individual accounts.

▪══▪

Quicknotes

ADMINISTRATIVE PROCEDURE ACT Enacted in 1946 to govern practices and proceedings before federal administrative agencies.

▪══▪

City of Los Angeles v. Manhart

Department of Water and Power (D) v. Female employee (P)

435 U.S. 702 (1978).

NATURE OF CASE: Appeal from decision favoring employees in an employment discrimination action related to pension benefits.

FACT SUMMARY: Because the Los Angeles Department of Water and Power (Department) (D) required its female employees to make higher monthly contributions to the employee retirement fund than male employees, due to the fact that women as a class live longer than men, Manhart (P), on behalf of women employed or formerly employed by the Department (D), sought an injunction and restitution of excess contributions.

🏛 RULE OF LAW
It is unlawful to discriminate against any individual with respect to compensation, terms, conditions, or privileges of employment on the basis of race, color, religion, sex, or national origin.

FACTS: Based on a study of mortality tables and its own experience that women, as a class, live longer than men, the Los Angeles Department of Water and Power (Department) (D) required its female employees to make larger contributions to its pension fund than its male employees. Benefits under the Department's (D) retirement plan were funded entirely by contributions from the employees and the Department (D), augmented by the income earned on those contributions. No private insurance company was involved in the administration or payment of benefits. Because employee contributions were withheld from paychecks, a female employee took home less pay than a male employee earning the same salary. Since the effective date of the Equal Employment Opportunity Act of 1972, the Department (D) has been an employer within the meaning of Title VII of the Civil Rights Act of 1964. In 1973, Manhart (P) brought this suit in the district court on behalf of a class of women employed or formerly employed by the Department (D). The suit prayed for an injunction and restitution of excess contributions.

ISSUE: Is it unlawful to discriminate against any individual with respect to compensation, terms, conditions, or privileges of employment on the basis of race, color, religion, sex, or national origin?

HOLDING AND DECISION: (Stevens, J.) Yes. It is unlawful to discriminate against any individual with respect to compensation, terms, conditions, or privileges of employment on the basis of race, color, religion, sex, or national origin. It is now well recognized that employment decisions cannot be predicated on mere "stereotyped"

impressions about the characteristics of males or females. This case, however, involves a generalization that the parties accept as unquestionably true: women as a class do live longer than men. It is equally true, however, that all individuals in the respective classes do not share the characteristic that differentiates the average class representatives. Many women do not live as long as the average man; and many men outlive the average woman. The question, therefore, is whether the existence or nonexistence of "discrimination" is to be determined by comparison of class characteristics or individual characteristics. The statute's focus on the individual is unambiguous. It precludes treatment of individuals as simply components of a racial, religious, sexual, or national class. Even a true generalization about the class is an insufficient reason for disqualifying an individual to whom the generalization does not apply. That proposition is of critical importance in this case because there is no assurance that any individual woman working for the Department (D) will actually fit the generalization on which the Department's (D) policy is based. A statute that was designed to make race irrelevant in the employment market could not reasonably be construed to permit a take-home pay differential based on a gender classification. Even if the statutory language were less clear, the basic policy of the statute requires that the focus be on individuals rather than on fairness to classes. Individual risks, like individual performance, may not be predicted by resort to classifications proscribed by Title VII. The Department's (D) practice constitutes discrimination and is unlawful unless exempted by the Equal Pay Act of 1963 or some other affirmative justification.

▶ ANALYSIS

The Court observed that it was true that while contributions were being collected from the employees, the Department (D) could not know which individuals would predecease the average woman. Therefore, according to the Department (D), unless women as a class were assessed an extra charge, they would be subsidized, to some extent, by the class of male employees. However, the size of the subsidy involved in this case is open to doubt because the Department's (D) plan provided for survivors' benefits, and female spouses of male employees were likely to have greater life expectancies than the male spouses of female employees.

■▬■

Continued on next page.

Quicknotes

GENDER DISCRIMINATION Unequal treatment of individuals without justification on the basis of their sex.

TITLE VII OF THE CIVIL RIGHTS ACT OF 1964 States that it shall be an unlawful employment practice for an employer to fail or refuse to hire or otherwise discriminate against any individual with respect to his employment because of such individual's race, color, religion, sex, or national origin.

■══■

Flemming v. Nestor

Secretary of Health, Education, and Welfare (D) v. Retiree (P)

363 U.S. 603 (1960).

NATURE OF CASE: Direct appeal from decision holding § 202(n) of the Social Security Act unconstitutional.

FACT SUMMARY: After Nestor's (P) Social Security old-age benefits were discontinued when he was deported as an alien who had once been a member of the Communist Party, he challenged the constitutionality of the section of the Act that allowed termination of those benefits.

🏛 RULE OF LAW
Old-age, survivor, and disability insurance benefits payable to an alien individual who is deported after September 1, 1954, under the Immigration and Nationality Act for having been a member of the Communist Party may be terminated.

FACTS: Nestor (P), an alien, immigrated to the United States from Bulgaria in 1913, becoming eligible for old-age benefits in November 1955. In July 1956, he was deported for having been a member of the Communist Party from 1933 to 1939. Soon after Nestor (P) was deported, his benefits were terminated, and notice of termination was given to his wife, who had remained in the United States. Membership in the Communist Party was one of the benefit-termination deportation grounds specified in § 202(n) of the Social Security Act. The district court held that § 202(n) was unconstitutional, and Flemming (D), Secretary of Health, Education, and Welfare, appealed directly to the Supreme Court.

ISSUE: May old-age, survivor, and disability insurance benefits payable to an alien individual who is deported after September 1, 1954, under the Immigration and Nationality Act for having been a member of the Communist Party be terminated?

HOLDING AND DECISION: (Harlan, J.) Yes. Old-age, survivor, and disability insurance benefits payable to an alien individual who is deported after September 1, 1954, under the Immigration and Nationality Act for having been a member of the Communist Party may be terminated. The district court erred in holding that § 202(n) deprived Nestor (P) of an "accrued property right." Nestor's (P) right to Social Security benefits cannot properly be considered to have been of that order. To engraft upon the Social Security System a concept of "accrued property rights" would deprive it of the flexibility and boldness in adjustment to ever changing conditions that it demands. It was doubtless out of an awareness of the need for such flexibility that Congress included in the original Act, and has since retained, a clause expressly reserving to it "the right to alter, amend, or repeal any provision" of the Act. Thus, a person covered by the Act does not have a right to benefit payments as would make every defeasance of "accrued" interests violative of the Due Process Clause of the Fifth Amendment. This is not to say, however, that Congress may exercise its power to modify the statutory scheme free of all constitutional restraint. The interest of a covered employee under the Act is of sufficient substance to fall within the protection from arbitrary governmental action afforded by the Due Process Clause. When dealing with a withholding of a noncontractual benefit under a social welfare program such as this, the Due Process Clause can interpose a bar only if the statute manifests a patently arbitrary classification, utterly lacking in rational justification. Such is not the case here. The sanction here is the mere denial of a noncontractual governmental benefit, and no affirmative disability or restraint is imposed. Reversed.

DISSENT: (Black, J.) This action takes Nestor's (P) insurance without just compensation and in violation of the Due Process Clause of the Fifth Amendment. The fact that the Court is sustaining this action indicates the extent to which people are willing to go these days to overlook violation of the Constitution perpetrated against anyone who has ever even innocently belonged to the Communist Party.

▶ ANALYSIS

In explaining why Social Security old-age benefits do not represent "accrued property rights," the majority observed that each worker's benefits, though flowing from the contributions he made to the national economy while actively employed, are not dependent on the degree to which he was called upon to support the system by taxation. Thus, the noncontractual interest of an employee covered by the Act cannot be soundly analogized to that of the holder of an annuity, whose right to benefits is bottomed on his contractual premium payments. In his dissenting opinion, Justice Black noted that the section of the Act under which Nestor's (P) benefits were terminated was passed 15 years after he had last been a Communist and 18 years after he began to make payments into the federal old-age and survivors' insurance trust fund.

■◼◼

Continued on next page.

Quicknotes

DUE PROCESS CLAUSE Clauses, found in the Fifth and Fourteenth Amendments to the United States Constitution, providing that no person shall be deprived of "life, liberty, or property, without due process of law."

SOCIAL SECURITY ACT Federal law creating the Social Security Administration, which is charged with the administration of a national program where contributions from employers and employees are held until the worker retires or is disabled, at which time they are paid out.

■━■

United States Railroad Retirement Board v. Fritz

Employer (D) v. Employee (P)

449 U.S. 166 (1980).

NATURE OF CASE: Appeal from finding of unconstitutionality of § 231b(h) of the Railroad Retirement Act of 1974.

FACT SUMMARY: When Congress restructured the railroad retirement system to eventually eliminate "windfall" benefits to railroad employees who were eligible for retirement benefits under both the railroad retirement system and Social Security, Fritz (P) and other railroad employees sought a declaratory judgment that § 231b(h) of the Railroad Retirement Act of 1974 was unconstitutional.

🏛 RULE OF LAW
Railroad benefits, like Social Security benefits, are not property since they are not contractual and may be altered or even eliminated at any time.

FACTS: The Railroad Retirement Act of 1974 (Act) fundamentally restructured the railroad retirement system. Under the prior statute, a person who worked for both railroad and nonrailroad employers and who qualified for railroad retirement benefits and Social Security benefits received retirement benefits under both systems and an accompanying "windfall" benefit. The payment of windfall benefits threatened the railroad retirement system with bankruptcy by 1981. Congress therefore determined to place the system on a "sound financial basis" by eliminating future accruals of those benefits. Congress also enacted various transitional provisions, including a grandfather provision, § 231b(h), which expressly preserved windfall benefits for some classes of employees. In restructuring the Act, Congress divided employees into various groups for the purpose of eventually phasing out the windfall benefits. However, the retirement rights of railroad workers that had become "legally vested" were preserved. An employee who was fully insured under both the railroad and Social Security systems as of the changeover date was deemed to have "legally vested rights." In other words, Congress made a choice as to where the line was to be drawn for the purpose of eliminating windfall benefits over the course of time. Fritz (P) and others filed this class action in the district court, seeking a declaratory judgment that § 231b(h) was unconstitutional under the Due Process Clause of the Fifth Amendment because it irrationally distinguished between classes of annuitants. The Railroad Retirement Board (D) contended that the classification was not arbitrary because it was an attempt to protect the relative equities of employees and to provide benefits to career railroad employees. The district court held the section unconstitutional, and this appeal followed.

ISSUE: Are railroad benefits, like Social Security benefits, not property since they are not contractual and may be altered or even eliminated at any time?

HOLDING AND DECISION: (Rehnquist, J.) Yes. Railroad benefits, like Social Security benefits, are not property since they are not contractual and may be altered or even eliminated at any time. The plain language of § 231b(h) marks the beginning and end of this Court's inquiry. There, Congress determined that some of those who in the past received full windfall benefits would not continue to do so. Because Congress could have eliminated windfall benefits for all classes of employees, it is not constitutionally impermissible for Congress to have drawn lines between groups of employees for the purpose of phasing out those benefits. The only remaining question is whether Congress achieved its purpose in a patently arbitrary or irrational way. The only eligible former railroad employees denied full windfall benefits are those, like Fritz (P), who had no statutory entitlement to dual benefits at the time they left the railroad industry but thereafter became eligible for Social Security benefits. Congress could properly conclude that persons who had actually acquired statutory entitlement to windfall benefits while still employed in the railroad industry had a greater equitable claim to those benefits than the members of Fritz's (P) class who were no longer in railroad employment when they became eligible for dual benefits. The task of classifying persons for benefits inevitably requires that some persons who have an almost equally strong claim to favored treatment be placed on different sides of the line, and the fact the line might have been drawn differently at some points is a matter for legislative, rather than judicial, consideration. Moreover, the distinctions drawn in § 231b(h) do not burden fundamental constitutional rights or create "suspect" classifications, such as race or national origin. The language of the statute is clear, and it must be assumed that Congress intended what it enacted. Reversed.

CONCURRENCE: (Stevens, J.) Congress had a duty to eliminate no more vested benefits than necessary to achieve its fiscal purpose. The timing of the employees' railroad service is a "reasonable basis" for the classification as well as a "ground of difference having a fair and substantial relation to the object of the legislation."

Continued on next page.

DISSENT: (Brennan, J.) As the legislative history repeatedly states, equity and fairness demand that Fritz (P), like his coworkers, retain the vested dual benefits he earned prior to 1974. A conscientious application of rational basis scrutiny demands, therefore, that § 231b(h) be invalidated.

▶ ANALYSIS

Persons who split their employment between railroad and nonrailroad employment received dual benefits in excess of the amount they would have received had they not split their employment. For example, if ten years of either railroad or nonrailroad employment would produce a monthly benefit of $300, an additional ten years of the same employment at the same level of creditable compensation would not double that benefit but would increase it by some lesser amount to, say, $500. If that 20 years had been divided equally between railroad and nonrailroad employment, however, the Social Security benefit and the railroad retirement benefit would each be $300, thus producing a $100 "windfall" benefit. Under a prior agreement between Social Security and the railroad, the entire cost of the windfall benefits was being borne by the railroad system.

■══■

Quicknotes

DUE PROCESS CLAUSE Clauses, found in the Fifth and Fourteenth Amendments to the United States Constitution, providing that no person shall be deprived of "life, liberty, or property, without due process of law."

GRANDFATHER CLAUSE An exception to a new law or regulation, exempting those already doing something to continue to do it, even though the activity is contrary to the new law or regulation.

■══■

Califano v. Goldfarb

Secretary of HEW (D) v. Employee's widow (P)

430 U.S. 199 (1977).

NATURE OF CASE: Appeal from denial of application for widower's benefits.

FACT SUMMARY: When Goldfarb's (P) application for widower's benefits under the Federal Old-Age, Survivors, and Disability Insurance Benefits program was denied, Goldfarb (P) appealed.

> 🏛 **RULE OF LAW**
> Gender-based differentiation that results in less protection for the spouses of female workers required to pay Social Security taxes than the protection provided for the spouses of men required to pay Social Security taxes violates the Fifth Amendment.

FACTS: Hannah Goldfarb worked as a secretary in the New York City public school system for almost 25 years until her death. During that entire time, she paid in full all Social Security taxes required by the Federal Insurance Contributions Act (FICA). When she died, her 72-year-old husband, Leon Goldfarb (P), who was a retired federal employee, applied for widower's benefits under the Federal Old-Age, Survivors, and Disability Insurance Benefits (OASDI) program. His application was denied on the ground that he did not meet one of the requirements for such entitlement because he had not been receiving at least half of his support from his wife when she died. Califano (D), Secretary of HEW, contended that "the denial of benefits reflected the congressional judgment that [because] aged widowers as a class were sufficiently likely not to be dependent upon their wives . . . it was appropriate to deny them benefits unless they were in fact dependent." Goldfarb (P) appealed.

ISSUE: Does gender-based differentiation that results in less protection for the spouses of female workers required to pay Social Security taxes than the protection provided for the spouses of men required to pay Social Security taxes violate the Fifth Amendment?

HOLDING AND DECISION: (Brennan, J.) Yes. Gender-based differentiation that results in less protection for the spouses of female workers required to pay Social Security taxes than the protection provided for the spouses of men required to pay Social Security taxes violates the Fifth Amendment. The gender-based distinction made by § 402(f)(1)(D) operates to deprive women of protection for their families, which men receive as a result of their employment. The differential treatment of nondependent widows and widowers results from an intention to aid the dependent spouses of deceased wage earners, coupled with a presumption that wives are usually dependent. The only

conceivable justification for writing the presumption of wives' dependency into the statute is the assumption that it would save the government time, money, and effort simply to pay benefits to all widows rather than to require proof of dependency of both sexes. Such assumptions do not suffice to justify a gender-based discrimination in the distribution of employment-related benefits and violate the Due Process Clause of the Fifth Amendment. Affirmed.

CONCURRENCE: (Stevens, J.) This discrimination against a group of males is merely the accidental byproduct of a traditional way of thinking about females.

▌ ANALYSIS

In response to the instant case, Congress repealed the dependency requirement for widowers and husbands. However, the government pensions of retired federal and state workers were to be offset by what they would receive as a spouse of a deceased Social Security recipient. Not providing for such an offset would have created a fiscal problem for the Social Security trust fund. The end of this particular gender-based discrimination was phased in over a five-year period.

∎▬∎

Quicknotes

DISCRIMINATION Unequal treatment of individuals without justification.

DUE PROCESS CLAUSE Clauses, found in the Fifth and Fourteenth Amendments to the United States Constitution, providing that no person shall be deprived of "life, liberty, or property, without due process of law."

∎▬∎

Vallone v. CNA Financial Corp.

Employees (P) v. Employer (D)

375 F.3d 623 (7th Cir. 2004).

NATURE OF CASE: Appeal of judgment for employer.

FACT SUMMARY: An employer reneged on a welfare benefit, and those employees who retired early and depended on the benefit sued the employer.

🏛 RULE OF LAW
An employer does not violate the Employee Retirement Income Security Act (ERISA) by terminating retirees' "lifetime" health-care benefits that were offered through an early retirement program.

FACTS: Continental Insurance Company (Continental) offered a voluntary special retirement program to employees who had 85 years of combined age and service. The special program included a monthly health-care allowance, which represented, employees were told both orally and in writing, a "lifetime benefit." Employees were not told that the benefits were irrevocable. The plaintiffs are the Continental employees (P) who accepted early retirement under the special program in early 1992. The health-care allowance was also offered to retirees (P) who were not part of the special program, but who retired under the company's normal retirement plan. Continental's normal retirement plan included a reservation of rights clause that gave the employer the power to amend or revoke benefits at any time, before or after retirement. This reservation of rights clause was incorporated into the early retirement program, even though the program documents did not contain the clause, since the early retirement program modified the employer's normal retirement plan and did not purport to stand as a separate plan. Continental was acquired by CNA Financial Corp. (D) in 1995. In 1998, CNA (D) informed all early retirees that the health-care allowance would be terminated.

ISSUE: Does an employer violate ERISA by terminating retirees' "lifetime" health-care benefits that were offered through an early retirement program?

HOLDING AND DECISION: (Cudahy, J.) No. An employer does not violate ERISA by terminating retirees' "lifetime" health-care benefits that were offered through an early retirement program. Under ERISA, employers are generally free to adopt, modify, or terminate welfare plans at any time for any reason. The presumption is against the vesting of welfare benefits—welfare benefits vest only if plan documents state in clear and express language that the benefit is vested. The health-care allowance was a welfare benefit, not a pension benefit, and no documents stated in clear and express language that the

benefit was vested. In addition, the normal retirement-plan documents contained a reservation of rights clause that stated that Continental could amend, revoke, or suspend coverage at any time, even after retirement. The benefits in the early retirement program were subject to the reservation of rights clause in the normal retirement-plan documents. The retirement-program documents made clear that the normal retirement plan was the baseline program to which the program's enhancements would be made. In addition, the retirement-program's covering memo specifically incorporated the normal retirement plan and its reservation of rights clause. In addition, CNA did not breach its ERISA fiduciary duty in eliminating the health-care allowance. In the Seventh Circuit, a breach of fiduciary duty exists if fiduciaries mislead plan participants or misrepresent the terms or administration of a plan. There was no evidence of any intent to purposefully mislead employees. The plaintiffs' fiduciary duty claim has no support.

▶ ANALYSIS

The court stated: "What this case comes down to, in the end, is the distinction between 'lifetime' and 'vested' welfare benefits—a legal distinction that understandably escaped many of ... employees who elected to take early retirement under the [early retirement program]. It is also a distinction that, as we have pointed out above, only relatively recently became important." Given its importance now, early retirement programs must generally spell out the distinction if the employee is to be properly informed of his or her rights.

■═■

Quicknotes

BREACH OF FIDUCIARY DUTY The failure of a fiduciary to observe the standard of care exercised by professionals of similar education and experience.

■═■

In re SPECO Corp.

[Parties not stated in casebook excerpt.]

Bankr. S.D. Oh., 195 B.R. 674 (1996).

NATURE OF CASE: Motion to confirm modification of collective-bargaining agreement under a reorganization plan.

FACT SUMMARY: SPECO, a debtor in possession, sought to unilaterally terminate the payment of retiree benefits under its collective-bargaining agreements.

RULE OF LAW
A debtor in possession is not permitted to modify or cease the payment of employee retirement benefits.

FACTS: SPECO, the debtor in possession, had retiree benefits costs of approximate one million dollars per year. SPECO entered a collective-bargaining agreement with the union in an attempt to restore SPECO to profitability and to reduce its costs. However, the subsequent agreement did not reduce SPECO's costs in relation to the retirement benefits. SPECO filed a petition for relief under Chapter 11 of the Bankruptcy Code. Then SPECO proposed to provide the retiree benefits as part of an employee K/ESOP plan. Under the proposed plan, SPECO would be converted into a company owned by its employees and management. The retirees would receive a lump-sum payment and utilize those distributions to purchase stock in the new company. Money would also be placed in a trust fund in order to pay for future medical benefits. The union rejected the proposal. SPECO submitted a second offer proposing that its duty to provide retiree medical benefits be eliminated from the provisions of the agreement due to the financial strain that it placed on the company.

ISSUE: Is a debtor in possession permitted to modify or cease the payment of employee retirement benefits?

HOLDING AND DECISION: (Clark, J.) No. A debtor in possession is not permitted to modify or cease the payment of employee retirement benefits. Traditionally, a debtor in possession was able to reject a contract to provide health benefits to its retirees under the Bankruptcy Code. However, Congress enacted § 1114 requiring the debtor in possession to continue those payments at their pre-petition amounts, except where the trustee or authorized representative of the beneficiaries agree to their modification, or the court orders such modification after notice and a hearing upon the motion of the trustee or authorized representative. Under § 1114(g)(1), the court is authorized to enter an order for modification of retiree benefits payments if the trustee has made a proposal satisfying the requirements of subsection (f). If the debtor attempts such a modification, under § 1114(f) the trustee is required, subsequent to filing an application for the order seeking modification, to submit a proposal to the authorized representative of the retirees providing for the modifications necessary to the reorganization plan, assuring that all parties are treated equitably and providing the necessary information to evaluate the proposal. Following the filing of the application, the court may conduct a hearing to determine whether the modification should be enforced. Here, SPECO failed to satisfy the requirements of § 1114(f)(1). While SPECO provided complete and accurate information regarding the proposal, it failed to demonstrate that the modification was necessary to effectuate its reorganization plan. Rather, SPECO had not yet submitted a plan of reorganization based on the fact that it had not yet decided whether to reorganize or to liquidate. Furthermore, SPECO failed to demonstrate that all parties would be treated equitably. SPECO did not wish to pay its retirees any benefits under the proposal and did not provide information regarding its proposed treatment of its other creditors. Thus, SPECO's proposed modifications are contrary to the purposes of § 1114 and therefore are not enforceable.

ANALYSIS

Note that the court ended its inquiry after having concluded that the requirements of § 1114(g)(1) had not been satisfied. However, the court additionally noted that SPECO failed to satisfy the requirements of § 1114(g)(2) as well. That provision requires the court to enter the order for modification where the retirees' authorized representative refuses to accept a proposal for modification without good cause. The court concluded that the retirees' rejection of a proposal that they relinquish their rights to health benefits with nothing in consideration could not be construed as constituting a lack of good cause.

Quicknotes

CHAPTER 11 BANKRUPTCY A legal proceeding whereby a debtor, who is unable to pay his debts as they become due, is relieved of his obligation to pay his creditors through reorganization and payment from future income.

COLLECTIVE BARGAINING Negotiations between an employer and employee that are mediated by a specified third party.

DEBTOR IN POSSESSION Refers to a debtor in a bankruptcy code Chapter 11 or Chapter 12 case.

Continued on next page.

GOOD CAUSE Sufficient justification for failure to perform an obligation imposed by law.

LUMP SUM PAYMENT A single payment as opposed to installments.

■=■

Common Latin Words and Phrases Encountered in the Law

A FORTIORI: Because one fact exists or has been proven, therefore a second fact that is related to the first fact must also exist.

A PRIORI: From the cause to the effect. A term of logic used to denote that when one generally accepted truth is shown to be a cause, another particular effect must necessarily follow.

AB INITIO: From the beginning; a condition which has existed throughout, as in a marriage which was void ab initio.

ACTUS REUS: The wrongful act; in criminal law, such action sufficient to trigger criminal liability.

AD VALOREM: According to value; an ad valorem tax is imposed upon an item located within the taxing jurisdiction calculated by the value of such item.

AMICUS CURIAE: Friend of the court. Its most common usage takes the form of an amicus curiae brief, filed by a person who is not a party to an action but is nonetheless allowed to offer an argument supporting his legal interests.

ARGUENDO: In arguing. A statement, possibly hypothetical, made for the purpose of argument, is one made arguendo.

BILL QUIA TIMET: A bill to quiet title (establish ownership) to real property.

BONA FIDE: True, honest, or genuine. May refer to a person's legal position based on good faith or lacking notice of fraud (such as a bona fide purchaser for value) or to the authenticity of a particular document (such as a bona fide last will and testament).

CAUSA MORTIS: With approaching death in mind. A gift causa mortis is a gift given by a party who feels certain that death is imminent.

CAVEAT EMPTOR: Let the buyer beware. This maxim is reflected in the rule of law that a buyer purchases at his own risk because it is his responsibility to examine, judge, test, and otherwise inspect what he is buying.

CERTIORARI: A writ of review. Petitions for review of a case by the United States Supreme Court are most often done by means of a writ of certiorari.

CONTRA: On the other hand. Opposite. Contrary to.

CORAM NOBIS: Before us; writs of error directed to the court that originally rendered the judgment.

CORAM VOBIS: Before you; writs of error directed by an appellate court to a lower court to correct a factual error.

CORPUS DELICTI: The body of the crime; the requisite elements of a crime amounting to objective proof that a crime has been committed.

CUM TESTAMENTO ANNEXO, ADMINISTRATOR (ADMINISTRATOR C.T.A.): With will annexed; an administrator c.t.a. settles an estate pursuant to a will in which he is not appointed.

DE BONIS NON, ADMINISTRATOR (ADMINISTRATOR D.B.N.): Of goods not administered; an administrator d.b.n. settles a partially settled estate.

DE FACTO: In fact; in reality; actually. Existing in fact but not officially approved or engendered.

DE JURE: By right; lawful. Describes a condition that is legitimate "as a matter of law," in contrast to the term "de facto," which connotes something existing in fact but not legally sanctioned or authorized. For example, de facto segregation refers to segregation brought about by housing patterns, etc., whereas de jure segregation refers to segregation created by law.

DE MINIMIS: Of minimal importance; insignificant; a trifle; not worth bothering about.

DE NOVO: Anew; a second time; afresh. A trial de novo is a new trial held at the appellate level as if the case originated there and the trial at a lower level had not taken place.

DICTA: Generally used as an abbreviated form of obiter dicta, a term describing those portions of a judicial opinion incidental or not necessary to resolution of the specific question before the court. Such nonessential statements and remarks are not considered to be binding precedent.

DUCES TECUM: Refers to a particular type of writ or subpoena requesting a party or organization to produce certain documents in their possession.

EN BANC: Full bench. Where a court sits with all justices present rather than the usual quorum.

EX PARTE: For one side or one party only. An ex parte proceeding is one undertaken for the benefit of only one party, without notice to, or an appearance by, an adverse party.

EX POST FACTO: After the fact. An ex post facto law is a law that retroactively changes the consequences of a prior act.

EX REL.: Abbreviated form of the term "ex relatione," meaning upon relation or information. When the state brings an action in which it has no interest against an individual at the instigation of one who has a private interest in the matter.

FORUM NON CONVENIENS: Inconvenient forum. Although a court may have jurisdiction over the case, the action should be tried in a more conveniently located court, one to which parties and witnesses may more easily travel, for example.

GUARDIAN AD LITEM: A guardian of an infant as to litigation, appointed to represent the infant and pursue his/her rights.

HABEAS CORPUS: You have the body. The modern writ of habeas corpus is a writ directing that a person (body) being detained (such as a prisoner) be brought before the court so that the legality of his detention can be judicially ascertained.

IN CAMERA: In private, in chambers. When a hearing is held before a judge in his chambers or when all spectators are excluded from the courtroom.

IN FORMA PAUPERIS: In the manner of a pauper. A party who proceeds in forma pauperis because of his poverty is one who is allowed to bring suit without liability for costs.

INFRA: Below, under. A word referring the reader to a later part of a book. (The opposite of supra.)

IN LOCO PARENTIS: In the place of a parent.

IN PARI DELICTO: Equally wrong; a court of equity will not grant requested relief to an applicant who is in pari delicto, or as much at fault in the transactions giving rise to the controversy as is the opponent of the applicant.

IN PARI MATERIA: On like subject matter or upon the same matter. Statutes relating to the same person or things are said to be in pari materia. It is a general rule of statutory construction that such statutes should be construed together, i.e., looked at as if they together constituted one law.

IN PERSONAM: Against the person. Jurisdiction over the person of an individual.

IN RE: In the matter of. Used to designate a proceeding involving an estate or other property.

IN REM: A term that signifies an action against the res, or thing. An action in rem is basically one that is taken directly against property, as distinguished from an action in personam, i.e., against the person.

INTER ALIA: Among other things. Used to show that the whole of a statement, pleading, list, statute, etc., has not been set forth in its entirety.

INTER PARTES: Between the parties. May refer to contracts, conveyances or other transactions having legal significance.

INTER VIVOS: Between the living. An inter vivos gift is a gift made by a living grantor, as distinguished from bequests contained in a will, which pass upon the death of the testator.

IPSO FACTO: By the mere fact itself.

JUS: Law or the entire body of law.

LEX LOCI: The law of the place; the notion that the rights of parties to a legal proceeding are governed by the law of the place where those rights arose.

MALUM IN SE: Evil or wrong in and of itself; inherently wrong. This term describes an act that is wrong by its very nature, as opposed to one which would not be wrong but for the fact that there is a specific legal prohibition against it (malum prohibitum).

MALUM PROHIBITUM: Wrong because prohibited, but not inherently evil. Used to describe something that is wrong because it is expressly forbidden by law but that is not in and of itself evil, e.g., speeding.

MANDAMUS: We command. A writ directing an official to take a certain action.

MENS REA: A guilty mind; a criminal intent. A term used to signify the mental state that accompanies a crime or other prohibited act. Some crimes require only a general mens rea (general intent to do the prohibited act), but others, like assault with intent to murder, require the existence of a specific mens rea.

MODUS OPERANDI: Method of operating; generally refers to the manner or style of a criminal in committing crimes, admissible in appropriate cases as evidence of the identity of a defendant.

NEXUS: A connection to.

NISI PRIUS: A court of first impression. A nisi prius court is one where issues of fact are tried before a judge or jury.

N.O.V. (NON OBSTANTE VEREDICTO): Notwithstanding the verdict. A judgment n.o.v. is a judgment given in favor of one party despite the fact that a verdict was returned in favor of the other party, the justification being that the verdict either had no reasonable support in fact or was contrary to law.

NUNC PRO TUNC: Now for then. This phrase refers to actions that may be taken and will then have full retroactive effect.

PENDENTE LITE: Pending the suit; pending litigation under way.

PER CAPITA: By head; beneficiaries of an estate, if they take in equal shares, take per capita.

PER CURIAM: By the court; signifies an opinion ostensibly written "by the whole court" and with no identified author.

PER SE: By itself, in itself; inherently.

PER STIRPES: By representation. Used primarily in the law of wills to describe the method of distribution where a person, generally because of death, is unable to take that which is left to him by the will of another, and therefore his heirs divide such property between them rather than take under the will individually.

PRIMA FACIE: On its face, at first sight. A prima facie case is one that is sufficient on its face, meaning that the evidence supporting it is adequate to establish the case until contradicted or overcome by other evidence.

PRO TANTO: For so much; as far as it goes. Often used in eminent domain cases when a property owner receives partial payment for his land without prejudice to his right to bring suit for the full amount he claims his land to be worth.

QUANTUM MERUIT: As much as he deserves. Refers to recovery based on the doctrine of unjust enrichment in those cases in which a party has rendered valuable services or furnished materials that were accepted and enjoyed by another under circumstances that would reasonably notify the recipient that the rendering party expected to be paid. In essence, the law implies a contract to pay the reasonable value of the services or materials furnished.

QUASI: Almost like; as if; nearly. This term is essentially used to signify that one subject or thing is almost analogous to another but that material differences between them do exist. For example, a quasi-criminal proceeding is one that is not strictly criminal but shares enough of the same characteristics to require some of the same safeguards (e.g., procedural due process must be followed in a parole hearing).

QUID PRO QUO: Something for something. In contract law, the consideration, something of value, passed between the parties to render the contract binding.

RES GESTAE: Things done; in evidence law, this principle justifies the admission of a statement that would otherwise be hearsay when it is made so closely to the event in question as to be said to be a part of it, or with such spontaneity as not to have the possibility of falsehood.

RES IPSA LOQUITUR: The thing speaks for itself. This doctrine gives rise to a rebuttable presumption of negligence when the instrumentality causing the injury was within the exclusive control of the defendant, and the injury was one that does not normally occur unless a person has been negligent.

RES JUDICATA: A matter adjudged. Doctrine which provides that once a court of competent jurisdiction has rendered a final judgment or decree on the merits, that judgment or decree is conclusive upon the parties to the case and prevents them from engaging in any other litigation on the points and issues determined therein.

RESPONDEAT SUPERIOR: Let the master reply. This doctrine holds the master liable for the wrongful acts of his servant (or the principal for his agent) in those cases in which the servant (or agent) was acting within the scope of his authority at the time of the injury.

STARE DECISIS: To stand by or adhere to that which has been decided. The common law doctrine of stare decisis attempts to give security and certainty to the law by following the policy that once a principle of law as applicable to a certain set of facts has been set forth in a decision, it forms a precedent which will subsequently be followed, even though a different decision might be made were it the first time the question had arisen. Of course, stare decisis is not an inviolable principle and is departed from in instances where there is good cause (e.g., considerations of public policy led the Supreme Court to disregard prior decisions sanctioning segregation).

SUPRA: Above. A word referring a reader to an earlier part of a book.

ULTRA VIRES: Beyond the power. This phrase is most commonly used to refer to actions taken by a corporation that are beyond the power or legal authority of the corporation.

Addendum of French Derivatives

IN PAIS: Not pursuant to legal proceedings.

CHATTEL: Tangible personal property.

CY PRES: Doctrine permitting courts to apply trust funds to purposes not expressed in the trust but necessary to carry out the settlor's intent.

PER AUTRE VIE: For another's life; during another's life. In property law, an estate may be granted that will terminate upon the death of someone other than the grantee.

PROFIT A PRENDRE: A license to remove minerals or other produce from land.

VOIR DIRE: Process of questioning jurors as to their predispositions about the case or parties to a proceeding in order to identify those jurors displaying bias or prejudice.

Casenote® Legal Briefs